Published 2016 by Computing Literature, Morgantown, WV 26506 / Rochester, NY

Cover design by Teo Spiller

ISBN-13:   978-1-943665-36-5   (pb)
                978-1-943665-38-9   (elec)
                978-1-943665-37-2   (pdf)

ACKNOWLEDGMENTS

I would like to thank Sandy Baldwin, the founder and editor of Computing Literature book series for enabling me to publish this book with this groundbreaking edition. I am also grateful to Kwabena Opoku-Agyemang for helping me in the process of editing, proofreading, design, and preparing the index. In addition, I thank Baldwin's other assistants, notably Charell Davis, who were engaged in preparing this book. I would like to express my gratitude to Philippe Bootz, the co-editor of Computing Literature book series, who is the key person in Europe in providing support and organization of European e-literary community. My profound gratitude is owed to Markku Eskelinen and Raine Koskimaa whose invitation to their Cybertext Yearbook project in the early 2000s paved the road for my exploration of electronic literature and digital textuality. I would like to give a special mention to my Slovenian colleagues Srečo Dragan, Narvika Bovcon, Mojca Puncer, and Aleš Vaupotič who encouraged me in my out-of-the box attitude to media art and cybertextualitity. Much has been gained from our talking things over, sharing comments and remarks on new media phenomena. And this book would not have been possible without the support and encouragement of my dear girlfriend Maja Murnik.

Janez Strehovec

CONTENTS

INTRODUCTION

The 20th century was in every way a cinematic one. A number of parallels can even be drawn between the industrial organization of work at the assembly line—rationalization in the sense of training the worker's movement, which is coordinated with the rhythm of the machine— and the cinematic way of organizing moving images. "Early cinematic montage extended the logic of the assembly line[...] to the sensorium and brought the industrial revolution to the eye" (Jonathan Beller). This means that even the Fordist assembly line presupposes cuts, montages, and a sequencing of movements as though it were a film whose moving images had become an example for a number of basic cultural contents—from avant-garde procedures on stage to the introduction of the copy and paste commands in a number of computer tasks—and even for a way of thinking. The key achievements of the humanities in the 20th century were defined by watching films and reading about cinematic procedures, from Benjamin to more recent thinkers such as Deleuze, Virilio, and Manovich.

Today we seem to be entering a new cultural paradigm which by no means ignores film, but introduces it into a new fundamental dispositif[1] of the present-day individual in an interface culture. This new dispositif is characterized by the paradigm of a ride, i.e. no ordinary "ride," but a highly accelerated ride—a thrill-ride—which intensely stimulates the passenger's sensorium at every moment. The moment the ride starts, the individuals find themselves in a situation where everything that is essential is placed in the field of vision directly in front of them, i.e. in the closeness of the mobile cockpit. A ride on a roller coaster, as the paradigm device for such an experience, is not only organized in theme parks but is becoming the model for the type of rides taken by today's individuals on a daily basis. The logic of this model is applied to the trendy contents of regular, as well as popular culture. And these rides are also entering film, especially the kinds created using 3-D technology that are intended to be shown in movie theaters (with the commercial/brand names XpanD, IMAX 3D, Dolby Digital 3D, and Real 3D). The film/ride concerns both the logic of organizing images and the special technical backgrounds that enable a unique experience

---

1 Dispositif is used to refer to both the machine or apparatus and institutions around it.

for the viewer/passenger. This experience integrally stimulates the viewer's senses to a greater extent than viewing films in cinemas equipped with traditional technology (e.g. Avatar). The core of the ride is not exhausted by one traveling far away and for good, i.e. by riding somewhere away from home with the purpose of finding a second home far, far away. No, the ride is based on the pleasure that one is no longer here and yet not quite there, i.e. that one is in-between. This in-betweenness can be very long or short, but in any case must be full of action, i.e. it requires that one receives a certain number of stimuli with a high amplitude, generally higher than the average that defines one's everyday experience. When the in-betweenness is short, the frequency of the stimuli must be especially high, the awake state heightened: the passenger finds themselves in a state that can be neither here nor there and that must not last too long, for they would physically not be able to receive that much stimuli in such a short time unit were this state to drag on. Such a short in-between is present in the programmed rides at theme parks that are limited to merely a few minutes.

Moving images can be considered as in-between rides. With various means of transport one watches a film and, since a ride is an intensifying activity, stars in it. During the ride everything revolves around you—the passenger. Even if no one says that you are the principal actor in that event, you yourself believe that you are: you are the agent of that intensive trip that resembles a computer game. The ride is not controlled merely by the operator or group of operators that controls the ride's machinery, but also by the passenger who as a participant in the ride is granted a great deal of competence during the ride itself. After all, the ride is there for the passengers; they and not the operators/pilots are the true subjects of the ride. The ride is not silent and amorphous; it is a partner that addresses the passenger who opts for it as a state in which he/she will be able to experience a number of stimuli.

This short excursion into film and rides was carried out in the introduction to a book that focuses on problems regarding electronic literature (or e-literature) and its attitude towards new media art. E-literature belongs to algorithmic culture and is discussed in connection with contemporary social paradigms; however, the mention of both film and the film-ride is not such a great departure from e-literature. Electronic literature, enabled by new media, is by no means situated in an area foreign to film and the film/ ride in particular. The author of this book spent some time in the 1990s following hypertext fiction, a genre that was the most distinct and media-covered part of literary writing in e-media (at least in the USA); however, in the effects of hyperlinks and mazes, which are at work in a hypertext with literary features, he discovered merely one of the possibilities of writing using new media. He found a bigger challenge for the contemporary reader/user in those new media textual practices that focus on movement, which result in a film of words. The latter is composed of units, which over a decade ago the author had already named word-image-movement, i.e. the verbal signifier-in-motion. What is crucial is that in the moment when text enters a moving form it begins to behave like a film, i.e. a film of verbal contents, presenting a challenge to theory which in turn abandons the field of literary peculiarities and begins to direct itself towards effects concerning the cinematic organization of textual contents.

When observing the text/film one soon discovers that what was written in the above on film and the film/ride also applies to kinetic text. This too appears as content-in-motion, which is founded on the play of light and shadow, on fast or slow cuts, close-up, and montage. Electronic text with literary features is part of today's digital culture; other procedures that are also relevant to it extend from the field of film to digital video, digital music, computer games, digital architecture, and locative media. All this is characterized by sampling, mixing, remixing, and mash-ups as much as montage and (fast) cuts. This shift concerns both the creativity of authors in this field, who apply procedures that are typical of DJ and VJ culture, and the feedback and behavior of the public, which is recruited for the field of e-literature among fans of club culture, software culture, new media art, and artistic activism.

When e-texts with literary features and effects begin to be placed close to films and new media, they enter a world whose main quality is speed, which implies a special grouping, defined by greater or lesser speed, acceleration, ride, and race. Without being familiar with the software that generates contemporary textuality, William S. Burroughs wrote in The Invisible Generation:

Take any text, speed it up, slow it down, run it backwards, inch it, and you will hear words that were not in the original recording; new words made by the machine different people will scan out different words of course but some of the words are quite clearly there and anyone can hear them words which were not in the original tape but which are in many cases relevant to the original text as if the words themselves had been interrogated and forced to reveal their hidden meanings (218).

Burroughs was fascinated with the capabilities of the tape recorder, whose functions he metaphorically applied to textual material. The essay from which this quote was taken dates back to 1962, and everything in it focuses on the technical manipulability of text, which experienced an actual bloom only with the new generation of technologies, namely those that are based on computers and digitization. In any case Burroughs's reference to speed is important and links him to Walter Benjamin, who understood the role of speed in a therapeutic sense, namely in this context:

In technology, a physis is being organized through which mankind's contact with the cosmos takes a new and different form from that which it had in nations and families. One need recall only the experience of velocities by virtue of which mankind is now preparing to embark on incalculable journeys into the interior of time, to encounter there rhythms from which the sick shall draw strength as they did earlier on high mountains or on the shores of southern seas. The "Lunaparks" are a prefiguration of sanatoria. (One-Way Street)

Speed is what brings things to clarity, to an experimental and accelerated state, when they start behaving differently from when they are in motion, i.e. traveling and simultaneously endangering, which the German expression Erfahrung used by Walter Benjamin alludes to etymologically: the expression contains both fahrt (ride) and gefahr (danger). In a certain way both of these components are also contained in the English term "experience" since, when one experiences something, one moves and if one goes (too) far, one becomes endangered. Speed is also experienced in e-literary texts (for example in animated poetry), when one "rides" the tapes of words-images-in-motion. At the same time, with regard to text/film, one tries to capture and perceive that which has not yet been included in the ride, what is not accelerated and is outside the field of vision, but is also essential for the basic understanding of such a text.

Therefore this book analyzes e-literary text in the sense of a textual film-ride; however, the issues connected with this are by no means the sole content of this book. Such a text is viewed as part of the expanded concept of textuality, which includes both verbal and non-verbal signifiers. Such a text challenges readers to complex experiencing, which is by no means exhausted in the reading-as-we-know-it in the sense of decoding units of meaning, but in integral experiencing, which also includes kinesthetic and motor arrangements. Hence the chapter "Cycling as Reading a Cityscape" was included, in which the city is discussed in the role of a textscape (in the sense Manovich's database), which is being discovered during the act of cycling, deploying the bicycle as a user-friendly interface. Along the expanded concept of textuality, the manuscript also addresses the issue of play and game that is essential for a basic understanding of present technoculture. By taking into account the very nature of the game in terms of philosophical investigations the chapter on the event space on the move tries to answer one of the basic issues posed by the Wark's "Gamer Theory": can we explore games as allegories for the world we live in?

The e-literary text is understood through interactions with new media art. The text shares not only the presentation space but also the fundamental concepts and design principles with new media art. Thus, several chapters emphasize the paradigm of new media art and e-literature as a form of research. The argument focuses attention on "the aesthetics of closeness" and raises questions about how defamiliarization (ostranenie in Russian Formalism), an important device of contemporary art, functions in the environment of new media art and e-literature.

The language of e-literature is seen as cyberlanguage, i.e. language that is essentially defined by changes deriving from online communication and social networking. Many of the findings described by David Crystal in Language and the Internet (2001) undoubtedly apply to cyberlanguage as well. Language is a social, historical, and consequently a changeable category; when e-writers refer to language, their engagement also touches on the social essence of language itself. The social mediation of language is not the only point in which e-literature abandons its self-reference and autopoiesis; however it is essential for e-literature, just as for similar new media art, that it is broadly integrated into contemporary society and thus also affected by the shifts of the fundamental social paradigms in the present. Today we are not merely the contemporaries of the paradigm shifts in the field of theory (in particular of philosophy) that direct one from the linguistic and cultural to the body and biopolitical. In fact, our reality has long been defined by peculiarities regarding life in a post-industrial, spectacle, information, and breaking-news driven society. This area is given attention in the final chapters of this book when terms are introduced that pertain to the integration of e-literature in contemporary society, namely e-literary service, derivative writing, e-literary world, elevator pitch, and performance. In referring to the e-literary world we have argued that the making of an e-literary piece is not enough; it is also necessary to present it in the community, find an audience and critics and theorists who will refer to it. Outside of the e-literary world many e-literary pieces do not have much of a chance.

E-literary practice has integrated not only certain concepts of film but also procedures shared with other fields. E-literature is likewise at least indirectly influenced by contemporary corporate capitalism. One encounters the will for abstractness, which is expressed in the practice of e-literature as a pure play with form, as a fascination with software and special effects, as an abandonment of the taking of sides in social reality, in which exploitation, racism precariousness, segregation, and the terror of a minority over the majority often triumph. When comparing e-literature with new media art it can be seen that the first has a noticeable deficit when it comes to activism, hacktivism, and feminism, i.e. when it comes to a more critical attitude towards social reality. This is surprising, since the early hyperfiction phase of e-literature showed enough promise (for example Shelley Jackson's "The Patchwork Girl"). Perhaps it is precisely hypertext with its explicit nonhierarchical structure that is the appropriate form for feminist authors, which has also been proved by the reactualization of this practice in Susan Gibb's Blueberries (2009).

The book concludes with a chapter on e-literary criticism which focuses attention on the uncertain nature of the field in question, on its fragile institutionalization and the constant movement along the line connecting digital textuality with hypertext and the new media. Yet the power of e-literature lies precisely in this uncertainty, which is also connected with the difficulty in defining the field and may even be its advantage over literature-as-we-know-it, which in a way has fallen asleep, adapted to the market, and abandoned the avantgardist, experimental direction and the neo-avantgardist quests characteristic of the 1960s and '70s.

Janez Strehovec

1 FROM E-LITERARY TEXT TO E-LITERARY SERVICE AND PERFORMANCE

The concept of technoculture, alongside expressions such as interface culture, cyberculture, software culture, digital culture, new media culture and algorithmic culture, does not point to a culture based on techniques and technologies of traditional industrial society. Rather, these expressions refer to cultures shaped by the applications of smart devices and software as one of the key factors of an information society (Manovich, 2008). Technoculture applies the techno principle to take artificial and synthetic progress to the limits, challenging the extreme edges of perception—as the example of techno (house, hip-hop) music does to music. Interface culture (Johnson, 1997) focuses on the role of interfaces in an individual's perception and function. Cyberculture presupposes classical cybernetics and second order cybernetics as fundamental to monitoring and controlling cultural contents. Software culture focuses on software platforms (Goriunova, 2011) that have a creative role in the networked culture and art. Digital culture refers to trans-coding from analogue to digital and the consequences it has at the level of archives and in data distribution. New media culture derives from the logic of the database and processes of mixing and remixing cultural contents (Manovich, 2001). Algorithmic culture includes all the features of the previously mentioned cultures and expands them throughout the area of social and cultural algorithms implemented by state-of-the-art software.

Nothing taking place in new media art and culture is excluded from the social text and context, determined by the findings of contemporary sciences, new media, and technologies, as well as a networking-supported economy and post-political politics (Virno, 2004). In the age of globalization, one-dimensional, globally established modes of participation and behavior are distributed and exchanged by means of new modes of digitalized economies and with the paradigm of cultures shaped by "being-in-technology."[2] This situation implies new forms of human perception and experience, and novel ways of embodiment and corporeality.

---

2 E.g. McDonaldisation, CNNisation, Microsoftisation, Benettonisation,

The concept of "being-in-the-world" can be traced back to Martin Heidegger who described the relationship between humans and new forms of technology in the following way:

> The hydroelectric plant is not built into the Rhine River as was the old wooden bridge that joined bank with bank for hundreds of years. Rather, the river is dammed up into the power plant. What the river is now—namely a water-power supplier—derives from the essence of the power station. (Heidegger, 1977:7)

The hydroelectric plant is set in contrast to a windmill that turns around in the directions of the wind, and a bridge that joins one bank of the river Rhine with the other. This comparison is set in terms of something essential and fatal. A hydroelectric plant turns the power ratio in nature upside down by producing something artificial within the river. Heidegger's example belongs to the second industrial society paradigm. However, its logic functions here to articulate the triumph of artificial over the natural, exercised more clearly in the post-industrial information society of the 20th and 21st-centuries. Crucial concepts such as management, control, manipulation, moving, connecting, networking, consulting, and monitoring no longer apply to the so-called first nature, but to second nature and even to "third nature," i.e. to the cybernetics of the first and the second order. In Heidegger's example, first nature is used to name the river, second to name the hydroelectric plant, and the third to name the reproduction of the river at the level of theory and art, for example, the Rhine as a scientific text built on the specificity of its ecology and its representations, a new order taking the place of the river by means of words, sounds, or images.

> The new media image is something the user actively goes into, zooming in or clicking on individual parts with the assumption that they contain hyperlinks (for instance, image-maps in Web sites). Moreover, new media turn most images into image-interfaces and image-instruments. The image becomes interactive, that is, it now

---

Googlesation and other trends imposed by transnational corporations and their brands.

functions as an interface between a user and a computer or other devices (Manovich, 2001:183).

Digitally coded images, sounds, or words placed within an interactive dispositif controlled by software and available on static or mobile "screenic" devices become manipulable, i.e. one can step in, zoom in, modify, and combine them into new wholes.

What is crucial here is that in the literature-as-we-know-it, which privileged verbal signs, gives way to other (e.g. non-verbal) signs as well as to machinic and posthuman codes. Digital words as the material basis of electronic literature are considered an emerging field of creativity in new media (Wardrip-Fruin 2009, Eskelinen 2012, Funkhouser 2012). Such words coexist with digital sounds, moving images, as well as 3D virtual objects. In this opening chapter we seek to broaden a discussion on contemporary technoculture, interface culture, and algorithmic culture by addressing some key particularities of electronic literature that might possibly be understood as a dry run for explaining the basic issues of the new media literacy. When we approach e-literature, we need to emphasize that this field has outgrown its early phase of hyperfiction[3] (and hyperpoetry) and has begun to articulate itself through textual practices characterized by new media specificities. Here hypertextuality [4] is merely one of the features co-existing with a number of other qualities, forms, and processes, including software, textual instruments, gaming, VJ-ing, mash-ups, virtual reality, special effects, social networking, virtual architecture, Second Life poetics,

---

3 The genre of hyperfiction goes back in 1987, when one of the pioneers in this field, Michael Joyce published Afternoon, A Story (at Eastgate.com)

4 The age of hyperfiction is the first significant movement in the history of e-literature (with the works by Judy Malloy, Michael Joyce, Stuart Moulthrop, Shelley Jackson, Carolyn Guyer, Deena Larsen among others). It stimulated hypertext theory (David J. Bolter, P. Landow), which has borrowed also from the philosophy and theory of French Poststructuralism (e.g. Barthes, Kristeva, Derrida), although within this movement the basic concepts were not defined in the dialogue with e-literary text and e-textuality. Rather than taking into account the specificity of e-text, poststructuralist criticism brought to the fore the materiality of experimental textual practices, the destabilized role (or even the death) of the author, the shift from work to text (e. g. Barthes's distinction between what he calls the readerly and the writerly text), as well as the intertextuality, transtextuality and paratextuality.

and locative media. We also find that literariness and narrative tend to be jeopardized in these works, while the logic of databases and post-literary effects step into the limelight. Media (Kac, 2007) and new media poetry (Morris and Swiss, 2006) are the particular experimental fields of e-literature where we can observe those transformations, which determine literary creativity at the very point at which it leaves the printed page.

These post-hypertext works of e-literature, to call them by their technical term, encourage new ways of reading that intervene in a broader space of perception and apprehension of new media creativity. In order to understand a text shaped in the form of a poetry generator, and in order to read a text formulated as a film of words that enter the visual/reading field from various directions, it is not enough to understand hypertext effects. For a suitable explanation of poetry generators, one at least needs a basic grasp of software, while understanding a text-film may well require turning to the film theory (Strehovec, 2010: 81). The new generation of post-hypertext e-literature occurs at the intersection of new media art and new forms of digital textuality, and points to a field beyond literature-as-we-know-it, that is, to an uncertain, experimental field marked by emerging new media specificities and investigations into the place and fate of the word in a time of new media and digital literacy. To go beyond mere abstraction, let us list some genres of this type of creativity: animated and kinetic poetry, textual generators, text-based modifications (mods) of video games, textual electronic installations, software textual art, Second Life textual projects, textual VR applications, textual applications in locative media, text-centred techno-performances and holopoetry. We are undoubtedly dealing with textual phenomena that abandon the printed page and migrate to the field of new media. In the case of holopoetry, this means that a poem is "organized non-linearly in a three-dimensional space and that even as the reader or viewer observes it, it changes and gives rise to the new meaning" (Kac, 2007: 129).

In order to approach this new field, let us first provide a basic description of the very nature of the new generation of digital textuality with artistic and literary features plugged into the world of new media. Within the paradigm of new media, the text is digitally coded and saved in memory devices, programmatically surveyed and manipulated, and displayed on computer screens and other screenic devices. This is the foundational premise that challenges us to re-think the reading, apprehension, and comprehension of texts. When the text is on-screen, it is opened up for reading with the aid of a computer mouse, scroll bar, and other instruments for its manipulation. It is also important that the reader enters it with a cursor, a textual avatar, which demonstrates the reader's presence in the textual landscape. When the reader is in front of the screen, surrounded by steering and controlling instruments, they are in a nomadic cockpit, meaning that what is in front of them is also accessible in kinesthetic arrangements. And before the reader is a sophisticated textscape with principal units we will attempt to understand by reference to the image of new media, which, when dealing with textscape articulated through spatial grammar, also provides a suitable framework.

The shift from hyperfiction to more sophisticated e-literature shaped by the new media specificity of "post-hyperfiction e-literature" stimulates novel theoretical approaches that focus on issues opened up beyond hypertext theory (Landow, 1994). The year 1997 saw a notable turn in e-literary theory, which increasingly took media specificity into account with the publication of Espen Aarseth's Cybertext and Janet H. Murray's Hamlet on the Holodeck. These books, along with the start of some crucial events in this field in the next years—conferences such as Digital Art and Culture, E-Poetry Festival and Conference, and the publication of journals and yearbooks such as Dichtung Digital, Electronic Book Review, Cybertext Yearbook—contributed to the very beginning of a new phase in e-literary theory and criticism. Essential to this new phase is an understanding of the e-literary field associated with theoretical approach to new media shaped-cultural and artistic contents (e.g. computer and video games). On the other hand, the software advances and popular plug-ins, the growth of the World Wide Web, and the new generation of e-textuality, e-poetry and e-narrative have also stimulated novel theoretical approaches that highlight the ergodic, event-based and gaming nature of e-texts. In terms of methodology, media specific analysis (Hayles 2002), digital processing (Wardrip-Fruin, 2009) and ludological approach (Eskelinen, 2012) comes to the fore, as well as Bolter's and Grusin's concept of remediation.

DIGITAL TEXT AND THE PARATEXTS

Electronic literature utilizes the digital text that, in nature, differs from printed text and texts on other, non-digital media. Digital text is generated and controlled with software, stored in memory devices, and manipulated with various interfaces, rather than just being a "more or less lengthy sequence of verbal utterances more or less containing meaning" (Genette, 1997: 3). Such a text is often non-sequential, without the hard and fast lines between the inside and the outside, process-like (text as event) and based on the play of the verbal and non-verbal signifiers. It is presented on the screens of static or mobile screenic devices and distributed via several media. Often, its creation is not merely the result of the creativity of one author or the collaboration of author and programmer, but its authorship is connected with artistic and creative platforms. Such texts can also be influenced by texts that are simultaneously generated on networks and encountered by the individual as a flâneur armed with mobile screenic devices (e.g. Bauer's and Suter's AndOrDada, 2008).

Digital text belongs to the paradigm of new media, for which it is crucial that the cultural contents are defined by database logic as a non-linear structure that is distinguished from narrative, organized with regard to chains of cause and effect (Manovich, 2001). One enters digital text at random; it is not read from the first page to the last. One encounters the organization of a website that contains a new configuration of paratexts in the form of menus, instructions, comments, hyperlinks, permalinks, tags, blogrolls, buttons, other navigational devices and posts (in the case that such a project is also added a weblog), which direct even the random user/ reader to the experiencing and reading that is characteristic of that text. In the new mediascape both the text and the paratext are intertwined due to the performance-like mode of textual condition, which presupposes the real-time interactions between the text, paratexts and the reader-user. One example is Mark Amerika's FILMTEXT, whose units are equipped with a menu that includes individual sections of this piece, the intro and credits. Very particular paratexts are also found in video games, e.g. icons, basic instruction on gaming and progressing, information of levels, score, numbers, and progress bars.

The user/reader approaches a digital text within an interactive fashion, which is why she needs as many cues as possible that react to her kinaesthetic actions via interfaces. When addressing digital text, one encounters an expanded concept of the text, which can only be properly understood by considering the number of factors that define its nature and which are by no means merely intertextual, but rather the result of a series of interactions with the environment, including feedback loops and the influence of extratextual components, including the paratexts. "And paratexts are important not only for the process of textual reception but also for text productions; they function as indicators to be aimed for, as structures of literary expectations." (Stanitzek, 2006: 32) Literary expectations direct us to the horizon of expectations introduced in Hans Robert Jauss's reception theory, which deploys the reader's significant role in the life of literary works. The reader is expected to enter a literary text armed with the data, knowledge and experience gained from her previous interactions with other texts. This horizon encompasses the cultural and social norms and historical implications of a given time and place, and also situates the work in relation to others. Also paratexts considered as devices that mediate a text to the reader, even in terms of the threshold (Genette, 1997: 3) might be understood as the essential component of such horizon.

This also means that paratexts are by no means a marginal matter (even though in the paradigm of print they are often defined by the very physical margin of the text, for instance the book cover); they do not merely play the role of a supplement; they also enable and profile the reader's understanding and perception of the text, the reader's navigation through textual levels and even influence what one should call attention to and what one should push aside or move to the background. Jonathan Gray, who updated Genette's views on paratext using TV shows, discusses also the challenge raised by the Cameron's movie Avatar with the following words: "the New York Times's review, the trailer you saw a month ago, what Aki Kaurismäki said about it—these are all still constitutive of how you regard the film that you haven't yet seen. Much of the text is the paratext..." (Gray, 2010, n.p.).

Jonathan Gray argues that numerous users of contemporary media contents are getting their cues from the trailer, the reviews, the posters, the credits etc. It is important that Gray mentions reviews (for instance the New York Times review), which means that intellectual contents (including interviews and authors' statements) also define the user's approach to a (new) media project. Even certain special features of software, which are otherwise essential for new media contents, can be interpreted in the sense of paratext (Galloway, 2012: 76). It should be mentioned that Genette paid a great deal of attention to prefaces in the sense that "the most important function of the original preface, perhaps, is to provide the author's interpretation of the text or, if you prefer, his statement of intent" (Genette, 1997: 221). By doing so he anticipated the role of the author's statement in the present, particularly in the case of new media art and e-literature, where it actually becomes a statement of intent, which is essential for the user's correct approach to the project. Hence, in the case of (new) media contents, paratexts and extras (e.g. the documentation of performances and activist events) are not really that extra and "para"; on the contrary, they often affect our understanding retroactively. It is only after one reads the reviews and interviews with the authors of the performance that one develops a more complex attitude towards it, which means that the paratexts have reconfigured the meaning that was constructed by the viewer/user upon encountering it for the first time.

In his Paratexts: Thresholds of Interpretation Genette ascertains the historical and consequently changeable nature of paratextual components in terms that "the ways and means of the paratext change continually, depending on period, culture, genre, author, work, and edition…"(p.3), which he interprets as a flexible area between inside and outside and in the process even mentions the understanding of paratext as a screen that mediates between the visible and hidden components. This mention of a screen is by no means alien to e-literature, which distinctly belongs also to the interface culture (Johnson, 1997; Galloway, 2012); however, as has already been addressed in the case of Mark Amerika's FILMTEXT, in the present we are contemporaries of a series of new paratexts that are essential for entering events which are being realized by reading/navigating e-literary projects. Rather than being just stable components, the new media paratexts as thresholds (and interfaces) are becoming also paratextual practices, actions, re-enactments and events.

When looking at Genette's concept of the paratexts that accompany printed books of fiction, it is clear that certain paratexts (ranging from the format and type of print to the title and preface) also function in e-texts (that are otherwise about the size, form, and color of the writing and not about the print). Furthermore, a series of new paratexts can be seen that relate to software, algorithm, and hardware units that enable the storage and distribution of e-texts, interfaces and devices intended for controlling and manipulating the text. In any case, what we should be clear on is that we are moving around in the world after books and after print. Book covers are most certainly no longer the borders of the (literary) text, which has now been given a much more complex identity (i.e. through the collaboration of authors and programmers). In the case of poetry generators the author likewise no longer has complete control over the e-poems, which are often organized as textual instruments (for example Torres' **Poems in the middle of the road**), but the reader/user can greatly and substantially alter (write in) it. The digital text is also not a completed unit, tied to the artifact, but is articulated as a network (texts by authors plus texts generated in mobile or online networks), as event and performance, which means that it is an entity in time, which most certainly includes the appearance of paratexts as instructions that can enter at higher levels of the experiencing of an e-literary project.

Genette understands paratexts in the sense of "accompanying productions," which frame, surround and extend the text in terms of "extras," which contextualize e-literary projects and enable their presentation to an audience, to the expert public and to institutions. A series of such "extras" contributes to that what has been called the **e-literary world**, which is essential for the e-literary text to receive an appropriate institutional context (Strehovec, 2012).

Of primary interest in the e-literary world are theoretical and critical writings (in the role of Genette's epitexts) that introduce the readers/users to e-literature and which are essential for their reception. That is: from the very beginning e-literature has been accompanied by great theoretical reflection. The latter is necessary for its understanding, while at the same time its creators require many theoretical foundations. Numerous practitioners in this field are also theoreticians; moreover, e-writers and theoreticians in this field work hand in hand with each other and meet at every important event (festivals, readings, conferences). An observer of this field may sometimes get the impression that there is more theory (though heterogeneous and profiled with different approaches) here than there are relevant e-literary pieces.

This fact is mentioned because the reviews, documentation and statements of authors in terms of new media paratexts are not the only ones essential to the basic understanding of this field; for the perception and cognition of individual projects it is important that one is acquainted with many expert works (texts, monographs), not only from the narrow field of e-literary criticism and e-literary studies, but also from new media art, video games, software studies etc. The reader/user certainly benefits from knowledge of software and new media literacy including the navigational skills. An important example of new media paratext is the instructions that relate to the manipulation of e-text, especially when organized as a game. In order to enter Nelson's Nothing You Have Done Deserves Such Praise the reader/user must be familiarized with the "directions" (which are considered as a new media paratext, too), which are based on the use of arrow keys, so that left-right signifies move and the up arrow causes the avatar to jump.

When the reader/user first encounters electronic literary projects and is not skilled in new media art, and is not familiar with the contemporary theoretical (first and foremost philosophical) paradigms, and does not master many skills of new media literacy, the reader/user faces great difficulties. She is unclear about how to enter such piece and does not know what to look for in it. She completely misses the core of an e-literary project by following the horizon of expectations, profiled by literature-as-we-know-it, and overlooks the complex algorithm that is, as a rule, active in an e-literary project and which demands from her a much more active role than she holds when reading printed texts.

The reader/user's familiarization with the author's statement and reviews is necessary for her to enter e-literary project. If she becomes acquainted with them only later on, she will realize that her knowledge of the piece must necessarily be corrected and that once again (perhaps even several times) she will have to approach it and encounter it. Paratextual features, connected to the printed literature (Genette) and the media, must therefore be complemented by new "extras", paratextual acts, re-enactments and tags that are derived from context and the world of e-literary projects, and directed towards new theoretical paradigms, software, and lifestyles. Furthermore, the new media paratexts are important also in the form of menus and instructions that facilitate orientation and the progress in traversing across the e-textscape, which means that they are also essential for navigating and controlling the e-literary text. Whereas many new media paratexts are regarded as the audience (and fandom) productions, the e-literary paratexts are the professional ones; they are as a rule generated by programmers, writers, scholars, researchers and critics. Such a turn toward the theory is based in the very nature of electronic literature, considered as an emerging field, which stimulates enjoyment in its theoretical endeavours rather than in decoding and perceiving its aesthetical and literary features.

E-literature is in its core very conceptual and radical in that its the most compelling and innovative projects share the goal of calling into question the very specificity of literature as we know it. They also destabilize common ideas about digital writing and the smooth functioning of technological advances. They do so by opening up new forms of textual organization (e.g. cinematic) by reflecting on how software conditions our basic understanding of online textuality through literary scripts, by pointing to the changes caused by algorithmic culture, and by intervening in online processes of digital writing and reading.

E-LITERARY TEXT AS A PART OF ALGORITHMIC CULTURE

It is essential that we place our introductory understanding of e-literature with algorithmic culture, because this placement will show us that e-literature is a sufficiently unique area that it cannot be explained as simple continuation of the literature-as-we-know-it by other means, but only as a novel field of new-media shaped creativity. This requires finding new concepts that often arise from non-literary disciplines (i.e. from new media, film theory and social theory). Technoculture after the first decade of the 21st century, defined by the expansion of social networks, is highly algorithmic, meaning that contemporary cultural contents require an algorithm approach. Here we are dealing with two classes of algorithmic applications, namely, with the one based on the requirement that an individual-user needs to know the algorithm, which is the basis of certain cultural content (i.e. video game) in order to enter and understand it, and with the other class referring to the smart algorithms of hardware systems, which nowadays perform (i.e. in social networking) tasks that significantly affect the epistemological field.

An example of the first class is playing video and computer games, where the player's success is conditioned by his or her knowledge or reconstruction of the (secret) algorithm that at work in the game. "To play the game means to play the code of the game. To win means to know the system. And thus to interpret a game means to interpret its algorithm (to discover its parallel 'allegorithm')" (Galloway, 2006: 90-91). This issue has also been addressed in Manovich's **The Language of New Media**: "As the player proceeds through the game, they gradually discover the rules that operate in the universe constructed by this game. They learn its hidden logic—in short, its algorithm." (p. 222). Galloway and Manovich formed these claims when they were faced with the video games, however, their statements of the algorithmic nature of video games may also be used in explaining the features of e-literature pieces, particularly those shaped as the text-based installations. The user (similar to a video gamer) is in the real world, where they carry out a number of motor tasks in front of the screen, while at the same time manipulating and controlling its (virtual) avatar presence in the screen. They are here and there, jumping between the real and the cyber modalities, because e-literary works challenge non-trivial, problem-solving encounters with their users requiring an algorithm approach (e.g., the Bouchardon's **Toucher**, which makes the user to deploy various interfaces to enter this piece).

An example of the second class are algorithms used for organizing and managing users' participation, behavior, and ways of thinking in major social networks and on the Internet. Ted Striphas argues the following:

When I began writing about "algorithmic culture," I used the term mainly to describe how the sorting, classifying, hierarchizing, and curating of people, places, objects, and ideas was beginning to be given over to machine-based information processing systems. The work of culture, I argued, was becoming increasingly algorithmic, at least in some domains of life. (Ted Striphas, 2011)

Such algorithmic culture is at the heart of today's Internet culture and social networking, where a series of algorithms essentially defines an individual's behavior and decision-making, perception and thinking, socializing and participation. Google PageRank is a useful illustration: a technology that determines the importance of a webpage by looking at what other pages link to it. Similarly, Facebook's algorithm EdgeRank, which determines which of your connections is the most important to you and thus appears most frequently, and which kinds of content should appear higher than others.

Algorithmic culture is defined by when cultural contents are organized by algorithms that are controlled and managed by software, and therefore require an algorithmic, problem-solving thinking and related and organized ways of functioning. Algorithmic thinking presupposes procedures that are formed with as economically and carefully selected steps as possible, and which solve the problem and help reach the objective. This is about a culture, which adds to C. P. Snow's division of two cultures—namely: the culture of natural scientists and the culture of literary intellectuals—a third culture (Vesna, 2001) and tries to overcome the traditional division and the related (social, cultural) conflicts.

This description of some of the properties of algorithmic culture introduces us to the issues opened up by e-literature (e.g. user/reader's non-trivial approach in decoding the e-literary work, e-reading as problem-solving activity). Instead of looking for links with traditions—with literature included in the culture of literary intellectuals—it makes more sense to search for connections of e-literature with similar areas of algorithmic cultures, and especially with new media art as well as with other technocultural practices (e.g. VJing and video games). In particular, new media art is a field, which, with its forms and internal logic, affects the novel practices of e-literature that are articulated beyond hyperfiction. At the same time, some the text-based installations and performance projects may also be understood in the context of new media art (digital art, Internet art).

Can we discuss e-literature in similar terms to video and computer games: as a field of algorithmic culture par excellence? A number of e-literature pieces can be understood as sophisticated cyber tools (i.e. poetry generators), the understanding of which requires a non-trivial effort from its readers-users. They too are forced into decoding the algorithm that is in the background of such projects, and their entry into the work often requires an algorithmic approaches—in the sense that a user creates an efficient procedure on how to approach such works and to effectively enter into them on his/her own. In addition, an algorithmic approach also connects video games with e-literature, where one of the useful concepts and paradigms is not only gaming, but also **textual instruments** (Wardrip-Fruin's term) which apply the intrinsic logic of a game.

ON THE LITERARY SPECIFICITY OF E-LITERATURE

Although often defined as an umbrella and technical term, e-literature involves literary components even in its name, so the question needs to be raised: what precisely is the literary nature of this kind of creativity in new media? Can it still be considered literature or has it already developed into something else? Is the literary in such a literature just a pure formality that is getting more and more obsolete and volatile, giving way to other more media specific features? In searching for theoretical foundations that can match the question of the literary nature of e-literature, one might apply the concept of literaturnost ("literariness") that was introduced in Russian Formalism at the very beginning of the 20th century. Literariness, according to Roman Jakobson, Viktor Shklovsky, Yuri Tynianov, Boris Eikhenbaum, Grigory Vinokur and others, is defined as the sum of special linguistic and formal properties that distinguish literary texts from non-literary texts. The crucial device of literariness is defamiliarization, understood as a series of deviations from ordinary language. Instead of considering literature as a reflection (mimesis) of social reality, Viktor Shklovsky and his Formalist followers considered it in terms of linguistic dislocation, or a procedure of "making strange." As described by Shklovsky in "Iskusstvo kak priem" ("Art as device" 1917), ostranenie ("defamiliarization")—as a typical device of all literature and art—serves to present a familiar phenomenon in an uncommon fashion for the purpose of an aesthetic perception, which is an aim of art. Facing a text with literary features means being struck with both "artistic" language and the order of things designated such language that deviate from our common expectations based on everyday verbal experience.

In introducing the concept of defamiliarization, we are aware that it works in e-literature only to a certain extent, and that it needs to be continuously refashioned by the use of the new media devices, with a special regard to the software features of digital texts. At the beginning of the 21st century, we are witnessing the blurring of boundaries between disciplines and fields, between institutions and networks, i.e., literature and everyday life are no longer easily differentiated categories, creating another problem in introducing ostranenie. It is also self-evident that Russian Formalists were not concerned with questions of digital textuality, digital literature, or the Web in general; however, unlike many traditional literary devices such as form, content, genius, style, aesthetics, the lyrical subject, etc., Defamiliarization enables one to grasp (and define) the e-literary author's effort in arranging her material in a very uncommon fashion.

Therefore, what are we dealing with regarding the concept of defamiliarization in the field of e-literature? Defamiliarization in terms of e-literature means that the authors arrange the subject's feelings, sensations, dreams, projections, linguistic attitude, experience, events, and atmospheres in an unfamiliar way in order to ensure a non-habitual and non-automatic perception of an individual's intimate realm as well as of her language, views and ideas. Briefly, their key aim is in making strange conventionally understood feelings, conditions, human fates, and individual's being-in-the world. They try to grasp the reader's attention span in a very persuasive fashion and within a very limited time interval, and because the modern individual is easily distracted, distinctive particularities of language need to be set up in very striking manners. In doing so, the authors use the specificity of new media, their special effects, and they try to organize the "linguistic" elements in a way that deviates from the language of commercial websites, online journalism, and Web 2.0 portals, although this often appears to be a difficult procedure. Along with stylistic and narrative devices, a big emphasis is put on software-based solutions that often deviate from conventional software applications (e.g. Galloway's claim for the "alternative" algorithm). Web based textual pieces with artistic or literary functions diverge from textual objects applied to ordinary websites and disturb even the user's perception and cognition.

The literariness in e-literature refers first and foremost to making cyber-language strange. We therefore can see that many digital pieces defamiliarize our expectations of what digital texts look like, what they are about, and the order of tasks performed in them. For example, in Mark Amerika's FILMTEXT, genres of film, computer games and text are made strange by presenting cinematic, gaming, and textual phenomena in an uncommon fashion. Natalie Bookchin's The Intruder defamiliarizes our expectations and ideas about video games and gaming behavior (instead of making a progression to a higher game level and keeping a score, we are interested in gaining the meaning, ideas, and feelings of the extraordinary). Komninos Zervos's animated poem Beer alienates the visual appearance of the stable lines of the traditional lyrical poem by placing the emphasis on the digital morphing of single nouns and their letters. Eugenio Tisselli's Degenerative website project[5] undermines our belief in a website as a stable medium, while Simon Biggs's text installation reWrite disturbs the reader's habitual expectations of how the authorial text is organized by enabling an artificial condition, which allows the reader to observe themselves reading endlessly self-generating texts.[6] Finally, Michael Joyce's hyperfiction Afternoon, a Story defamiliarizes the genre of the novel-as-we-know-it. It is self-evident that each of these projects also defamiliarizes the world, events, language, ideas, and scenes referred to in them. In such pieces we are facing "making-strange" as a distinctive effect achieved by the literary pieces and artworks that are shaped through new media, thereby disrupting our habitual perception of the world while enabling us to see even the cyberspace-based things afresh. In short, digital texts bring something into the language, into its organization (e.g., on Websites), and into reading that did not exist before. The emotional capital of such projects that initiate and

---

5 The key point of this project about the malfunctioning of high-tech is corrupting the website by means of clicking its URL. Each time the site is visited, one of the characters that make up the html code is either deleted or replaced. This causes a step-by-step degeneration, not only of the site's content but also of its basic structure.

6 The essential cues on how to approach this sophisticated language installation are found in the author's statement available at: <http://hosted.simonbiggs.easynet.co.uk/rewrite/statement.htm>.

stimulate a distinctive form of psychological change and feelings also belongs to literariness in new media: they initiate and stimulate a distinctive form of psychological change and feelings.

Therefore, the e-literary text defamiliarizes our expectations of what digital "language" looks like, of how a special feeling of a digital word is shaped, and of what the crucial features of the literary genre are within the paradigm of cyberculture (e.g., feedback loops, customization, the new media-shaped materiality and even physicality i.e. of on-the-screen displayed text as well as the user's textual control and navigation).

We have seen that the concept of defamiliarization works only to a certain extent in e-literature, but there are also other theoretical devices that need to be employed in this field in order to get a glimpse of its "literariness." One of them is Roman Ingarden's concept of metaphysical qualities that also addresses a particular atmosphere, arranged in the arts in literature in order to demonstrate its deviation from the everyday life.

Life flows by—if one may say so—senselessly gray and meaningless, with no regard for the great works which might be realized in this antlike existence. And then comes a day—like a grace—when perhaps for reasons that are unremarkable and unnoticed, and usually also concealed, an "event" occurs, which envelops us and our surroundings in just such an indescribable atmosphere [...] These "metaphysical" qualities—as we would like to call them—which reveal themselves from time to time are what makes life worth living, and, whether we wish it or not, a secret longing for their concrete revelation lives in us and drives us in all our affairs and days. Their revelation constitutes the summit and the very depths of existence [...] Independently of whether in themselves they have positive or negative value, their revelation is a positive value in contrast to gray, faceless, everyday experiences [...] they reveal a deeper sense of life and existence in general [...] Their realization, however, is, as we have phrased it, a "grace" [...] In real life, as we have said, situations in which metaphysical qualities are realized are relatively quite rare [...] Art, in particular, can give us, at least in microcosm and as reflection, what we can never attain in real life: a calm contemplation of metaphysical qualities. (Ingarden, 1973: 291-293)

When today, while being a part of the rhythm of algorithmic and cybernetic culture, one hears these thoughts by Ingarden, one gets the impression that they come from a world that is very much of the past, but one that most certainly was not and is not alien to traditional art and literature. In addition, it is essential to the understanding of literary culture, which belongs to the so-called high and elite culture. The essence of the above-mentioned thought by Ingarden is that there is something mysterious and even metaphysical in our lives, which is revealed in the so-called metaphysical qualities that are characteristic of a very special atmosphere, and reveal to us the deeper meaning of life and existence. This atmosphere envelops an event that occurs suddenly in the routine course of life. When it occurs to an individual, it signifies a true breakthrough and retreat from everyday, dreary boredom. The revelation of metaphysical qualities presents the summit of life, however, it is essential that these qualities are rarely revealed in life and that the only area in which we can calmly contemplate them is art. With this finding, Ingarden connects art with something that is highly existential and concerns an individual's "Dasein," meaning that art can be justified precisely with the fact that something extremely important and irreplaceable is being realized within it. The fact alone that it provides for calm contemplation of metaphysical qualities justifies the existence of art, as without it we would not have insight into something that is fundamental to our existence.

When trying to direct our attention from the horizon of metaphysical qualities to e-literature and the reality of present-day digital and algorithmic culture, we find ourselves in an awkward position, as we are being addressed in a language that we understand less and less. Furthermore, this position demands from us an ability which we believe is becoming more and more distant; namely, what is expected of us is that which is conveyed by "a calm contemplation of metaphysical qualities." What is becoming increasingly alien is precisely "a calm contemplation," for digital culture by no means involves contemplation: the calm mode is alien to it, while the direct participation in an events—that is the complex experience of its—is gaining in importance. This event is itself crucial, for it is no longer an Ingardenian one, that is, no longer something that occurs rarely, on the day of occurrence—like a grace—and is therefore enveloped by something extraordinary. On the contrary, in new media art and algorithmic culture everything occurs on purpose; events are artificially set up, arranged and programmed. New media art and algorithmic culture need events—as time extensions and intensities of physical arrival on the scene of stagings—for it is through them that the essential components of their practices are articulated. The point of algorithmic culture is not the contemplation of cultural contents independent of the observer but experiencing-within-an-event (term coined by the author of this book); it is not the contemplation of qualities but their rule-driven making. In addition, the so-called metaphysical qualities no longer directly present a stimulus to the creativity of e-writers. Instead of these qualities, matters concerning software, interfaces, and the processes themselves are gaining ground. "Rather than defining the sequence of words for a book or images for film, today's authors are increasingly defining the rules for system behavior" (Wardrip-Fruin 2009: 8). The core of an e-text too lies not in the sum of the components that comprise it, but in the relations between them, in code and rules, algorithms and instructions on how to set up functionality. E-literary text might be considered even in terms of a concept of post-literarism, which demonstrates that the dominance of literary coded verbal signs is at stake within the new media arts and culture.

Experiencing-within-an-event requires intensive participation, that is, someone who participates in an event, for instance, an actor, performer, or user. Hence, new media art thoroughly addresses and strikes its users (not merely spectators, observers). The same is true for e-literature, in which the traditional reader is being replaced by a hybrid reader-viewer-listener-toucher in the role of the user, who is a crucial actor in the events of e-literature as a field that, similarly to video games, requires a nontrivial effort in order for its user to follow the algorithmic logic at work within it.

TOWARD 3D INSCRIPTIONAL SURFACE

E-literary theory presupposes the shift from the analysis of pure linguistic signs to the broader materiality of textual and extra-textual signifiers, which posit this theory in a closer relationship with new media art theory. To enter the world of e-literature one needs a special approach which requires abandoning of the traditional way of reading, and therefore also of logic, as developed by Roman Ingarden in his phenomenological aesthetics of a literary work of art. When mentioning such a way, one touches at least fleetingly upon the phenomenological aesthetics which described the transition to the level of aesthetic experience as a far-reaching and radical turning-point with a practical and natural attitude. The e-literary attitude also requires certain "cyber-reduction" in the sense of the reader's/user's shift from the usual practice of textscape decoding. An e-textuality user needs to stay at the visual aspect of the text, at the digital word-image itself, and not use it as a pure means to something entirely different, to literary worlds, which was the topic of Roman Ingarden's The Cognition of Literary Work of Art:

> there is the question of the degree to which we really sensibly perceive and must perceive the individual paper and the individual flecks of ink themselves in the concrete reading of a printed book. Are we not rather immediately disposed to apprehend the typical forms of the printed "words" or the typical verbal sounds, without bringing to consciousness what the individual written signs look like? (Ingarden, 1973a: 177)

In e-literary textuality the emphasis is not only on the decoding of a meaning. A hybrid reader-viewer-listener is also curious about what each individually written sign looks like. Therefore, the visual features of a signifier and the spatial syntax of the text units come to the fore.

Print-based analog texts (excepting those experimental works within the framework of Concrete and Visual poetry) are spread out in planes, particularly across pages (of journals, magazines, printed books), which means that their "life" is limited by two dimensions. With digital texts incorporated into a screenic dispositif, we encounter a much more complex structure, which is by no means limited by a text in squares and rectangles, but rather by a text that is spread out (actually constructed by software) in the shape of a cube, cone, or a more complicated three-dimensional configuration (for example, in the works of e-authors such as Aya Karpinska, Daniel C. Howe, Rui Torres, Mary Flanagan, and John Cayley). The cube (as a stable one, rotating or floating) is a significant form in electronic literature, functioning as a 3D inscriptional surface that emphasizes the transition from the 2D surface of the printed page to more sophisticated structures. Contemporary software suites enable this presentation of textual units, particularly when we can experiment with a text using the VR platform Cave (the case of Wardrip-Fruin's et al. Screen and Cayley's Torus). The text extends statically when displayed in virtual bodies, but it can also be arranged kinetically in bodies as well as in two-dimensional forms, as is the case with animated and kinetic poetry (pieces by Kim Brian Stefans, Philippe Bootz, Stephanie Strickland, Komninos Zervos, Claire Dinsmore, and J.R. Carpenter). In this case, the text can flow from top to bottom, from left to right and vice versa, and we even come across texts that enter the reader's visual field from different directions. Today, we are facing a complex dispositif of a digital text, which challenges the reader with a non-trivial task. The reader may read it successfully, but they may also be rejected; some of the text becomes comprehensible while the reader misses others; They are led into a one-way street or a tunnel with no light.

Post-hypertext e-literature challenges the reader's bigger activity, which might be considered an aftermath of big changes in the very design of experimental e-textuality.

> When avant-garde or experimental works (among which hyperfiction likes to be counted) are approvingly called demanding, it is useful to keep in play the coercive connotation of the term: such works insist on our attention and our engagement more fully than do more conventional works. The relationship between the freedom of the author in forming a work and the freedom of its readers in receiving the work can be described as a simple function: the more liberties the author takes in giving shape to the work, the more forcefully are readers enlisted in its construction. (Chauli, 2005: 608)

Rather than taking into account just the reader's significant role in the life of literary works in terms of their efforts in "filling" the semantic blanks and gaps (Iser, 1979) or spots of indeterminacy (Ingarden, 1973b), the new media shaped (literary) texts stimulate even more sophisticated readers' operations.

When we mention reading as a non-trivial task, let us add that we thus define it in terms of an algorithmic culture (Galloway 2006) where actions are organized and directed by means of algorithmic, problem-solving thinking. Upon encountering works of e-literature, the reader is also placed into an unsafe position in which he/she must fashion her own algorithm in order to progress in the reading/experience of such a text. In this she can be either successful or rejected, that is to say, she is also faced with the message "reading is over" (similar to the message found in unsuccessful video gaming). We can understand algorithmic culture as a third culture (Vesna, 2001) based on the bridging of differences between the cultures of literary intellectuals and scientists (i.e. Snow's notion of two cultures).

> Artists using technology are uniquely positioned in the middle of the scientific and literary/philosophical communities, and we are allowed "poetic license," which gives us the freedom to reinforce the delicate bridge and indeed contribute to the creation of a new mutant third culture. By utilizing tools familiar to scientists and collaborating with the scientific community, we are getting closer to an atmosphere of collaboration and mutual respect. (Vesna, 2001: 122)

J. R. Carpenter's work Along the Briny Beach (2011) is an example of an e-literary text that demands non-trivial effort from the reader in order to be decoded. This is based on a poetry generator that gradually generates verses from the top to the bottom, doing so in an even rhythm so that the reader can comprehend the text with no trouble. This work, according to the author's statement, generates a coastline.

> The source code loads the following variables: Land Sea Write Erase Walk Liminal Space. The variable _Read_ is assumed to be client-side. The function _Writing and Erasing_ returns: Edges Ledges and Legible Lines caught in the Double-Bind of Writing and Erasing. Onload: Write Coast. (Carpenter, 2011)

The source code for the poetry generating component of Along the Briny Beach is based on "Taroko Gorge," by Nick Montfort.

Alongside the text (let us call it the basic text) rendered along a vertical axis, there is also a moving text on four levels which enters the basic (generated) text from the right and is spelled out in four sizes approaching at varying speeds. These lines are quotations from Elizabeth Bishop, Joseph Conrad, Lewis Carroll, and Charles Darwin. They are moving lines, which approach horizontally from the right and which must be read and viewed in order to gain an impression of this poem-event's content, that is to say, the content of a poem with an emphasized temporal dimension. This is not merely the simple generating of text (as is the case with Monfort's "Taroko Gorge," whose portion of source code the poet uses as a base); rather, the basic flow of text, which unfolds on a vertical axis, is continually interrupted by the text that appears from the right, and is performed by javascript. Reading this poem thus depends on scanning the "growing" basic text and the text on four levels that appears from the right. The text on the right side is not equal, since one line presents an encounter with text that rapidly enters from the right in a sequence of images of Briny Beach and is difficult to read (it is, in fact, also made up of quotations). In this piece, it appears as if the text itself is some sort of a beach, a presentation of Briny Beach and simultaneously its metaphor, which is to say that the shifting of elements on the sandy beach (various colors are used in the background and in the text) and the shifting on the level of the unpredictable entrance of text from the right that is moving at different speeds, the way waves tend to go hand in hand within the event of this text.

What is crucial here is also the spatialization of text in terms of sophisticated multi-layered structure, which presupposes the insertion of novel spaces (opened up with the lines entering from the right) that might be considered as an interval or a gap bringing into the space of text around the vertical axis the outsider contents. Such an insertion is also about the meaning and the very particular intellectual atmosphere, which is spread around the text. As an arrival of unfamiliar, strange and unsafe, the spatialization also implies the possibility of conceptualization in terms of arranging the meaning as an enigma, and in form of the non-identical and non-mediated (e.g. the uncanny). It is here essential that the e-literary text, which is not articulated sequentially, encourages "ideographic thinking" (Kac, 2007: 129), which differs significantly from linear thinking. More can be read from this text by those who are familiar with programming, who can read what is above or below and who know which programming operations generate precisely this textual output. The perception of e-literature does not include just reading (and not just reading in terms of the user's more intensive bodily activity based on textual arrangements that tactually strike her), but also the basic cognition of the software applied and the procedures that enable such a textual practice.

> If anything, a user without knowledge of html could be more confused by looking at the code, and might mistakenly believe some sort of generator should be present when in fact <meta name> tag simply states the name of the html editor used to create the page (Funkhouser, 2012:191).

In referring to his e-literary work Set of U (2004) Philippe Bootz also argued that so-called meta-rules deployed in organizing the textual material in this piece

> are not "technical rules," but the expression of a complex esthetical intention that lies in programming and can only be perceived by looking at the program. This intentionality is not addressed to the reader but to a "meta-reader": reading is a limited activity that is unable to give a complete knowing of the work. (E-Lit. Collection 1, online).

Since we understand post-hypertext e-literature in the context of significant connections with new media art, let us note that Along the Briny Beach can also be explained as a platform, an open work of textual relations (Umberto Eco, 1989), or a textual instrument which enables various readings and performances that add something new to the online version of the text (for example, Along the Briny Beach 1.1, 1.2, 1.3, etc.). One of these possible versions was realized in J.R. Carpenter's and J. Fletcher's performance in the framework of the event "Words in Motion" at the De Balie cultural centre in Amsterdam on December 9th, 2011. With the term "textual instrument" we mean "a tool for textual performance which may be used to play a variety of compositions" (Wardrip-Fruin, 2003), which conceptually means flexibility, as an "open work" platform that enables various performances (akin to, if we dip into the field of new media art, Marko Peljhan's project Makrolab[7]).

One of the key features of post-hypertext e-literature is that the reader-user is less and less engaged in understanding the symbolic nature of works and in decoding of meaning, while her interest becomes focused on a new series of (rich sensory) experiences by which she expects to be addressed as directly as possible. The reader-user demands from the e-literary text that it strikes her with its visual and tactile effects and that it arouses his/her motor stimuli. The reader-user, who is more and more a rider, expects literary and artistic content to be organized in the kind of form (a "package") that she encounters in attractive products of the entertainment industry, that is to say, she expects that they also strike and intoxicate her as if they were a roller-coaster ride or a movie (e. g. James Cameron's *Avatar*, 2009).

The "more" in the sense of tactile and motor arrangements in the practice of reading/riding is accompanied by a sort of "less" on the level of the reader/user's focus on semantic and symbolic features of post-hypertextual literary projects. We are encountering jumpy reading in the sense of a progressive scanning of textual components on-screen, which means that this type of reading is extremely vulnerable to distractions and interruptions. The reader-user keeps herself busy with a number of tactile and motor tasks. These have been already characteristic of reading hyperfiction with the aid of a mouse or touch-pad. In the moment when "our urge to click" (Mangen, 2008: 410) is upgraded by the "urge to ride," the reader-user comes across even more sophisticated corporeal procedures which challenge her attention span and destabilize her concentration. She is placed into a "jetzzeit," an operational realtime where her experience is continuously provoked by expectations directed toward what is yet to come, when she will react to the current state with the aid of an interface. The reader-user is continuously

---

7 In 1997, Slovenian artist Marko Peljhan presented his mobile lab for telecommunications Makrolab at Documenta X show in Kassel, Germany. The core of this project is in organizing a research platform, which enables artistic, tactical and scientific creativity for artists and activists whose projects focus on the issues of digital and satellite culture, including radio waves, atmospheric data and electromagnetic spectrum.

distracted by both expectations on the level of mental activity and by the physical activity required for her participation in the event of such a text.

The textual occurrence even in terms of rich corporeal activity is found in Simon Biggs' **Bodytext** (2010) as a textual performance work that involves speech, movement, and the body. A dancer's movement and speech are re-mediated within an augmented environment employing real-time motion tracking, voice recognition, interpretative language systems, projection and granular audio synthesis. The acquired speech, a description of an imagined dance, is re-written through projected digital display and sound synthesis, the performer causing texts to interact and recombine with one another through their subsequent compositional arrangement. What is written is affected by the dance whilst the emerging recombinant descriptions determine what is danced. The work questions and seeks insight into the relations between kinesthetic experience, memory, agency, and language.

Here the emphasis is placed on "moving around the text," which undoubtedly directs us toward the concept of reading as riding, which foregrounds topological feature (at the expense of the pure semantic one). "Moving around" is actually the basic way one approaches new media content(s): it implies tactile arrangements and method, which demonstrates that the user is often not in charge, and this unstable condition generates the readiness for being "in search." The "moving around" also resembles Iser's concept of the wandering viewpoint discussed in The Act of Reading (1978) as a device that relates to the switching between various textual perspectives; however, such a wandering refers more to the instability in terms of meaning generated by the interplay between modified expectations and transformed memories, whereas in the e-literary text wandering is a physical act of wandering the text, traversing it, and possessing it through a process of movement.

READING ON A TECHNOLOGICAL PLATFORM

New media texts are intended for screenic presentation, which is why we always read them on a very specific technological platform that (over)determines the accessibility of the text, its manipulability, and its ways of reading.

The crossing over from the text's physical presence to its digital expanse on the screen presents theorists of reading with certain problems.

> The reading process and experience of a digital text are greatly affected by the fact that we click and scroll, in contrast to tactilely richer experience when flipping through the pages of a print book. When reading digital texts, our haptic interaction with the text is experienced as taking place at an indeterminate distance from the actual text, whereas when reading print text we are physically and phenomenologically (and literally) in touch with the material substrate of the text itself. (Mangen, 2008: 405)

It is certainly true that in the process of reading we are not in direct physical relation with the e-literary text (we do not touch the pages, nor turn them), yet this is by no means a drawback. On the contrary, e-text is there in a very subtle interface-shaped dispositif, so that we are in a certain sense closer to it than we are on the printed textual platform, which presupposes merely a sort of rudimentary turning of the pages. Let us note here that turning the pages, touching the paper, and even sensing its scent, undoubtedly signals the presence of a text in the reader's physical proximity; however, these activities are accompanied by the reader's powerlessness to simply reach into the text and manipulate it. With an e-text, however, we encounter the following: a subtle, interface-based presence of the reader/user in the text itself, and considerable manipulability of the text, which is available to the reader/user as a standing reserve (Heidegger's term) for various types of manipulation.

The reader's manipulation of digital text is already well known (simply think of the copy-paste procedure), but what is, as we have called it, the subtle presence of the reader in the text? We are thinking of her identification with the cursor as a flickering avatar, which marks the reader's position in the textscape. In the text formulated by new media, the reader is in fact where the cursor is, while the latter is in near proximity to the word itself and to its atomic units—letters. Furthermore, the cursor is not there as a coincidental ornament but is an active factor that can erase a letter, add a new one, or insert a punctuation mark—that is to say, alter the text from the inside in such a way that its operations can be concealed (it is impossible to do this with a printed text). Rather than being a simple opposition, the digital and the tangible are linked by new media technologies that enable subtle forms of, let us say, the digital tangible. The digital tangible is not something concrete: we are not dealing with visible operations, but with very subtle ones. The touch (sense) at work with the digital tangible is a "sense theoretician," since it is a sense that does not grab in a rough physical relation but functions precisely through its avatar in the textscape. The term "sense theoretician" was coined by Karl Marx in the following context:

> The forming of the five senses is a labour of the entire history of the world down to the present. The sense caught up in crude practical need has only a restricted sense. For the starving man, it is not the human form of food that exists, but only its abstract existence as food [...] The care-burdened, poverty-stricken man has no sense for the finest play; the dealer in minerals sees only the commercial value but not the beauty and the specific character of the mineral: he has no mineralogical sense [...] The eye has become a human eye, just as its object has become a social, human object—an object made by man for man. The senses have therefore become directly in their practice theoreticians. They relate themselves to the thing for the sake of the thing, but the thing itself is an objective human relation to itself and to man. (Marx, 1844)

What is crucial in Marx's notion of the human senses is the very historical (e.g. changeable) attitude to them. They mutate across their history, and this point is also of significance at this moment, when we draw upon the senses engaged within the present interface culture and their deployment in the cognition of digital literature.

One of the significant works in this field, which stages the material/immaterial problem as well as the subtle issue of touching within the interface culture is Serge Bouchardon's Toucher (2009). "Touching" means exploring through a certain curiosity which generates the touch as a sense of proximity and of movement (the touching hand gets more information when it moves around the object). In Toucher the shift from immediate touching to an interface-mediated and driven one is thoroughly demonstrated: the touching in this piece requires interface mediation by mouse, microphone, and webcam. Such a subtle touching experience reveals a lot about the way we touch multimedia content on screen, as well as the reading of e-literary contents. We enter them by interfaces, reading mutated to interface reading (e.g. mouse reading). The reader of this piece is actually the user, provoked to access the text by means of sophisticated interface-shaped procedures that include various modalities of touching.

- the erotic gesture of the caress with the mouse;

- the brutality of the click, like an aggressive stroke;

- touching as unveiling, staging the ambiguous relation between touching and being touched;

- touching as a trace that one can leave with a finger dipped in paint; and

- touching from a distance with the voice, the eyes or another part of the body. (Bouchardon, 2009)

This piece demonstrates that its reading is first and foremost shaped by the interface sophisticated experience, which stimulates various senses and puts the reader-user into the riding adventure that stimulates several senses and provokes reader/user's corporeal and kinesthetic participation. Therefore, the interface shaped reading of Toucher might be considered a risky activity culminating in the production of an event that is not a homogeneous one but is determined by the intervals in which the user/reader has a chance to modify the basic condition of reading by deploying several interfaces.

Such an interface-shaped reading also affirms the crucial role of interface(s) in digital art:

The interface is the basic aesthetic form of digital art. Just as literature has predominantly taken place in and around books, and painting has explored the canvas, the interface is now a central aesthetic form conveying digital information of all kinds. (Pold, 2005)

What is crucial in this notion is the emphasis on the interface as an aesthetic form, meaning that the traditional concepts of style, creativity, genius, and value give way to concepts taken from the interface (including algorithms, software, and problem solving services).

New generations of digital devices most assuredly provoke new forms of perception and action. With a stylus or touch pad we can come into very direct, although virtual, contact with the word, contact that is much more immediate than using a typewriter, which means that these devices once again establish an immediate relation between the body (in fact, the hand) and the word. This is why they are not subject to Heidegger's critique intended for the fate of the word in a time of the typewriter.

The hand is, together with the word, the essential distinction of man [...]Man does not 'have' hands, but the hand holds the essence of man, because the word as the essential realm of the hand is the ground of the essence of man [...] The typewriter tears writing from the essential realm of the hand, i.e. the realm of the word. The word itself turns into something "typed." (Heidegger, 1992: 80)

Heidegger was unsettled by the fact that the typist uses a keyboard set in front of her, that she touches only the keys while the text that is created is over "there" and is separated from direct contact with the hand so that the individual letters that constitute it are not physically touched. The directness between the hand and the text may be lost with the typewriter, but, in the opinion of the author of this text, digital screenic devices once again enable the proximity of the hand and the text. This proximity now takes place in more subtle and virtual forms (even tele-forms). For example in touching the virtual keyboard on tablets (e.g. iPad), digital phones, and PDAs, or in the touch of an individual letter through a word processor with the use of a cursor.

Heidegger's objection in fact belongs to a broader context of a critique of cybernetic culture, which supposedly destabilizes our sensory experience and our perception of near and far, of here and now (Virilio, 1997).

Yet these allegations miss the core of the problem, which lies in the fact that in our current algorithmic and interface culture, which takes place in augmented reality (characterized by the intertwining of the given-real and the virtual), we are contemporaries of the modification of sensory experience that has mutated from the condition of direct sensation into a new modality marked by action and sensation conducted through interfaces. Physical tangibility has been replaced with the virtual, and with mixes of both. Real and virtual modes have become intertwined, tele-labour and long-distance sensation enrich our activities as we know them.

ALGORITHMIC CULTURE AND THE SERVICE OF E-LITERATURE

E-literature is embedded in today's reality and its fundamental social and cultural paradigm shifts. This may be described as a transition from industrial society to post-industrial (and informational), from labor in material production to immaterial work, from factory to corporation, from (material) product to logo, from an artifact economy to an economy of the performative, from production to prosumption (the consumer is addressed, one's feedback is considered), from an economy of products to an economy of experiences and adventures, from linguistic and discursive to biological and political, from an aesthetic culture to culture as an economy of spectacular events, from the literary culture to the culture of algorithms and processing.

Algorithmic culture emphasizes performativity, knowledge, event-driveness, software, and by interface-shaped perception. Despite the fact that strong tendencies towards autopoiesis and self-reference can be detected within it, its embeddedness into modern society is noticeable as well. This means that parallels can be drawn between the processes inside it and the key paradigms of the post-industrial society to which the post-Fordist organization of labor is essential. Let us mention Natalie Bookchin's Mass Ornament as an example of a new media piece that directly refers to the organizational principle of present-day labor. This video installation choreographs hundreds of YouTube dance videos to create a dazzling artwork that also questions contemporary isolation and connection via screens, cameras, and technology. Bookchin clipped and combined hundreds of video clips from YouTube and set them to the soundtracks from two 1935 films, Busby Berkeley's Gold Diggers and Leni Riefenstahl's Triumph of the Will.

> Also, just as the Tiller Girls dance embodied characteristics of Fordism and Taylorism, the YouTube dance, with its emphasis on the individual, the home, and individuated and internalized production, embodies key characteristics of our economic situation of post-Fordism. If Fordism once described a social and economic system that focused on large-scale factory production, post-Fordism describes a shift away from the masses of workers in the same space, to smaller scale production by workers scattered around the world. [...] If the machinery of the Fordist era was mechanical, post-Fordism is digital. The vehicles for production today are information and communication technologies, rather than conveyor belts and assembly lines. (Kane, 2009)

Post-industrial society is a society in which the significance of services (with a great deal of knowledge and skills) is growing. While the shift from artifact to service activity is by no means alien to e-literature, where a number of readings are organized as new media performances (for instance, on textual instruments). These are arrangements of particular contents in time with the purpose of solving a problem or the introductory conflictive state that appears as the generator of events. The concepts and qualities that essentially determined literature-as-we-know-it (for instance, metaphysical qualities, literariness, generating lyrical atmospheres) are no longer in the forefront of e-literature. Instead, the importance of algorithmic organization, of problem thinking, software, networking, expressive processing, and performativity is growing.

As a rule, e-writers no longer begin creating a piece after being stimulated by one sensation or another derived from experience (for instance, during natural phenomena or social events). They hardly even use their imagination with matters regarding aesthetics. Instead, that which has an impact on them from the start is the task presented to them by language itself and the code of the field in which they are involved and addressed, i.e., e-literature itself and its reader-user. Reading in itself is a task worth engaging in on the level of the creation of such pieces. In addition to the already mentioned authors and projects (for example Bouchardon's Toucher), let us point out the piece by Rui Torres Poems in the middle of the road (in Portuguese: Poemas no meio do caminho) organized as a set of combinatory texts programmed in a way that allows the reader to dynamically change the paradigms that feed the original syntax of the poems. The essential part of this e-poem is a set of instructions related to the very procedures of reading in terms of user/reader's tasks (read, open, combine, interact, recreate, constitute, take apart and save) meaning that the reader is expected to form his/her own algorithm in order to complete a task posited by algorithmic e-literary text. Besides altering the poems, the reader is expected to save her versions on a weblog and discuss on it via blogging.

In dealing with Poems in the middle of the road the reader is faced with different reading possibilities, depending on her navigational decisions. There are two available versions: the horizontal and the vertical. The horizontal version is a 3D panorama including video that the reader can drag; the vertical version uses html to allow the reader to read and play with the texts in a more conventional and simple way. This Torres piece could also be considered as the e-literary service that relates to the very act of reading under the new media condition. The user/reader is challenged with various possibilities, and they are expected to experience them within themselves as algorithm shaped procedures. Rather than taking a part in a semantic game of signifiers (basic components of e-literary text) the user/ reader is challenged to execute various algorithms and procedures relating to the very code that generates such a digital textuality with literary scripts. In short, the reader's reading is getting more and more of the not-just-reading (Strehovec, 2007), as a more corporeal and sophisticated activity that stimulates all the senses, and even provokes motor responses.

Such a user/reader's approach is based on the very nature of digital verbal contents that smoothly co-exist with non-verbal signifiers within the same cultural or artistic arrangements. They might be considered as platforms of relations articulated by signifiers of various origins. We should also not forget that the nature of contemporary reality is characterized by a sophisticated mosaic design, where interfaces shape events and produce memorable perceptions. The web site as a popular medium is an example of mosaic features in present contemporary culture: in today's culture, it has the same paradigmatic role that the MTV music video clip had in the 1980's. The web site (as a simple platform by which many e-literature pieces are accessed) demonstrates the non-conflictual co-existence of verbal and non-verbal contents, meaning that the visual (as the privileged feature in postmodern culture) ceases to be foregrounded on websites, at the expense of non-verbal signs.

2 NEW MEDIA ART AS RESEARCH: ART-MAKING BEYOND THE AUTONOMY OF ART AND AESTHETICS

This book considers electronic literature as a broad and diverse field of textual practice which calls into question the very nature of the letter, word, text, the lyrical, narrative, and the literary, all under the condition of new media. It does so by opening up new ways of textual organization (e.g. cinematic one), by reflecting on how software conditions our basic understanding of on-line textuality with literary scripts, by pointing to the changes caused through algorithmic culture, and by intervening in on-line processes of writing and reading which push aside the specificity of new media. We can address new media art as a practice, as another field of creativity in new media which—in similar vein to e-literature—calls into question the established canon, and which is weak in terms of institutions and marketing. In this chapter we aim to explore some of its basic features.

Due to its extreme diversity and plurality, art at the beginning of the new millennium undoubtedly represents a problem for philosophy and theory of art, cultural studies, and aesthetics, as well as for authors and audience. Much of the recent works set in the social contexts of art are no longer "works" in terms of artistic tradition, but rather are concepts, software projects, computer mediated situations, computer game patches and VR, or augmented reality installations. The works of art which count today are therefore often "would-be-works of art" which appear at the intersection of art, techno-science, technology, new media, social networking, design, politics, and lifestyle.

The abandoning of the institution and canon of traditional works of art, and the abandoning of the method of its creation is especially noticeable in the new genres of works which are formed in close connection with techno-sciences, technologies, and new media. Here we mean works of electronic art, notably in the genres of computer music, graphics and animation, holography, hyperfiction, interactive installations, interactive digital cinema and television, interactive drama, virtual reality as art, virtual architecture, net art, techno-performance, machine theater, locative art, tactical media, and computer game mods. Producers of these works often do not have (merely) an artistic training. Instead, they are scientists, programmers, activists, and technologists who possess knowledge and skills of new media. And their works are actually not artworks in the traditional sense but rather they are precisely "would-be-works of art" that are set in the social contexts of art. This setting means that institutions of art (viz. criticism, history and theory of art, aesthetics, museums and galleries, new media art communities) still consider them art-like even though they exist in a perhaps controversial form. However, major changes in art connected to the influence of science, technology, and new media by no means concern merely the visual arts and do not restrict themselves merely to art "hardware." We can observe the subtle influence exerted by the new media, especially through the organization of space and time. For example, in literature, specifically in Postmodern fiction, where the genres of musical video-spot, websites, and television serials have an "underground" influence. The organization of windows in hypertext even impacts the codes of print in book-space (for example, in Astro Teller's e-mail novel Exegesis and Irwine Welsh's short story The Acid House).

Questions that arise at this point include: how do we think of the fateful turns that today accompany the controversial features of artworks? How can we come closer to the works of art in through the medium of thinking? How is this possible in the case of works of art which are no longer works in the sense of tradition but rather would-be-works in the social contexts of art? How can we understand new artistic articulations, the exclusive generator of which is no longer the artist's imagination but which appears at the intersection of the artist's creativity, techno-science, smart technologies, new media, new mythologies, design, and even techno-lifestyle?

Starting with the introduction of historical avant-garde (a term coined by Peter Bürger), it was already the case that no activity other than the production of art could so uncompromisingly allow so many different, even subversive and transgressive, orientations and movements. Even attacks on the institution of art (in terms of critique, and subversive transition to a position of "counter-art") do not destroy art, but paradoxically supply it with new energy and strength (e. g. Duchamp's ready-mades). Looking at the greats of aesthetics and cultural theory shows us that these turns and paradigm shifts towards would-be-works of art were not overlooked. Let me remind you of the opening sentence in Aesthetic Theory by Adorno: "It is self evident that nothing concerning art is self-evident anymore, not its inner life, not its relation to the world, not even its right to exist" (1). It seems that this notion is a starting responsible for many contemporary artists and e-literati who begin their art-making right at the zero point—the non-self-evident-ness of art and e-literature in the present. Heidegger's The Principle of Reason offers this far-reaching claim:

> Strictly speaking, we may indeed be barely able, as we will see, to speak of objects any more. If we pay attention, we see that we already move in a world where there are no more objects [...] That in such an age art becomes objectless testifies to its historical appropriateness, and this above all when non-representational [gegendstandlose] art conceives of its own productions as no longer being able to be works, rather as being something for which the suitable word is lacking. (pp. 33-34)

Heidegger therefore lacked the expression for what I have referred to as would-be-art. And Walter Benjamin left us in suspense as well, even though he directed his attention towards the fatal change of the function of art in his essay "The Work of Art in the Age of Mechanical Reproduction":

> In the same way today, by the absolute emphasis on its exhibition value the work of art becomes a creation with entirely new functions, among which the one we are conscious of, the artistic function, later may be recognized as incidental. (34)

According to Benjamin the artistic function of works in the social places of art can in due time become incidental, and the same applies to the aesthetic function of work, for "in the hyper-aesthetic world of everyday life art, is no longer used for bringing beauty to the world. That was already done by designers of cities with the greatest success" (Welsh, 1996: 205). Art is thus itself a historical and therefore changeable phenomenon. It is no coincidence that in The Transparency of Evil, the sociologist Jean Baudrillard "profanely" applied Hegel's notion about the end of art to activities in modern art:

We see Art proliferating wherever we turn; talk about Art is increasing even more rapidly. But the soul of Art—Art as adventure, Art with its power of illusion, its capacity of negating reality [...] in this sense, Art is gone. Art has disappeared as a symbolic pact, as something thus clearly distinct from that pure and simple production of aesthetic values, that proliferation of signs ad infinitum. There are no more fundamental rules, no more criteria of judgement or of pleasure. In the aesthetic realm of today there is no longer any God to recognise his own. (14)

An interesting claim with respect to the philosophical problems of the end of art is found too in Barthes's The Pleasure of the Text: "Art seems compromised, historically, socially. Whence the effort on the part of the artist himself to destroy it" (408). And finally Hegel's statement on this issue: "For us art counts no longer as the highest mode in which truth fashions an existence for itself. We may well hope that art will always rise higher and come to perfection, but the form of art has ceased to be the supreme need of the spirit" (103). Rather than referring to the end of art in terms of its production and dissemination, Hegel addressed the end issue in terms of art's ability to fit the supreme demands of Absolute Spirit.

A common denominator of these notions is found in the changeable nature of the social function of art (Benjamin), the agony of its objective character (Heidegger), and even relativization of its existence (Hegel, Adorno, Barthes, Baudrillard). However Baudrillard, completely in the vein of Hegel's notion from his Lectures on Aesthetics, ascertains the disappearance of art only in the sense of something historically important, for, in the sense of a "profane" culture of postmodernism, a recycling of the recent art forms increases. Art is a problem, an enigma at the beginning of a new millennium. That is, it can no longer be considered to be a self-evident issue. Art today is not gone; it continues in different, even more extraordinary forms that often develop in symbiosis with developments in the theory of art. This emergent creative practice is articulated in would-be-works of art and placed at the intersection of art, techno-sciences, techno-lifestyle, new media, and social networking. It is set in a reality becoming more and more hyper-textual, simulated, techno-stimulated, "clickual," and playful.

At this point the question needs to be raised on the subject of would-be-works of art. Who is it? Where to find them? This is an individual who is balancing between real and virtual space, physical presence and tele-presence, who has a vulnerable physical body leaning between "actual" and cybernetic egos—meaning that they are actually already a multiple ego who performs in different places and worlds. This is an individual who lives in a world of continuous hybrid, synthetic, imagined, and fictional events among which it is harder and harder to decide and choose. The motto clara et distincta is diminishing into the fog of pixels on the media highway from which an individual manages to escape into individualized ecstasy stimulated by events of the techno paradigm. This is a person who weaves into their self-awareness, both the plot and closure of Borges's The Garden of Forking Paths, and who perceives the reality in the rhythm of cinematic fast cuts and MTV videos. Their home is at once roller-coaster simulator and ejection seat. And they are that individual who is, after all, in their core only a person with one final physical death and with obvious pain (physical and virtual), who is put in the web by means of multiple egos and would-be-existences. This individual will be looking for an event which will, just like a loamy pot that bears the traces of the fingers of an ancient potter, show the traces of their authentic existence. They will fight for a name, for the part of a name, for the pain and scrap of pain, for silence and their individualized part in it. This individual enjoys the creative uncertainty of their art-making, this risky and horrible ride into the maelstrom of actual and virtual events without any simply given solutions. And today they are rarely alone: instead of one creative individual caught into the techno-paradigm, there is a group or collective of authors; in fact, in terms of art-making institutions, Olga Goriunova has even developed an artistic platform.

TOWARD ART-MAKING BASED IN NEW MEDIA

New media (virtual reality, augmented reality, software, virtual architecture, hypertext, special effects, digital cinema, web, social networks, tactical media, computer games, mobile telephony, GPS...) contribute to the proliferation of new art genres and forms. Some of theses forms include net art, software art, generative art, locative art, hacktivism-oriented art projects, digital installations, computer games as art, techno-performance, e-literature, and virtual architecture, all of which challenge contemporary cultural studies and criticism, and pose questions on the very nature of such phenomena. While traditional and even modern arts generally attempt to hide their use of technology—the specificity of art-making technological devices does not enter the traditional art theory—new media-based projects place technology out in the open by highlighting the hardware and software components of their production (e.g. Flash art, Flash and javascript digital poetry). Such projects are less and less about making completed artifacts that are "kunstwerks" by nature, and more and more about processes, goal-oriented and problem-solving activities, activism, immaterial entities, relations, performances, software, research, and services.

In a very limited sense, the new media art is a part of contemporary art, understood as a broader field of artistic activity than so-called modern art defined by aesthetic modernism and its proclamation of the separation of the art field from the social and other parts of a given reality. The profound changes in the field of art-making are also the result of constant efforts of contemporary artists to define the field of their own quests and creations anew and time adequate. The new art is considered as a problem, an unsafe field, an enigma, but it has not vanished nor has it been abolished. In terms of quantity, there is more art than ever. For example: the Rhizome online Artbase alone includes more than 2100 new media art pieces! The only mistake is that we are often looking for it in the wrong places (in traditional places) and we still judge art as it is today by concepts and canons gained from experiencing art as-we-know-it, namely as an activity linked only to artifacts (such as book, statue, painting, and also symphony and film) and to certain site-specific institutions (galleries, museums, theatres, libraries, etc.).

Today we are coming across the new media art projects that occur at the intersection of contemporary art, networked economy, new politics or postpolitics (often beyond the state institution-driven), technoscience, and new lifestyles. New media art pieces are often only one click away from the Web-embedded sites and portals of political organizations, big corporations, and e-commerce, meaning that we are facing a different situation than what used to be common within the modernist paradigm based on differentiation of the artistic realm from the social. The very nature of art is being steadily interrogated and conceptualized anew, and the artistic nature of art is getting more and more instant, fluid, and temporary. In a similar fashion, one can talk today about the temporary art projects as entities that have artistic signification and justification for a very short period of time, as in Hakim Bey's term "temporary autonomous zone" (1985). Such projects spring up in a very limited time, but, given the different times and contexts, they can gain quite different signification and functions. They are multi-functional and their creators can, by means of their artistic training and experience, execute other projects, not strictly in art realm-based tasks (as demonstrated by net artists such as Vuk Cosic).

While traditional aesthetics begin by exploring the specificity of a work of art and its crucial features (form, genre, creativity, author, and aesthetic value), new media art theory finds the artwork itself to be a non-self-evident issue; it could be considered (as already mentioned) a would-be work of art. Rather than being a stable and aura-based object. It is a process, an artistic software, an experience, a service devoted to solving a particular cultural or non-cultural problem, a research, an interface—all of which also demands from its user the ability for associative selection, algorithmic (logical) thinking, and for procedures pertaining to DJ and VJ culture, such as (re)mixing, cutting, sampling, filtering and recombination.

Art has mutated. It has given up its "natural state" as a complete and stable work of art (artifact) and has lost its aesthetic feature. In terms of the "beautiful," such truly aesthetic objects and processes are much more common in fashion, sports, the jet set, commercials, pop music, computer games, and even politics than in most of contemporary art. The aesthetic in the sense of intensive sensual stimulation is much more common in theme parks and their attractions (e.g. roller coaster and Star Wars simulators, bungee jumping, water park adrenaline devices) than in art. Art's tradition-ally conceived functions in terms of representation, narrative, and aesthetic education have also been often left aside. The key question facing the art projects from the very beginning of the twenty-first century to today is no longer "What is art?" but "When is art?" Or, even more directly: "What conditions must be fulfilled that an event, a program, a process, or an ar-tificial world as a complex structure of relations begins to function as an artwork?" This shift and redirection also omits art's ontology as the first and decisive field of art theory and instead represents the transition towards art theory as a critical social and political theory of power institutions judging the art field and distributing power in it.

THE ART PROJECT AS PROCESS

In the field of net art, digital art, installations art, software art, locative art, virtual architecture, e-literature, new conceptual art, art activism, and tech-no-performances we face the art of would-be-works, absent works, process-es, net activism events, art worlds, artistic services, artistic software pieces, artistic digital games (patches), and locative art projects. The new media art formed by computer hardware and software brings forth various forms of digital arts, among which the most developed are net art and software art (e.g., art of artistic interventions into programming and scripting languag-es), all with a strong influence on this turn towards the fluent, the process, the non-material, the event, the conceptual, and the performative. For this kind of redirection and repurposing in the art field, it is undoubtedly char-acteristic that it omits traditional art's functions. Art pieces (these are in the present actually processes, actions, services, events, and programs) are as-sociated with the art-as-we-know-it merely by the corporate institution of art with its sense-defining and interpretative devices (art criticism, history, and theory) and by the reproductive and distributive artistic devices and networks. By this we mean art as an institutional umbrella embracing all possible phenomena in this area. Basically we are encountering extremely heterogeneous artistic contents, which are frequently completely non-artis-tic or even counter-artistic by their function. They are, however, declared as art by the authorization and justification of the institutions of art (e.g., museums, art criticism), which are created historically in the process of the differentiation of modern society.

However, in the current informational society (of Post-Fordist la-bour), the strict divide between the realm of arts and the social is at stake. The contemporary is faced with dedifferentiation as a process caused by the implosion of various modern socially separated fields. "The cultural realm is no longer 'auratic,' in Benjamin's sense; that is, it is no longer systemati-cally separated from the social" (Lasch 1990: 11). All the theoreticians of aesthetic art have insisted on the notion of a strict divide of the aesthetical from the social. The social "given'" reality is one, the realm of aesthetic art is something quite different—as has been the opening statement of any account on the social condition of modern art. In order to come closer to such a art vs. social reality problem, one could take into account Roman Ingarden's notion of anthropological and psychological aspects of such a divide, which implies that the reader possesses an ability for a very demanding and sophisticated switching between both fields. Entering the aesthetic art realm demands one's readiness for a very special, non-self-evident condition in the following terms:

> The appearance of the original emotion [i.e. as a starting point of aesthetic experience] in a person's stream of consciousness produces, above all, a certain check in the preceding "normal" course of experiences and modes of behavior in regard to the objects surrounding him in the real world. (Ingarden 1973: 191–2)

Since the break of the practical attitude caused with this check is very demanding in that it leads us far away from the conditions in which we normally are, in the same way the return to the normal conditions is demanding as well. Ingarden argues that "the return to the concerns of earlier life is often accompanied by discomfort, by a feeling of the pressing weight of life, from which the original aesthetic emotion had, to a certain extent, freed us" (Ingarden 1973: 193). Therefore Ingarden's final notion about the nature of such switching is not surprising: "The transition from the practical to the aesthetic attitude is perhaps the most thorough-going change in man's psychological attitude" (1973: 196).

Ingarden's notions can be perceived as extremely historical. They are bound to the time before new media-based interface culture became part of the most striking of today's art, when only rare situations, connected to art environments and encountering works of art, made the switch off from everyday reality which is possible based on the original aesthetic emotion. On the contrary, the readiness to work in different generations of reality, artificial worlds, and in hybrid times belongs to the current condition of a contemporary individual living and performing tasks in information society. She is constantly urged to switch among various modes of given and artificial realities and execute various modes of activities. It looks as if her horizon of expectations (Hans Robert Jauss's term from his aesthetics of reception) is used to meet the demands of participating in ontologically and technologically differently founded realities. Therefore the demands of entering synthetic spaces and times do not cause extra problems to such an individual. We are actually witnesses of a learned, routine readiness for such switching: the contemporary individual spends more and more time in hybrid (mixed and augmented) realities occurring in hybrid times and determined by the in-between mode.

When they are on-line, people constantly pass from one form of social activity to another. For instance, in one session, a Net user could first purchase some clothes from an e-commerce catalogue, then look for information about education services from the local council's site, and then contribute some thoughts to an on-going discussion on a list server for fiction-writers. Without even consciously having to think about it, this person would have successively been a consumer in a market, a citizen of a state, and an anarcho-communist within a gift economy (Barbrooke 2005).

Suddenly, various modes of realities and several forms of activities are at one's disposal; everything is on the move in a very smooth fashion, and is accessible as a standing reserve for possible manipulations as demonstrated by the Web's platform, which enables smooth moving and shifting among various websites by means of very simple navigational devices. The artists creating in such novel conditions are challenged with the radical questioning of the entire institution of art, and even with the broader dilemmas of creativity in terms of the contemporary social world, shaped by globalization, multiculturalism, the War on Terror, multitude, post-Fordist labor, and precarity. We are facing the condition where the only authentic art in the present is the one based on the extremely questionable, non-self-evident approach to its tasks and positioning within the social. Today, authentic contemporary new media artists challenge the entire institution of art with each of their projects: they do research, frame concepts, create new paradigms, and go to (and frequently beyond) the limits of their field. Today's institution of art is a challenging and advanced field because it takes under its umbrella all these various practices without difficulties; it even needs them, for its sense-defining (meaning-making) devices need these kinds of transgressions. Currently, artistic theory, critique, and history too often occur as the praxis of permanent revaluations and transgressions. They are even written in a form that anticipates future works and blurs the difference between fiction and facts. Arthur C. Danto, in considering the use of manifestos, touched upon this problem as follows: "as if the structure of the art world exactly consisted not in 'creating art again,' but in creating art explicitly for the purpose of knowing philosophically what art is?" (Danto 1997: 31).

BEYOND THE SACRED AND REPRESENTATIONAL FUNCTIONS OF ART

We have already mentioned that the traditional (or one could say "artistically aesthetic") function of a significant part of contemporary art (especially conceptual and new media) has become obsolete, or at least secondary. Today, to a very limited extent, traditional art takes part in production of cultural innovations, especially those establishing new cultural turns and paradigms. We can certainly agree with the following claim of Lev Manovich:

> Thus in my view this book is not just an anthology of new media but also the first example of a radically new history of modern culture— a view from the future when more people will recognize that the true cultural innovators of the last decades of the twentieth century were interface designers, computer game designers, music video directors, and DJs–rather than painters, filmmakers, or fiction writers whose fields remained relatively stable during this historical period. (Manovich 2003: 16)

This was written in his introduction to the New Media Reader, where computer scientists and technologists are proclaimed to be important artists of our era and new media technologies are considered to be the greatest present-day works of art. Is Manovich right? Is it questionable to declare all great innovations in the field of software works of art without any thorough reconsideration? However, if we think of the demands of cultural innovation, we can agree with Manovich. The mainstream culture of the last two decades is far less defined by contributions of traditionally-oriented artists than by profound changes in the field of communication, design, and perception brought about by theorists, engineers, and experts from the field of new media technologies and software, as well as scientists that created concepts for the new scientific picture of the world.

In this period, writers, poets, painters, and musicians working in the acknowledged, traditional art genres and media have somehow fallen asleep. On the other hand, artists who instantly started seeking artistic connections to new media technologies and started designing new genres and forms of the new media art—such as interactive installations, communication art, VR as art, as well as patches of computer games, electronic poetry, hyperfiction, software art, and net art—are praised as important cultural and artistic innovators.

So we ask ourselves: What is the new key function of contemporary art, and, above all, of art integrated with new media technologies? What is it that comes to the fore and makes traditional art's functions less important or even unimportant? Which are authentic places of today's art? Where must we look for works defining and expressing the new art's function?

Answering these questions makes us aware of the limitations deriving from generalization and introduction of stricter definitions. Both sharp and perfectly clear forms, on the one hand, and hard and fast lines, on the other, are rare among the fields, and, frequently, there are no ideal types—only a co-existence within in-between spaces of hybrid and mixed realities. We actually live in a culture of mixes, recombining, sampling, rapprochements, hybrid forms, in-between spaces, side-by-side integrations of separated fields, and repurposing of state-of-the-art technological platforms. The new functions of today's art, which we are trying to determine, are by no means ideal types. We would also be pretending by declaring them to be final and unchanging. However, by taking into consideration several events in the field of contemporary art—especially art integrated with new media—we can take a chance and expose research as a crucial function for understanding new media art paradigms.

Walter Benjamin's claimed traditional art emphasized cult value (it was based on a ritual). By contrast, in modern art the emphasis is on its exhibit value (Benjamin 1969), which can be complemented with a notion that the emphasis of the contemporary art—thus art integrated with new media technologies—lies on its research value. What do we talk about when we bring to the fore research value and research functions of art projects (actions, performances, and events)? First of all, we foreground a post-object new media artistic practice (which is to a certain extent influenced by molecular biology, informatics, robotics, communication sciences, networked economy, post-political politics, activism etc.) devoted to publicly accessed critical science and opposed to the official science, i.e. that executed just by means of professional scientists. The idea of public science is based on efforts of some artists or groups (e.g. Critical Art Ensemble) who "contribute to making the meaning of scientific initiatives immediate and concrete, as opposed to the vague abstractions they tend to be" (Critical Art Ensemble 2003: 135). Therefore, art is a research in order to show that research could be ordered and executed otherwise, not just within a frame of official science. Facing artistic research practices one can even find that they pioneer in a field, which currently considered to be "action research," i.e. a kind of novel, problem-centered, client-centered, and action-oriented activity. It involves the client system in a diagnostic, active-learning, problem-finding, and problem-solving process.

While traditional art theory has introduced concepts like form, content, creativity, author, style, genre etc., new media art scholarship and criticism has foregrounded theoretical devices like activism, hybridization, recombination, (re)mixing, artistic platform, repurposing, and researching. Even artists themselves are getting more and more familiar in their statements with the expressions like research or researching. Instead of forming and creating (from scratch) they find researching to be a proper term devoted to intrinsic description of their activity shaped within new-media conditions. Digital literature writer Mark Amerika argues that

> with FILMTEXT I take this surf-sample-manipulate research practice right into the belly of the beast, interfacing Hollywood with hypertext, video games with literary rhetoric, interactive cinema with image écriture. (Amerika 2004: 9)

FILMTEXT demonstrates that text-making in terms of new media paradigms is surf-sample-manipulate research practice. Rather than being an artist or author (written with capital letter), the textscape producer could be defined as a new media researcher dealing with issues of new media words and language.

The Slovenian art and activism inspired group KITCH officially titled itself as an Institute of Art Production and Research KITCH Ljubljana, meaning that both fields of art and research fit well together under the current condition. In the opening words of KITCH's statement, referring to its most current project "Permanent Waiting Room," one encounters the research in the following way:

> The art installation Permanent Waiting Room is an artistic conceptualization of a research process developed during a period of twenty months. It artistically disseminates theoretical statements of the project and contributes to the creative popularization and widening its basic idea among a wider public. (KITCH 2008)

This activism-oriented piece is about the fate of emigrants within the European Union, and its key idea is that the world is flat when it comes to money, capital flows, goods, and agents of globalization, but it is getting more and more closed and restricted for the people at the margins, i.e. the immigrants, the asylum applicants, and the inhabitants of those parts of the developing world that are blamed as the axe of evil.

Research is a crucial function of contemporary art, but it is by no means the only function of such art that is interesting to contemporary curators, critics, and scholarship. Beyond this function we meet several other functions, associated with contemporary art's heterogeneous nature and to the fact that its space is actually an event space, within which interactions between scientific, technical, political, and conceptual contents run. This

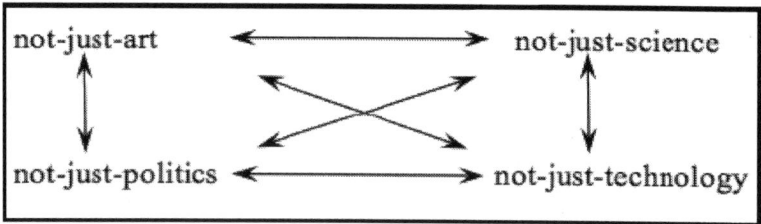

event space is about a play of the scientific, the artistic, the technical, the political, and the conceptual, including various shifts and transformations of its own constitutive links. The scientific, the technical, and the political are de-realized in social place of art; they take a role of the spectacle (new technologies, for example) or they are integrated with the fictive (science, when generating and trying out various models), while the artistic and the conceptual are realized to some extent in the social spaces. They receive realistic predicates; they take part in the process of debunking the purely fictive. Technoscience, new media technology, design, new economy (e-commerce), and politics are being redirected towards art, while art and the field of the conceptual begin to point towards a debunked reality. Ethical correctives and questionings become even more important than pure aesthetic features as is argued in Paul Virilio's book **Art and Fear** (2003).

The key issue regarding such art is how and under what conditions do we give art-like features to such interactions-processes-events-situations-installations? How do they actually differ from non-artistic processes? The question of form, which was dominant in traditional art (for form is an instance preventing empirical elements from intruding into artwork infiltrated and unprepared), has now become secondary or even redundant. The question of organization of components and context is of greater importance.

All kinds of elements taken out of technoscience, politics (activism, hacktivism),design, new economy, and lifestyles—which as such act dispersed, inconsistent, and arbitrary—meet in installations and artistic events as art worlds. At first glance these elements implicate relations and links that are as far away from artistic connections as possible. But in art, these components tread into tensile and compact relation with each other, arranged in a way to produce a whole being that is more than just a sum of its component parts. What is essential in such projects placed within in-between spaces is the question of relational organization, in other words: how to organize the components with regard to time and space syntax; how to repurpose the technological and media platform in a way that contributes to art-shaped findings; when to place or exhibit such projects; and finally, which function, depending on the situation, to set up into the dialogic relation with the research function—the dominant function of the art project as process, program, or experience. Other important functions are also density, energetic features, relations, and—observed from the viewer standpoint—participation. Therefore, the significance of such art projects-processes-performances is in relations and complex structures rather than in the transparency of their elements. The artist (or collective artists) always arranges a dry run of interactions which would take too long and would be too complicated in the non-artistic reality; in the artistic environments, however, they can function in a very fluid and even crystal clear form. It seems that a piece or process of art, conceived as an art world, establishes clear space for the articulation of pure laboratory and even archetypal interactions.

THE REALITY OF NEW ECONOMY, TECHNOSCIENCE, AND (POST) POLITICS

Although the (social) system of art—especially in its autonomous development in the nineteenth and twentieth century—is explicitly autopoeitic and self-referential, contemporary art seems to be a self-feeding machine which needs to reinvent itself with each movement and new genre, in fact such noticeable turns in contemporary art are possible in the presence of profound and essential shifts arising in other fields as well. Reality itself has mutated, too: it has passed through noticeable turns and shifts of paradigms, and nowadays we find that traditional concepts and devices for its understanding have become useless, even obsolete. All its important components are part of a new constellation defined by bio-politics, post-political politics, technosciences, globalization, multiculturalism, new empires, fatal social segregations, and new lifestyles. The solo play of the contemporary art would not be possible today if the "prime" (given) reality components and forces did not undergo such transformations. Technological and political processes occurred in the fields of science that lead towards an art-like nature of these fields and a destabilization and relativization of traditional forms. One could say this parallels the destabilization of artifacts in today's art and destabilizations of national state in the globalized (trans)politics, and the material wealth in (new) economics, and the project of discovering natural laws in technosciences.

Today we are witnessing the mutation of contemporary science as well. It has abandoned the project of revealing natural laws in terms of scientific decoding of nature's open book. By this we mean nature as representing the objectivity of a natural world as a stable given reality, based on inherent order, and that can be exactly observed, measured, and interpreted by means of information-based on empirical observations. At this point, consider Paul Feyerabend's claim from his essay The Nature as Work of Art (Die Natur als ein Kunstwerk), where he writes "nature is a work of art designed by generations of artists, who are considered as scientists today"(Feyerabend 1993: 278). We are dealing with a notion that makes a certain concept of objective nature, sustained in the traditional natural science, as relative and historic, for "what we find when researching nature [...] is not nature alone, but the way that nature responds to our efforts." (Feyerabend 1993: 286) Also the world of scientific research is on the move. In place of the profound specialization so prevalent within the modern science of twentieth century, there is a novel emphasis on the need to have creative work across the boundaries, disciplines and the "two cultures" divide.

Contemporary social reality is also defined by the a economy based on e-business globalization, networking, flexible Post-Fordist production, services, and information technologies. In the USA approximately four-fifths of employees no longer produce things. They are employed in professions requiring moving of things, handling or producing of information, and other intellectual services. Because the new economy is based on intangible capital, global smooth space transactions, close connections to the stock exchange and e-business (e-enterprises as Cisco Systems, Yahoo, Google, Amazon, etc.), and the "networked business model" (Castells 2002: 68), the stress is shifting from material wealth towards intangible, immaterial wealth (the latter grows faster within stock exchange processes than the material one), and towards intellectual services, among which can also be found art. Abandonment of the value of material production in the new economy and its devaluation and shift towards (intellectual) labor and services coincide with the frequently mentioned tendency accompanying contemporary art: the shift from a complete artifact to an artistic service. Various parallels can be drawn between the two fields today: the art (sub)system too frequently works as a stock exchange; it is faced with rapid evaluations of certain works and steep slumps of their value, meaning that it is no longer possible to explain anything in both fields by means of common sense. The shift from artwork as artifact to art service, which is as customized and oriented towards knowledge production as possible, reasonably connects both fields. Just as an example, we can mention that the stock exchange, e-business, trade marks, multinational corporations, etc., are also becoming a motif and topic of various artistic projects. Many contemporary artists have used various e-commerce strategies in order to form projects that are in their core critical to the capitalistic way of production and consumption. One among them is Michael Goldberg's "Catching a Falling Knife," which took place in Artspace, Sydney, between the October 17 and November 9, 2002. This field was also pioneering with net artists (e.g. Etoy and RTMark).

It is essential for today's reality, undoubtedly defined and articulated by the profoundly changed politics following the emptiness existing since Ground Zero of September 11, 2001. The globalization processes, based on new information technologies, multiculturalism, postcolonialism, and new colonialism, have significantly shaken up the basic concepts of politics and influence (the power of so-called parliamentary democracies) bound to the national state. In the world of different temporalities, i.e. temporalities in plural, we witness the coexistence of liberal forms of democracy, tied to capitalism, and the most extreme forms of nationalism, tribalism, and fundamentalism, which, even at the beginning of the twenty-first century, re-actualize forms of ethnic cleansing and ritual killings of their political opponents. If we draw a parallel with the art field again, the most crucial shift is absolutely connected to destabilization of national state in contemporary politics, for many decisions of international organizations (with no democratic mechanisms of control), multinational corporations, and the new and only leading world superpower, have much more far-reaching consequences for the everyday life of the citizens (and for shaping of their needs) than resolutions and decisions of their parliaments and other "democratic" institutions. Facing the issue of multitudes and the new political subjects in the present world of post-Fordist labor, Paolo Virno has introduced the term "post-political politics," which refers to various political activities beyond the state and its decision-making mechanism.

That is why in the milieu of such social turns, new political subjects come to the fore, which can even take over positions of traditional institutions of civilian disobedience. One of them is certainly activism, also carried out by some artistic groups (the Radical Software Group for example), especially those cooperating with technical experts in the field of new media, among which hackers are most important. Hacktivism, the term combining activities of hackers and political activists, is based on electronic civil disobedience (e.g. Hakim Bey, Critical Art Ensemble), and is practiced by those that believe that traditional social institutions are more vulnerable in their cyberspace forms than in their traditional representations bound to the physical world. The way hacktivists work is that hackers deliver weapons, while activists locate the targets against which the weapons are to be used. At this point let us mention actions directed towards blocking the servers of the opponent institutions, with what is clearly a unique cast, i.e. the so-called virtual sit-ins (e.g. SWARM action on behalf of the Zapatistas by means of Java script program Floodnet, produced by the Electronic Disturbance Theatre, 1998).

Today's art is by no means a simple derivative of a given reality; rather, both fields are in complex interactions with each other. Several processes and shifts of paradigm can be expressed with economic and political concepts. We can also discover qualities that can be explained on the basis of turns, which have already defined the contemporary art in the field of technoscience, new politics and new economy. Technoscience and new economy are becoming "artistic" to a certain degree, they reveal and represent less, and present more; they are to understood through the shift from mimesis to poiesis. And that is the reason why they can enter into creative interactions with contemporary (especially digital and Internet) art, which brings certain scientific and economic concepts forth, while art's traditional functions, especially aesthetic ones, inevitably sink into decline. In the present hybrid, augmented and mixed reality as a plural reality, based on interactions between given reality and artificial ones, the very function of art ceases to be a creation of fictional and aesthetic realities within reality.

Today we witness the interactions of "scientific art" and artistic technosciences, technologies as culture, and new forms of politics. Matthew Fuller coined the term "not-just-art" in reference to alternative browser Webstalker (1998). This seems the proper term for naming the nature of the contemporary art-of-in-between spaces with its would-be-artworks. Its "not-just" could be applied also in other fields. "Techno-science," which refers to other-than-science, could be called "not-just-science," and very similarly, terms like "not-just-technology," and "not-just-politics" could be introduced as well. The basic interactions in the area that enable art as research, technology as art and culture, and both artistic politics and artistic "techno-science" can be expressed with the following scheme:

Contemporary technosciences as a kind of artistic "soft sciences" are in dialogue with art, which consciously has given up the aesthetic (embellished, cosmetic) function and its role in hiding behind the social irresponsibility. Art has ceased to be placed beyond practice and everyday tasks, meaning it is becoming more and more lifelike, even in the sense as it has been defined by the performance artist Allan Kaprow by its opposition to "artlike art" (Kaprow 1993: 201).

THE HYBRID USER AS RESEARCHER

This is actually contemporary art returning from aesthetic would-be reality to the given, and by new media constructed and interpreted, event-driven reality, returning to reality (from the ontological point of view, it is a hybrid, mixed and augmented one) in which day by day everything is getting more and more real. As the field of the fictive is on the increase everywhere (even in technosciences, economy, advertisement, politics), as the logic of theme parks more and more infects the everyday life, contemporary art has started to deal with the "real" reality. Thus it started to develop a unique artistically-theoretical approach. Contemporary art projects produced in the traditional or new media (and therefore unstable) form are nowadays merely a part of a wider process of new knowledge, which means they take part in a broader stream of simultaneous theoretic production of cultural values in a sense that "research has become a center of cultural innovation: its results are radically influencing life and thought" (Wilson 2002: 3).

Contemporary, new media-based are projects deliver—when it is a matter of up-to-date issues of globalization and multiculturalism, surveillance, human rights, and personal data protection—new and entirely competent knowledge presented as an artistic surplus, which is complementary to the knowledge produced by natural science, humanities, and social sciences. We encounter issues of surveillance by taking into consideration contributions of social theory to this field, but our knowledge about this topic can be enriched also by artistic concepts of this issue in the form of artist actions and hacktivism and net art events. If contemporaries do not encounter and perceive some of the new media art projects they will know too little and only in abstract form; they can even overlook specific problems. This viewpoint can be expressed even more radically: we believe that today many difficulties regarding the issues of nation-state destabilization within globalization will fall away in the globalized political scene if politicians were adequately informed about the agony of the "state" in the field of art, notably the destabilization of artwork as artifact. Their view point would change if they considered the unique story of contemporary art, for example: Marcel Duchamp's intervention in the field by publicly exhibiting everyday artifacts as works of art.

These novel art practices (we can follow them in the performance art, in the genre of objects and installations, in activist based processes, and especially in net art) are creating new and changed demands for its audience. The user of this art is not affected only by multimedia and software requirements of new art, changing her into an uncertain and hybrid reader-viewer-listener. Her attitude is also defined by demands deriving from the complex concept of contemporary art and reality outside the art. Having only an aesthetic standpoint and thus the capability to switch to art-as-we-know-it mode is by no means enough. It is necessary to have the capability to smoothly switch to "given" reality and to perceive it in its entire complexity.

The traditional art receiver/observer, accustomed only to the aesthetic standpoint, is forced to suddenly take into account a broader field of mind and meaning. She has to adjust herself to demands of sophisticated interpretation. She has to shift from the beautiful appearance to concepts, issues of Zeitgeist and reality problems, from which contemporary art of the twenty-first century has been redrawn into the direction of forms of fascination and the drive of constant reproduction of the new. The user of contemporary art is therefore challenged to take part in an educational process and even to do interdisciplinary research. They need to know, understand, and perceive a lot to be able to understand such works, which usually do not give up only the fascination with new technologies but with technosciences, new economy, and new media communication as well. They always strive for a "more"—a surplus—and, why not, for a "less." They are directed towards the art's research function in the sense that contemporary art projects-processes-events give the users more time and space and wider semantic field for their answers. The user's activity frequently requires interpretation of already finished path in the direction of comprehended-experienced work of art. They draws sketches, schemas, and notes of already performed links, motion direction of certain objects-messages in their interactions during observing-reading-listening. They also need to perceive such a work more than only once. Her participation is often based on goal-oriented and decision-making activities.

The connection of contemporary art to the processes of new knowledge making and the necessity of a certain pre-knowledge for understanding of art projects-events-processes are expressed also in the importance of artist's statements for correct understanding of contemporary artworks. It seems that today's artists are literally forced to restore not only their work but also their author explication and interpretation of (exhibited or put on the Internet) the work of art. We can also notice that today visitors of contemporary art exhibitions and (multimedia) performances, even before viewing the work of art, read artist's statement. They are convinced that merely on the basis of their "naïve" viewing, they would know too little of the work of art, if they had not reached for its theoretic explication, meaning that with new media art, to the same extent as one's sensitivity, is also addressed her pure mind.

Art today is a highly contested, questioned, and politicized field—a field that has mutated. We are witnesses of great changes painful and shocking to the traditionalists. Although the world stage is weakening under the weight of old scenery, the play on it is irrevocably a new one. Life in the milieu of smart machines and on the basis of Internet communications (social networking) has irrevocably infected not only everyday life but our ways of thinking and perceiving as well. Procedures such as mixing, sampling, shortcutting into the databases, and compositing of elements into new wholes regarding the daring associations, in other words an activity characteristic for DJs in their procedures of synthetic music and VJs in making their visual palimpsests, is entering the everyday life where every individual frequently tries to follow the algorithm-program logic in order to perform certain tasks successfully (in playing computer games for instance). The logic of smart machines is getting under our skin and influences the way we think, communicate, and design. Even code languages for machines are being more and more integrated into the netspeak (as the language of the online communications).

NEW MEDIA ART AS A SERVICE-LIKE ACTIVITY

In this section we question the unstable nature of today's art processes and manifestations by stressing profound changes, both in the very nature of the art (a shift towards the research function of new media art and would-be-works of art), as well as in the recent world as it is defined by new political conditions, new (networked) economy, technosciences, and techno-lifestyle. The shift from industrial production and manufacturing artifacts to the service sector in the economy of post-industrial societies also affects contemporary art. Its social position also benefits from other shifts in contemporary societies (post-industrial, information, spectacle, event-driven, breaking news-driven and software). An example would be the increasing stress placed on knowledge, research, innovation, education, use of new technologies, communication, and spectacle. We are entering a world in which data and intangible, abstract entities, immaterial products and services, mobility, flexibility, decentralization, rhizome-like order of organization, and high-level professionalism are gaining importance. We have already mentioned that the role of the national state is at stake in the globalized networking-based politics, more and more affected by the multinational capital and international institutions, and similar shifts can be observed in science (destabilization and relativization of the concept of subject-independent nature, i.e. objective nature, natural laws and objective truth) and in new economy (the shift from the tangible wealth towards services and information).

Rather than being a production that objectifies itself into a material finished" product, the art-making embedded in a new condition of immaterial labor finds its own purpose in problem-solving and research activities, which bring something into the world that is not there: an alternative mode of knowledge coded in a way that discerns itself from the common scientific methods. Such activities are embedded in a present condition of post-Fordist labor and in a realm of immaterial production that privileges the intellectual and innovation-based services at the expense of finished material artifact. Paolo Virno, as a theoretician dealing with the new mode of intellectual labor, refers rightly to the artistic performance as an activity, which becomes the quintessence of the present labour in general:

> Let us consider carefully what defines the activity of virtuosos, of performing artists. First of all, theirs is an activity which finds its own fulfilment (that is, its own purpose) in itself, without objectifying itself into an end product, without settling into a "finished product," or into an object which would survive the performance. Secondly, it is an activity which requires the presence of others, which exists only in the presence of an audience. (Virno 2004: 52)

New media art is also more and more about processes, immaterial entities, relations, performances, software, goal-oriented and problem-solving activities, and services. We then encounter art that increasingly exceeds the manufacturing of artifacts and is crossing over to a field that can be called a service of art. Service of art is defined as a part of contemporary art (especially new media) that is crossing into the service sector of the (new) economy in a post-industrial, information, spectacle and software-society. Its services are—in terms of social justification—equal to those in the field of education, management, counselling, finance, politics, etc. They are then equal to the activities based on knowledge and professionalism and are as flexible as possible.

Contemporary art, especially new media as a service of art, directs us to the question, "what is a service?" It is by no means an artifact, a completed product, but it is essentially an activity, a praxis, a process, an exploration, and an intervention (inside things, states or processes). The service is not so much the manufacturing of things as it is a process of reshaping the thing, moving it, repurposing it, connecting it, and incorporating it into new relations, (re)combinations, and contexts. The service presupposes a problem, a challenge, or an order to be solved or executed. The performer of the service is always faced with a certain task and challenged to solve it in a sequence of steps chosen as economically as possible. The service therefore ends with a solution to the problem, or its removal, and not the manufacturing of an object.

The service always presupposes a procedure that has to be as rational as possible, economical, and divided into phases, steps, and the operational commands needed for it to be carried out. This kind of procedure—an exactly defined, planned procedure, executed through an economical sequence of steps—is called an algorithm. The algorithm has for quite some time no longer been an exclusive domain of the mathematical operations, it is the core of all sophisticatedly defined processes intended for performing certain tasks, solving problems, researching the state of things, etc. It would not be an exaggeration to say that artistic services are algorithmic by nature: the moment art begins to position itself beyond the aesthetic and becomes oriented towards tasks, research, and problem solving, it is forced to carefully elaborate the procedures and to define the instructions to be carried out in order to get to the solution quickly through economical phases. Those artistic services based on the use of computer technologies, intended for algorithmic functions, are especially, and explicitly, algorithmic.

A lot of new media art projects can thus be understood as interventions and services within different states of things. They have an algorithmic nature and are often stimulated by non-artistic motives—for example with regard to political, research, and communication needs and interests. An example of such a shift towards research based art, is the project-service "Free Range Grain" (2003) by Critical Art Ensemble, Beatriz da Costa and Shyh-shiun Shyu. This project took place in Schirn Kunsthalle Frankfurt, Germany, as part of the art show "At Your Own Risk," and was organized as a live, performative action placed in a portable, public lab devoted to test foods for the more common genetic modifications. People (the art show visitors, the audience) bring to the museum foods that they find suspect for whatever reason. The artists-researchers then test them over a 72-hour period to see if their suspicions are justified. The authors of this project claim, that "within a very brief period of time, anyone who is modestly literate can learn the fundamentals of scientific study and ethics" (Critical Art Ensemble 2002). As a result, even non-scientists could use highly advanced technologies and apply them in a public, democratic research.

Art understood as a goal-oriented activity constitutes the artist as the performer or executor of the artwork, but at the same time the artwork often includes the person who had placed the order for it, or at least the person who had initiated it. An example of this is the contemporary curators and art directors of big festivals and exhibitions, who—along with the "'Call for Entries"—often also define a theme to which the artists are supposed to respond with their practices. For example, at the 2002 CODeDOC project[8] at the Whitney museum in the USA, the curator Christiane Paul issued a call for software tenders, dependent upon an exactly defined order. The participating artists were prescribed the choice of programming and scripting languages. The code had to move and had to connect three points in space, could not exceed 8 KB, and had to be interpretative. The transfer from the artifact to the service of art and the artist as the one who executes the service (the service depends on certain instructions, software, and algorithmic approach) is also on its way to abandon the metaphysics of artistic creativity and genius. The artist is the one who executes service, performs certain tasks, solves problems, does research, defines commands, executes algorithms, and does not wait for the divine inspiration to come upon her.

The artistic service actually moves art closer to the new (networked) economy, that has customization as adaptation of the service to the user's preferences as one of its key concepts. The power to control, to navigate, to form, and to finalize that in the traditional paradigm belonged exclusively to the author, but is now also being transferred to the user. The term "user friendly," although worn out and trivialized, does have a certain content. It is, by no means, solely the artifact that is customized—it can apply to the service as well. A software artist can, for example, create a program as an open—as much as possible—scheme to be concretized and finalized by the users, according to their personal preferences. We are facing the condition as it was far-reachingly described by the musician Brian Eno in his interview with Kevin Kelly:

> What people are going to be selling more of in the future is not pieces of music, but system by which people can customize listening experiences for themselves. Change some of the parameters and see what you get. So, in that sense, musicians would be offering unfinished pieces of music—pieces of raw material, but highly

---

8 Christiane Paul, "CODeDOC," Whitney Artport, August 2002,http://artport.whitney. org/commissions/codedoc/

evolved raw material, that has a strong flavor to it already. I can also feel something evolving on the cusp between "music," "game," and "demonstration"—I imagine a musical experience equivalent to watching John Conway's computer game of Life or playing SimEarth, for example. (Kelly 1995)

Introducing lifelike art (Allan Kaprow's term) as service (intervention, open system, experience, research, communication...) also means the abolishment of the European modernism-based concept of art autonomy. It challenges the basic western art canon, by demanding that art be fully separated from the everyday reality and practical purposes. Such a turn also presupposes a broader art inclusion in everydayness, which appears to also be interesting and significant for other fields and disciplines. Today we are observing that the technosciences, design, social gathering, clubbing, and fashion are becoming more and more challenged by social functions, procedures, and interventions of contemporary art. As a striking and even intriguing example, genetics can be mentioned as a new discipline striving to gain artlike autonomy as it used to be applied within modernism. These efforts towards art like "licentia poetica" being a value in the field of science are provoked by surveillance strategies, pertaining to the genetics field, as they are executed by institutions of politics, media, and public morals.[9]

Defining new media art in terms of post-industrial service means that traditional artistic autonomy is left behind (together with its participation on the realm of aesthetic values), while other features and functions gain in importance. What counts, within this novel condition of art integrated with the broader field of the cybersocial and networked economy, is the capability of art for linking, creative participation, and doing research

---

9 One example of an art exhibition devoted to the topic of surveillance is the Open_Source_Art_Hack show in New Museum of Contemporary Art, N.Y. 2002. Hacking practices, open source ethics, and cultural production were explored in an interactive group exhibition of artists who openly undermined the programming of everyday software tools. "Open_Source_Art_Hack" featured a performance and walking tours by the Surveillance Camera Players; an installation by Knowbotic Research; a Free Radio Linux broadcast by radioqualia; a data body cloning project by LAN; a video by Harun Farocki; an anti-war game by Future Farmers' Josh On; a packet-sniffing application by RSG; an "ad-busting" project by Cue P. Doll; and, a streaming media workshop with Superflex and Tenantspin

together with the non-artistic subjects and organizations. Within such a novel condition, a question is raised: could the artist produce projects that contain both pieces considered to be art and commercial products with non-artistic use value? By considering art as (post-industrial) knowledge based service, art-making is actually challenged to produce pieces/works/projects that simultaneously participate an artistic realm and in other fields (e.g. politics, social, economy), meaning that they abandon the traditional notion of art's pure autonomy. Furthermore, current practices in contemporary art demonstrate that such a boundary-blurring platform foregrounds novel art-making, which is directed to not-just-art pieces.

Machiko Kusahara's (2008) most recent paper refers to Japanese artists involved in the process of making the so-called device art, which means that the device, designed in a playful fashion, becomes the essential content of the art piece, enabling it to be launched as a commercial product free of special maintenance. Device art can be sold both as art and as a device shaped for practical purposes. It gains practical use value or "device value." Such art could be placed beyond the limited context of museums and galleries, and presupposes artist's involvement in broader fields such as entertainment, design, and commercial production. It is based on artist's positive attitude to state-of-the-art technologies as the key foundation of new media art.

A very challenging approach to the current art versus economy problem is also found in the practice of Electroboutique founded by Alexei Shulgin and Aristarkh Chernyshev: both a laboratory for studying new strategies in art and a gallery-slash-gadget shop selling distorting screens and other high-tech toys (2005). Their new practice is called CritiPop due to a critical attitude to blurring art versus economy boundary issue. Such a commercial protest seems to be realpolitics in the today's social condition. Contemporary artists are challenged to make product that would fit well to both the realm of art and the economy (meaning it can be sold). Rather than dealing with modern art's big ontological (and ideological) problems of the human, the new media artists find their essential tasks in establishing the innovative and creative relationship to the market even in terms of inventing their own economy.

We wanted to create media works that were plug-and-play and zero-maintenance. Furthermore, we wanted to distance ourselves from media activism, which had hit a dead end. Since art equals consumption in the conditions of the unipolar capitalist world, we decided to make a commercial object. We put protest and critique in its body. That's how we arrived at our style, which we called commercial protest. Then we added exciting shapes and sound. And that's how we got CritiPop. (Droitcour 2008)

In the moment when the art (on the Web or beyond it) is just click or two away from the commercial, political, and social, artists are urged to reinvent their very personal and temporal tactics, even in terms of a kind survival kit, referring both to the institution of art and their individual existence.

Janez Strehovec

3 THE CLOSENESS THAT GROWS TOWARD THE USER

I n the present, we are witnessing a significant transformation in contemporary arts and textuality shaped by new media, perhaps as significant and profound as the transformation from traditional art to modern art. The diversification and plurality of art forms as well as their ontological status has undoubtedly presented a problem for philosophies of art, art theory, criticism, cultural studies, and aesthetics. In the previous chapter we saw that the vast majority of works and would-be-works that count today are no longer works in the mode of stable (material) artifacts. Instead, they come to us in the form of concepts, interactive net projects, computer-mediated installations, e-literary projects, tactical media, and techno-performances.

How can we come to an understanding of these works of art and e-literature (in previous chapters considered as services of art) and the radical turns (paradigm shifts) which brought them into being, and—at the same time—come to an understanding of the individual and her experience at the end of the millennium? How can we come closer to these projects, whose extreme forms and articulations profoundly impact our understanding of traditional works of art and, more poignantly, the institution of art today? It seems that these art projects could even be understood as a kind of dry run for new ways of perception, orientation, and sensitivity. Above all, these projects should be seen as a new means of communication in the world: a communication guided by techno-experience.

It is becoming increasingly difficult to find a common denominator for works of art that are set beyond art-as-we-know-it (e.g., beyond the book, beyond flat paintings, beyond the stage...), i.e. as projects turned toward expanded concepts of creativity within artistic institutions that take into account such issues as politics, lifestyles, net activism, alternative modes of communication, new media, techno-sciences, and even alternative forms of the social. We can approach the particularities of these projects only by recognizing the main features of the world that they thrive in, and by analyzing the crucial shifts which have shaped their aesthetics.

The paradigm of technoculture is crucial for the basic understanding of new media art and e-literature addressed in this chapter. Both fields owe their specificity to the recent advances of technical and new media features: they are a part of a broader complex of technoculture which rely on "techno" as a key principle. What is the meaning of this unusual denotation? "Techno" is not only a form of house and dance music, which developed from Acid House and Detroit Techno at the end of the eighties in the 20th century. In addition, it is a term used to indicate a new paradigm in the world under the sign of the artificial and shaped by new media experience. Specifically, the techno describes a massive shift from the natural to the artificial which is gaining advantage over what we have, up until now, accepted as our natural, given reality. The techno principle involves the following fundamental concepts: augmented reality (in terms of a given, "real" reality, and artificial realities coexisting in an interdependent complex relationship); the world as a pluriversum of the given world and artificial worlds; an interaction between Apollonian and Dionysian; the coexistence of the principles of order and ecstasy; mix as an ontological principle in the forming of synth realities (DJ as proto-artist and proto-designer); second-order artificiality (i.e. an artificial state between living and non-living); life-as-it-could-be on non-organic hardware; technology as culture, technology as politics, and technology as religion; augmented concepts of the person (multiple-egos, avatars); a transition from the mechanic to the bio; techno-science as a creative, artistic science; scientists as the creators (in terms of the techno-artist, his/her work might be considered as a totally scientific work of art and a total work of science); augmented and accelerated, techno-formed experience (enabled with the synth-senses formed by means of smart technologies); and cybernetics, especially second-order cybernetics, as establishing founding principles for the world of the artificial.

What are some of the main features of works of art created within the "techno" paradigm that, when comparing them to traditional works of art, allow them to be categorized as would-be-works of art which capture our attention and cause us to make a number of changes concerning perception and sensitivity? First of all, let us state some of the key concepts that have been introduced to us—concepts which determine the aesthetics of new media art: interactivity, tactility, immersion, and total-data-work of art

(Gesamtdatenwerk), participatory digital media, non-trivial reception, "ludic" (i.e. game-like) interactive environments, and time-based digital works of art. We should emphasize that new media arts are, by their nature, time-based and at their foundation occur in terms of an event (Massumi, 2011). Because, within the paradigm of the techno, time also has a distinctive spatial nature. Such a time is actually time-space, which leads us to the question of whether space, correlative with real time, can also be in some sense real, and therefore technical space. We answer in the affirmative to this question, namely in the context within which we shall add to the already mentioned main concepts of new media art (and e-literature) concepts which actually provoked this chapter: non-trivial and risky perception; the advantage of communication, research and political value over cult and exhibition value of new media artworks and e-literary pieces; temporal perspective, i.e. real time as a technical time-space; and spatial perspective as real closeness.

The perception of traditional works of art has become one of the most common activities in the Euro-American world and beyond. It reminds us of crowds hurrying toward attractive historical venues in big cities, toward theme parks and sports events—there are people crowding together in museums, galleries, theaters, and concert halls. Just let us think about the big museums of contemporary art (e.g., Guggenheim museum in Bilbao, Spain) that function as a hybrid of sanctuary and the shopping mall. The book also often serves as a companion of the innumerable passengers we meet on city buses, trains, or planes. The common feature of such encounters of the mass audience with traditional works of art and literature is that these consumers of art and literature (viewers, audiences, readers) have no major difficulties in "consuming" that which is familiar to them. It could be said that they got used to traditional art and literature. They "bring home" what is expected from the museums, theaters, and concert halls, where the attitude toward these works of art carries on, more or less, without conflict. The audience has learned to parry even the most shocking excesses—they are used to it after constant assaults by avant-garde or neo-avant-garde in the 20th century. Readers we meet on a train or on a plane would soon give up reading a more sophisticated article in a newspaper or magazine, but they would stick to reading a short novel until their drive or flight is over. The audience often has trouble understanding a more sophisticated article of non-fiction. They have difficulties in getting through a challenging scientific article or paper, but they get along great with fiction.

We shall use this example to point out a very different approach taken in the perception and cognition of new media artworks and e-literary projects. These pieces or processes usually demand a more sophisticated or even risky perception. A successful reader of a classic novel or a visitor of a traditional exhibition of visual arts might be disappointed or possibly even drawn back from an interactive VR installation or e-literature piece crafted as computer game patch or textual instrument. A traditional art audience often finds surfing through a more demanding project of net art to be an exhausting affair. In contrast to most traditional works of art, works of new media art contain a certain amount of risk, some obstacles in approach, and a readiness to go back and start again. It is essential to know that efforts must be made on the part of the audience to approach a work of new media art. Specifically, one must be up to date with certain advances in techno-sciences and have a certain knowledge of art theory—getting through the instructions for the use of new media technologies applied in an art project can often be an exhausting affair that resembles the problem-solving activity. One must be ready for an intellectual engagement which demands excellent motor and kinaesthetic skills, speed, and mental agility. Concerning video games and cybertext, Espen J. Aarseth claims that: "The cybertext reader, on the other hand, is not safe, and therefore, it can be argued, she is not a reader. The cybertext puts its would-be-reader at risk: the risk of rejection" (p. 4). The emphasis here is on rejection, which may even cause the user to feel frustrated or embarrassed. We could say that a traditional work of art tends to be much more user-friendly than the cyberarts. In general, new media arts do not appeal to trivial users, but instead, to those who are prepared for the risky perception and are able to overcome the insecurity of choosing between diverse possibilities without a simple "easy way" through a project. Such risky perception is stimulated with the very non-trivial nature of such artwork, i.e. with its design in the mode of the complex, non-trivial machine that means that the output is not a simple consequence of the input but depends on its social interactions and contingent behavior.

The significant features of new media arts, which today by all means fall under the paradigm of computer mediated communications, are their communicational and political (including activist and hactivist) functions. In "The Work of Art in the Age of Mechanical Reproduction," Walter Benjamin compares two fundamentally different kinds of art: traditional art (based on ritual), and modern art (based on politics). He argues that each has a corresponding type of value: cult value is fundamental for traditional art as exhibition value is for modern art. The very existence of a piece of art was the most significant factor for the works of art in the traditional art paradigm, e.g., the works of sacred art (although they were hidden, placed behind an altar, serving as agents between the profane and the sacred). In contrast, exhibition value is most important for modern works of art—to be put under the lights, to be shown. Today, it is evident that this comparison must be corrected by adding a third category and a corresponding artistic practice.

TIME IN NEW MEDIA ART

The value of works of new media art and e-literature is not derived from cult or exhibition but from communication and politics. Such art and literature are becoming the carriers of more and more dialogic, two-way, even multi-way cybernetic communication. The circulation of information in the form of links and feedback loops is essential due to the cybernetic nature of these works of art and literature. The orientation toward the communication features brings up the issue of communication in an artistic sense. To what extent is this art form liberated from traditional communication designs which are developed within the context of media and (trans)political communications shaped by big corporations? Can works of new media art be, as one of the results of intimate technology, the basis for an alternative form of communication—a non-profit and creative interaction between machine and human? Are there any modes of experiences developing within these arts which are more user-friendly to the general public—our "neighbors" in the on-line communication? Are we capable of assisting the novice, also in the form of a virtual agent, bot, or clone, in this form of communication, or do we enforce only the laws of the most experienced and the fittest? When mentioning the communication value of new media art, we should stress that its importance is growing through the increasing quality of message exchange. Online communications are becoming more and more individualized, to ensure that interactivity is not only a device of technical fascination but a procedure which contributes to richer perception and skills on the basis of play and knowledge.

The next problem of new media art is time. What is the nature of time in the cyberspace and augmented reality? Is it the time defined as Aion or Chronos, discussed in the context of Deleuze's work Logic of Sense? Is it the technical time introduced by Vilem Flusser's theory? Is it apocalyptic time like an uncertain gate, supported with expectations, through which a Messiah can enter at anytime? Or is it the real time characteristic of decision-making and function procedures which occur during the online processes?

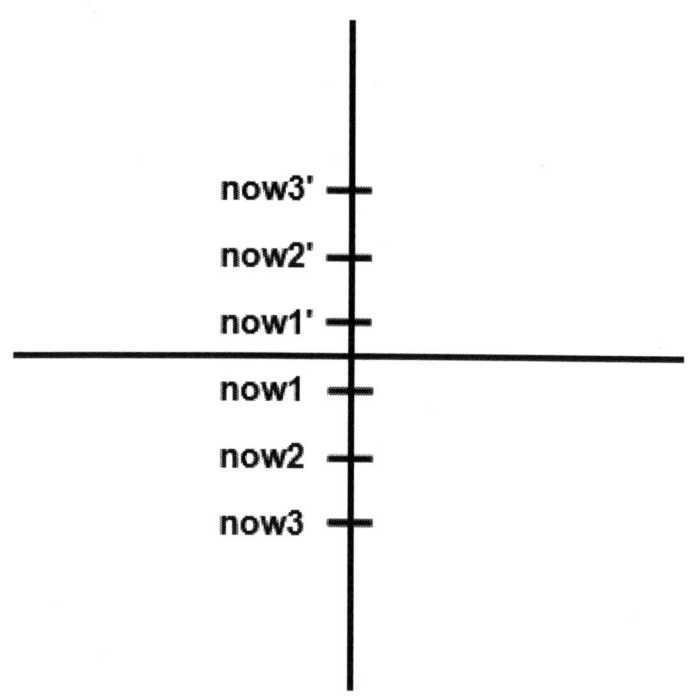

Figure 1

Illustrative examples for understanding time in new media art pieces, which are distinctly time-based, are the projects of e-literature which demand an active reader, directed toward reading as a supplement to original "textscapes" and the creative voids within. Navigation through words-images and words-bodies in "textscapes" takes place in a complex time. It seems that at the moment of linking (or turning the screens), "nows" start to load. These "nows" are torn out of temporal continuum and form a certain middle, which is suspended for reading within a "textscape." This is the between which is characteristic of the apocalyptic moment. One waits for the arrival of the unknown; the other wants it. It seems that we are dealing with uncertain time following something no longer and preceding something not yet. This is a time of expectation, a time for nourishing the deepest dreams and mythic visions. Everything is left open. The link or button simulates a narrow door through which the messianic "word" may enter. The situation of "nows" loaded vertically, and therefore spatially, from a point in linear time could be viewed in the diagram above.

With "nows" loaded vertically, time is stopped, causing words and images to be suspended, and vie for space with a competitive distribution of different times. New media art and e-literature are essentially connected to and dependent on smart machines, which were invented as "dams" to keep time from flowing away. State-of-the-art machines could actually be seen as ingenious devices for saving time. Video-recorders, samplers, and computers are all memory machines that enable us capture visual, audio, and textual recordings from different periods of time. All of these recordings are at our disposal (like Heidegger's "standing reserve"). In real time these periods of time can be recalled and used in a technical sense. In other words, real time does not flow away from us of its own will like time in the natural world. Time, within a machine, is made possible by its own technical manipulation (addition, subtraction, multiplication, division, and intensification) of times, and their various contents, centered around a vertical axis. Real time is artificial and in many ways anti-natural. It owes its very existence to technical memories. Jean-Francois Lyotard claims:

> The importance of the technologies constructed around electronics and data processing resides in the fact that they make the programming and control of memorizing, i.e. the synthesis of different times in one time, less dependent on the conditions of life on earth. (Lyotard, p. 62)

The stress is laid on technical time's independence of the conditions on earth, which points to an area of artificial which is also possible outside our planet.

Such a time is a pure time focused on the being-in-time, experiencing-in-time and listen-to-time. Being displayed around the vertical axis means gaining the spatial quality. In such a time various components of e-literature also appear—not as a means of representation and emotions, but as purified entities of the cyberlanguage itself. They are seen as the letters themselves in terms of being freed from departing from realistic, representational contents beyond them. They resemble the pure line in the abstract painting and the pure movement in dance. Examples for such a practice in e-literature are found in various John Cayley pieces, centered on the very letter as a basic component of such a textual practice (e.g., Torus).

Real time as technical time is not an exclusive short time, like a fleeting moment, perceivable only by machines. It is expansive and complex (in practice, it causes the feeling of augmented present). It is the time of all times (Lyotard's concept of "the synthesis of different times within one time"), and it can be broken up into pieces to serve as an excellent material for the arts, which have been exploring the complexities of time for ages. The real time creative process allows the artist to employ different times or some sort of saturation of times as a painter might choose from colors on his palette. Therefore, we never find ourselves without enough time to choose as some might expect. It is also true that times within the physical processes of a machine are not necessarily bound to existence; they can act as "times liberated from the day's leaden weight," defined only by their own intrinsic qualities, e.g., purified time of moving letters in e-literature.

Can we draw a similar parallel to the issue of space? Specifically, can we speak of a saturation of technical space within a technical-based complexity of cyberworks of art and e-literature? Can we imagine a space of all spaces: the synthesis of various spaces within one space, implying a radical saturation and, similar to technical time, the appearance of artificial? What would be the impact of this level of saturation on a viewer-user? What are the units of saturation causing the effect of complete immersion into the medium? What are the main features of the space between the user and the cyberwork of arts?

FILLING THE GAP BETWEEN THE WORK OF NEW MEDIA ART AND ITS USER-VIEWER

A traditional work of art can be understood as a window or as a departure point for the observer to step into the complex background of the work of art consisted of various levels of meaning. To understand this constellation we must consider the work of art, as discussed in Nicolai Hartmann's *Aesthetics* (1953), which is inspired by phenomenological aesthetics. The founder of this approach, who got his inspirations both from Husserl's concepts of phenomenology and Kant's (and Neo-Kantian) aesthetics, is Moritz Geiger, notable in his essays "Beiträge zur Phenomenologie des ästhetischen Genusses" (1913) and "Zugänge zur Ästhetik" (1928). An additional significant figure is Waldemar Conrad, who published his article "The aesthetic object" as early as 1908. Among the more important followers of this tradition, one should mention (besides Nicolai Hartmann, Roman Ingarden and Merleau-Ponty) Martin Heidegger, Eugen Fink, and Jean Paul Sartre, who are all close to this approach.

What do we talk about when we talk about phenomenological aesthetics? According to Moritz Geiger's book The Significance of the Art, a main task of phenomenological aesthetics is exploring aesthetic objects from their phenomenal aspect. They should be analyzed as phenomena by bracketing the issues of real existence (both the object and the empirical ego). Geiger even wrote on "the purification of reality into a sphere of unreality" (p. 205), and suggested that common structures (for instance, the essence of the sonnet as such or of the symphony as such) and not particular objects are the main concerns of aesthetic approach to the arts. Talking today about the web (with regard to web art) the main scope of phenomenological approach could be devoted to exploring the very nature of web media—the "webness."

Among key achievements of phenomenological aesthetics we call attention to its criticism of naive empiricism, psychologism, and naturalism (for example, as exclusion of interests of empirical self in aesthetic standpoint). Discerning between (literary) works of art as a schematic artifact and its concretizations—this is Ingarden's standpoint, which became real with hyperfiction, giving the reader much greater competence when encountering traditional texts in a printed, codex book—and the shaping of the original theory of ontological status of a work of art as a heteronomous formation, divided into layers, which participates in two areas of being, namely the real and unreal.

In particular, phenomenological aesthetics destabilizes traditional concepts of reality: given, natural, material reality is not everything, but along with it are would-be-realities, unreal actualities, and unrealities. What Gilles Deleuze says in the Logic of the Sense refers to the Alexius Meinong, who employed a phenomenology that identified impossible objects as having a particular nature of existence: "they are of extra being" (p. 35). And when we nowadays encounter net artworks we can find an augmented concept of reality which encompasses, let us say metaphorically, e-reality, dot com reality, and @-reality.

A typical example of phenomenological approach to the main features of a work of art is the aesthetics of the previously mentioned German philosopher Nicolai Hartmann. He introduced a radical distinction between the everyday activities in the sense of realization (stirring the lead weight of the real) and between the artistic approach, of which derealization is typical. Especially important is Hartmann's theory of the many-layered structure of the work of art: having real foreground and unreal background with a number of layers which go from more concrete towards the most abstract layers, towards the idea of the work. He found out six layers of background (in Rembrandt's self-portraits to be exact). The number of layers contributes to the richness and endurance of a work of art, while the beauty of the work lies in their relations.

Can we come closer to the particularities of new media cyberworks of art on the basis of Hartmann's approach? For instance, can Hartmann help us understand cybernetic installations by Jeffrey Shaw and Monika Fleishmann or web based e-literary pieces like Mark Amerika's FILM-TEXT? It is possible, yet a closer look reveals a number of fundamental changes. The complex unreal background has now narrowed solely to the abstract layer of the idea of artwork (new media artworks are close to the conceptual art). The real foreground has also narrowed (containing first and foremost hardware and software components), while there is a new sphere of intermediate layers, mediating between real and unreal, which is not only accessible by imagination, but is also influencing the user physically with special effects. Hartmann's layers have now moved closer to the observer and are no longer as abstract as in traditional arts; on the contrary, they include the stimuli of tactile, visual and kinetic origin.

The model for this new constellation is a hologram as an optical memory unit that, metaphorically speaking, grows towards the observer, filling the space between the wall and the eye. We witness here the effect of "closeness that grows towards the user," intensively filling the space between the installation (or the screenic interface) and the eye. Similarly, as we can talk about real time as an action time in online communications, we can, in order to understand cybernetic works of art, introduce the term "real space" as a technical space moulded with special effects such as hologrammatic closeness. Such space is shaped according to various geometries (Euclidian and Post-Euclidian) that enable the occurrence of objects with more than three dimensions. The shaping of a technical view aside these dimensions, which demands the eye's deterritorialized view, which now takes the position on the mobile axis between the nondiscerned front and back, up and down, left and right, and tries to see also the "dark side" of that object. The procedure Gilles Deleuze established alongside Bacon's painting, namely deterritorialization of the eye, which accompanies the liberation from the representational function of (post)modern art, comes to full value with the perception of e-literary pieces (e.g., Jim Rosenberg's Diagrams) that can even function as unreadable objects. Fredric Jameson, in his "Postmodernism" essay, pointed to the effects of new depthlessness that destabilizes viewers' optics, jerking the rug out from under their feet. Jameson used the examples of LA architecture as special effect, which he described as:

> a surface which seems to be unsupported by any volume, or whose putative volume (rectangular, trapezoidal?) is ocularly quite undecidable. This great sheet of windows, with its gravity-defying two-dimensionality, momentarily transfers the solid ground on which we stand into the contents of stereopticon (p. 70-71)

New media are productively stimulating perception. They invest perception with a technical view that enters everyday life more and more, for example, looking through the eye of a smart bomb and weather satellite (cam) eye. Kinetic e-literary pieces especially demand that the viewer/ reader takes virtually impossible position: Their view must fall in the depth of the screen and approach from the back side of the screen (dark side of the moon position) to the fleeing words.

Immersion as one of the fundamental new media or cyberarts aesthetic concept can be explained on the following schematic structure of a multi-layered work designed according to Hartmann's theory of a multi-layered work of art.

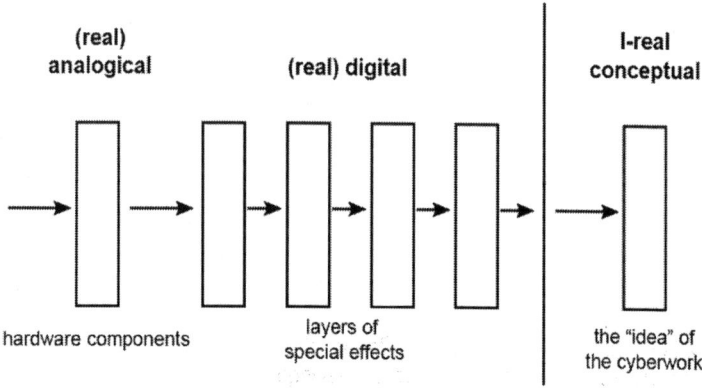

Figure 2

The direction of the arrows illustrates the direction of perception. The viewer/users' perception from the concrete layer of the work's basic structure over intermediate layers of special effects (e. g. tapes of moving words-images in animated poetry) moves towards the abstract layer of the idea of the work, which means that digital layers must be transparent. They are carried over hardware components and must enable the path to the idea, the concept, of the work. Unlike the traditional work of art, with new media work of art we are witnesses to a greater influence of direct sensory stimuli (transition from simulation to stimulation), because digital layers involve visual, audio, and tactile effects, typical of digital total-data-work of art. The more complexly formed and densely spread these layers—which contribute to the saturation of real space are—the more convincing are viewers/users' sensations of immersion into the "cyberwork" of art and e-literature.

The saturation created by the so-called real closeness of the holographic simulated field in front of our eyes, causes the user to experience total immersion. Due to the nonexistence of the distance between the organs of sight and the objects seen, we witness an immersion into the layers of special effects that are no longer objects in the traditional sense of the word. The objects are no longer placed in front of our line of sight but, instead, intermediate digital layers (designed by hi-tech effects) "stick" themselves to the sight itself. These virtual "would-be-objects," generated by new media technologies, stick to the viewer-user of a "visual system." Therefore, the very active sense in this situation is touch as well. This leads to a number of consequences in defining the nature of new media artwork, one being that its units are touchable—this holds true for both images and words—words of immersive digital literary pieces, i.e. touchable words, designed with different velocities.

The velocity of the cyberart image which assaults the view is an essential quality of immersion as a temporal activity. Immersion is fundamentally different from contemplation, which functions under the timelessness of static seeing. Entering the process of immersion, the user moves slowly or quickly, setting changeable goals on a journey through a 3-D landscape. New media artworks have a complexly structured, multi-layered foreground, which allows immersion into various layers (and back). However, herein lies the risky nature of such works of art. It is not a given that the user will find all of the layers of the foreground or that the journey through the holographic closeness will be successful. As often happens, the viewer-user is about to arrive at some sort of "vanishing point," causing a state of vertigo.

It is important to discuss one more effect of the saturation of technical space and the aesthetics of closeness: the loss of illusion, discussed in Jean Baudrillard's essay "Objects, Images, and the Possibilities of Aesthetic Illusion." Baudrillard argues that the issue that we called real closeness generates an "obscene rapprochement" of the artistic object and the user. A hi-tech and hi-fi art object often leaves little to the imagination. It has a perfect saturation, a surplus of elements, and special effects which crowd the space between the object and the user. We are witnessing works of art which allow the image and the image-word (in e-literary pieces put on the web) to close in on the user and say "more than should be said."

New media artworks are defined as would-be-works of art due to their intrinsic nature, which is defined by such technical features as real time existence and real closeness, non-representation (a break with the tradition of mimesis), interactivity, immersion, communication value, risky perception, and ludic nature (closeness to the features of game). This expression (would-be-works of art) was coined to point out the specificity of this new creative movement as an art praxis which abandons the codes of traditional arts (the arts-as-we-know-them based on the tradition of stable artifacts and approached by perception in the mode of remote contemplation), and directs us toward a new paradigm of communication and sensitivity (techno formed aesthesis). The essential prerequisites for this new paradigm are knowledge (particularly of the technosciences and of intimate technologies), technical skills in computer mediated communications, a sense of game, a readiness for risky perception, an awareness of global interconnectedness (abandoning hierarchical ways of thinking), and a strong sense of cyberethics based on a respect and responsibility for the person approached by online communications, and protecting the novice and weak participants in online communication.

4 AN EXPANDED CONCEPT OF TEXTUALITY: CYCLING AS READING A CITYSCAPE

One of the most talked about advances of digital technologies is their ability to create a displaced sense of place, of things, and of the human, calling into question individuals' everyday embodiment in physical settings and destabilizing the ways they connect to the environment and perceive its crucial features. Today, the users of digital technologies are driven to form their spatial and temporal experience from a variety of data. They are entering a mixed reality, which places virtual (screenic) contents into a very actual, physical environment. There is much to be gained from paying close attention to the intersection of smart technologies and the human that provokes special experience, enables novel techno-influenced perception, and opens up for investigation the very nature of one's sophisticated corporeal activity within interface culture. The contemporary individual participating in both given and artificial realities is faced by such novel conditions that it makes sense to discuss this cultural turn in terms of phenomenology, which—in turn—is challenged with various issues regarding one's corporeal experience stimulated with interface extensions, and regarding one's life within sophisticated mixed reality (i.e. actual realities).

Investigations into the ontological status of the work of art turned to phenomenological aesthetics, a movement largely underestimated within contemporary phenomenology. This early 20th century aesthetic theory derives from Husserl's phenomenological approach to the cognition, where the nature of the work of art is heterogeneous: besides its real foreground, it also contains a layer of unreal background. Analyzing the intentional world of artworks, phenomenological aesthetics likewise revealed such particular ontological forms as the unreal, quasi-real, and the as-if-real. And, last but not least, phenomenological investigations also raised the issue of the ontological status of pure artificiality. It considers impossible entities in our given reality, such as the centaur, the round square, wooden iron, etc. The being of these entities—as so-called impossible objects—is again quite particular in nature; one could say that their ontological status is shifted from

Janez Strehovec

the being towards nothingness. The French philosopher Jean Paul Sartre, having dedicated his thought precisely to nothingness—which in a way is essential to the being—reached farthest into these issues. In Being and Nothingness, Sartre distinguishes intermediate stages between fully positive realities and those whose positive nature is only appearance that conceals the chasm of nothingness. It is this very notion that first highlighted the existence of reality that includes the non-being within it.

The phenomenological approach to plural-mode being structures pertaining to fictional objects (i.e. objects of art and imagination), however, is not only typical of the theoreticians of phenomenological aesthetics, (e.g. Ingarden, Geiger, Fink). This field was equally familiar to Husserl, as the writings from his legacy testify, published in the XXIIIth volume of Husserliana (Collected Works), under the title Phantasie, Bildbewusstsein, Erinnerung (1980). His major concern in this book is fictional objects of imagination (German: Fikta) in the sense of as-if-real objects, and with this the specificity of unreality.

Nowadays ontology can still be written by referring to the philosophical tradition extending from Parmenides and Plato through to Husserl and Heidegger. However, this ontological movement can as well be enriched with the analyses of the ontological modality of the new-media entities, such as avatars (visual representations of a participant in a shared virtual community, i.e. an interface for the self) and virtual agents. And to these, one could also add investigations into spaces and times that define online communications and new-media activities within the contemporary social network (e.g. Web 2.0). As a result, new media generates what we shall term mixed reality as a "pluriversum," i.e. reality which encompasses both a given reality plus a vast field of virtual as well as other artificial or synthetic realities. The components of this reality are objects, which, in fact, are not fully and evidentially objects anymore, but are rather most fluid and dispersed entities, i.e. often only relations, actions, and data arrangements of quite provisional, instant existence. The key issues here are centered around the entities which take place in an instantaneous fashion and last only as long as certain special conditions are being satisfied. The moment this is no longer the case, the entities in question go out or can even be erased by pressing a delete key on the computer keyboard. New media, defined both by classical and second-order cybernetics, thus generates relational forms of existence whose being is likely to be something between stable being and pure nothingness.

TOWARDS MIXED REALITY AND ONTOLOGICAL PLURALITY

Cyberspace and "cybertime" are encompassed within mixed reality and therefore do not overlap with real space and time. As such, they call for comprehensive inquiries as well as noetic and noematic descriptions (terms borrowed from Husserl's phenomenology) of virtual entities, and in this they are already addressed by the phenomenological approach. What proves crucial here is the fact that phenomenology arises from ontological plurality and has no complexes about entities characterized by a very fragile and instant nature. This brings us to the following Herbert Spiegelberg's observation: "What is all-important in phenomenology is that we consider all the data, real or unreal or doubtful, as having equal rights, and investigate them without fear or favor" (Spiegelberg 1960: 892). Facing the specificity of currently popular cyberspace phenomena, we are now able to discern not only the as-if real (in this book dealt with along with the would-be-works of art) and the unreal, but—metaphorically speaking—also the e-real, the cyber-real, and the @-real as artificial modes of digital media which generate online would-be realities and which have become to a certain extent institutionalized in Second Life. The present mediascape increasingly blurs the boundaries between the given real-as-we-know-it and the artificial. The latter even appears to be the most prominent principle in the techno culture as a mainstream culture of information society.

One of the virtues of phenomenology is seen in its ambition to bring description as close as possible to the specificity of the medium in question. On the basis of phenomenological reduction and by considering the plural nature of objects (given as phenomena), it tries to disclose with great accuracy the special nature of the object under analysis, whether real or unreal. German philosopher Eugen Fink, in his investigations into the visual medium, has argued that "objects of the world of images are not objects in the real space, nor do they last in real time; they exist merely in the space of the world of images and in the time of the world of images" (Fink 1966:

74-75). Indeed, this is an instance of taking things for granted, typical of phenomenology; however, such an approach and orientation remains important even in the case of new-media objects, which fall under the concept of so-called augmented reality. If we think, for example, of avatars and virtual agents presented in cyberspace (e.g., in Second Life), we see that in fact they only exist in cyberspace and cybertime, they have cyberpast and cyberfuture, and they can only be the objects and subjects of cyberactions, that is, of the activities in the virtual worlds.

Consider the arguments of Vilém Flusser, the theoretician of telematic society, who pioneered analyses of the new media specificity of objects. In the section dealing with the hologram in Conceiving technology (Ger. Technik entwerfen), he remarks that these "pseudo-objects established by means of technology are no longer objects of the kind that can be negated by the subject, but rather they are projections, conceived from within the framework of a project" (Flusser 1998: 144). In the case of the hologram cube, he draws the conclusion that this is no longer an object that stands in space, but immaterial, pure appearance, pure "would-being" (Ger. Sollen). Another example of the phenomenological orientation in dealing with the specificity of a particular medium is also seen in the theory of the work of art as a stratified formation, i.e. a formation constructed of several different strata. This theory was developed by Nicolai Hartmann and Roman Ingarden, although its bases are found in Waldemar Conrad's "Aesthetic Object" essay. The work of art is thus not a monolithic formation, but has a polyphonic character, founded on the many-layered nature of its structure.

Life in contemporary mixed reality fosters the emergence of new forms of perception to fit the interaction with objects in cyberspace. These objects even call for a new sense to be created, namely the sense of the virtual, much in the vein of Karl Marx's notion of the mineralogical sense and the sense of beauty. This means that our consciousness needs to be cultivated so as to be able to handle the objects which we touch and control in virtual and other realities in a very subtle fashion (e.g., the reader of digital text is identified with the cursor grasping the individual letter of digital text, he/she is in the textscape there, where the cursor is).

Mixed reality (this term in contemporary new media studies also encompasses augmented reality and augmented virtuality) is, as a rule, accessible via interfaces. We can even talk about it in terms of interface culture, which is our contemporary culture of new media interfaces which generate special matrices (Johnson 1987). In turn, these enable typical and specific access to reality: one interface will run a distinctly particular movie in front of our eyes, while another will confront us with "another story," say, in the form of a computer game.

Furthermore, the use of a particular interface profoundly defines the structure and the form of an activity. By using a word-processor, for example, a text is organized and controlled in a different way than it would be organized if it was written with pencil or typewritten. Interfaces also enable us to apprehend space and time in formerly unknown ways and direct us towards new forms of representation. For example, consider interactive representation (typical of video and of computer games) which takes us from within the perspective of the perfect tense and places us into the imperfect tense referring to the pure present, and takes us from the standpoint of an observer to the position of the protagonist, the actor. The game, unlike the story, integrates us into real-time activities; it demands exercise, subtle hands-on-controls activity, skill, and experience, which means that it most persuasively employs all the senses—while creating a new one, i.e. the sense of the game. Games give us directions as to how to achieve mastery in a particular game and how to react quickly in risky situations, but, on the other hand, they only offer a limited and—in comparison to the narrative quality within the medium of the story—an impoverished view of the world, for now this view has been reduced to the mere goals of the game. Games are unmistakably centered around goals and motivated by results—all of which has nothing to do with the story and its subtle use of description.

ENTERING THE WORLD OF TECHNO-INFLUENCED PERCEPTION

"Mixed perception" emerges in parallel to mixed reality, shaped by means of the most advanced interfaces. This means that the perception of the contemporary individual is influenced by media, which is why she looks, listens, and touches—metaphorically speaking—in accordance with the principles of film, simulation, clicking, and hypertext. Not only film but also new media, with the Internet occupying an important place, crucially influence the perception, activities, and imagination of contemporary individuals, so that he/she—metaphorically speaking—sees, hears and touches to a certain extent more and in a different fashion than he/she normally would if they did not live in the world of interface culture.

Various technical goal-oriented activities, enabled with advanced smart technologies, generate certain manners of being-in-the world (in terms of Heideggerian ontology). Raising questions with regard to technology means posing both social and cultural questions, which refer to something essential in our primordial existence. In particular, new mobile technologies profoundly shape the way in which people communicate and perceive the reality. When we move around in our surroundings armed with the mobile screenic devices, we also perceive the data shown on the screen of such devices, meaning that both the visual and aural interfaces are integrated in our experience of the walking environment. Virtual data approaching from the remote context on the screen is related to and coordinated with our basic, non-mediated perceptions from the physical here and now. The digital technology "becomes a kinetic surface which is incorporated in the experience and understanding of different places" (Thrift 2004: 585). We face the novel condition that bodily movement (including walking, riding and stopping), real time visual (aural and tactual) perception of the physical environment, and screen mediated virtual data, are all integrated.

Such a condition and the rich experience enabled by it makes the users deploy novel modes of perception by combining both their tactile activity and procedures of seeing. By referring to one's ordinary use of mobile screenic devices, Heidi Rae Cooley has introduced the concept of "tactile vision" with regard to one's ability in activating procedures of seeing by the hand-on-controls activity. We face a condition of material and dynamic seeing involving eyes, hands, and screenic devices which enter one's nomadic cockpit. In discussing mobile screenic devices, Cooley introduced the distinction between window-ed seeing (as a practice of seeing through, i.e. a window) and the screenic seeing as a manner of more physical seeing that "encourages an experience of encounter" (Cooley 2004: 143) through the acquisitions of a sort of tangible experience.

In contemporary technoculture, seeing ceases to be a pure act of contemplative vision for a distanced viewer; on the contrary, it interacts with one's tactile activities enabling a dynamic oscillation between visual and tactile feedback. Vision is activated by the movement of hand. As a result, seeing (and reading) become tactile and the new generations of words-images called onto the screen by means of navigational devices generate a new circle of tactile and kinesthetic activity. Such activity provokes perception and stimulates and enriches one's experience.

We are aware that such an approach to contemporary techno-influenced experience and perception strongly differs from the traditional, more critical attitude to the world of perception framed by advanced media and technologies. Faced with the early age of print media and information, Walter Benjamin argued in his "Storyteller" essay that "experience has fallen in value. And it looks as if it is continuing to fall into bottomless. Every glance at the newspaper demonstrates that it has reached a new low..." (Benjamin 1968). According to Benjamin, the very nature of information, in his own terms, is that "its value does not survive the moment in which it was new," which strongly opposes the richness of experience derived from the story. Rather than sharing such a traditional and pessimistic approach to the world of information (e. g. information society) our essay seeks to broaden the knowledge of novel media shaped narrative, which enriches one's own experience and perception.

INTERFACE CULTURE REINVENTS THE BODY AND RESHAPES PERCEPTION

Whereas an early phase of cyberculture privileged pure mental operations of cyborg terminal identity discussed in terms of the mind vs. "cyber-mind" problem (e. g. the ideology posed by Gibson's proto-cyberpunk novel Neuromancer, 1984), by contrast, contemporary algorithmic culture is shaped through bridging of the gap between two cultures (Snow's term) and reinvents the mind/body problem by placing it within the condition of interface culture, which is underway in the basic condition of present individual. Rather than being pushed aside or left behind as it used to be within the cyberpunk ideology, the body of the present individual is armed with the nomadic screenic devices and gets more and more crucial, even in terms of reinventing its novel tasks and functions. The body as "our basic organ of having the world" (Merleau-Ponty 1998: 146) enters the novel ontological conditions of contemporary mixed reality, determined by hybridization and merging of in-between spaces and times which challenges novel ways of perception through linking and amalgamating different perceptive acts and procedures. The very nature of mixed reality demands mixed and hybrid techno-shaped perception, enabled with cooperation (and hybridization) of different senses, e.g., tactile vision, tactile hearing, not-just-seeing, and tactile scanning of surface on the move.

Maurice Merleau-Ponty's notion that "the world of perception is to a great extent unknown territory as long as we remain in the practical or utilitarian attitude" (Merleau-Ponty, 2004: 39) makes sense here, indicating the shift toward a more subtle artificial and sophisticated attitude that enables the richer perception. In this essay, in order to describe such an intimate and personal experience, which enables sophisticated techno-shaped perceptual acts, I draw on my everyday practice of cycling in my home city Ljubljana, which is experienced as a ride, enabled by the combination of two interfaces, namely the bicycle and the ride simulator such as can be found in present theme parks. For me, riding a bicycle is more than simply rolling on two wheels: once my urban ride starts, all that is essential in my life is in that moment, what's in front of me right now.

Thanks to a ride in real space, combined with a "co-imagined" ride in a simulator on the one hand, and the acquired "clicking" sensitivity of a trendy computer culture on the other, I can perceive the riding space in its complex entirety, which means that in the perceived space I can switch smoothly between the spheres of the real and those of the artificial, Thus, I can enjoy "the essence of the ride as such."

The ride as a rich temporal event is founded in my everyday experience. In other words, I am going to write about how I view the city and what I see in it, now that cycling complements both my everyday professional work in front of the computer screen and my excursions into trendy environments of the present-day entertainment industry (e.g. simulator races, SF-movies, VR-based games).

I cycle through the Slovenian capital Ljubljana, the city in which I live, in my own way, using a high gear which demands a heavy pushing on the pedals. The latter, offering crude resistance, allows me to experience the feedback of my own power. I am uncertain why I don't shift gears so as to make it easier for me, why I torture myself in this kind of way, and why, in fact, I am so ridiculous. For in pushing the pedals I keep unnecessarily bowing my head. But that's how it is: I have simply got used to cycling through the city in my own way. Pushing the pedals of my city-bike brings to my mind mouse clicking, say, in front of a screen featuring some slow 3-D computer animation into which I gradually penetrate by means of clicking. I have already pointed out that I push my bicycle slowly, so as to feel the maximum feedback of my generated power; it is for this reason that what I see in front of me does not open up as a traditional movie based on the sensitive chemistry of the film tape. There's no speed and no play of city lights involved. Instead, the view opens up for me in the sense of step-by-step, even see-saw-like penetration within the framework of gradual approaching. What is relevant here that the approach is in fact sequential, progressing to the rhythm beaten by the metronome and/or some other digital device.

Riding down Miklosiceva Street or Presernova Road, I not only cycle on them, but at the same time—metaphorically speaking—I also click on them to the rhythm of buildings approaching and receding. Whenever I cycle, I take the road as an imaginary zone-tunnel simulated by my own perception, which ends, say, near Ljubljana's famous Three Bridges. Thanks to the "clicking" pattern of approaching, structured in levels and steps, the tunnel of my perception is shaped as a telescope tube, offering numerous views across the landscape. Slow cycling also allows looking upwards and sideways, at the facades and pedestrians on the pavements flanking the two rows of buildings, and, of course, it allows looking down. The cyclist must look down, to the pedals, and look forward, a little ahead of the handlebar. She must direct an intense gaze also on the surface of the road and on the immediate surrounding terrain, which, however, lies at the same level, down.

In my imagination, I complement the ride down a real street with a ride through an unreal, "co-imagined" tunnel, as of the moment I receive a special stimulus. Viewing the surroundings I notice that acceleration causes the facades to be set in motion as if to create a movie featuring light-dark surfaces with their outlines getting lost. It is in this moment that I switch to the "tunnel-mode." Suddenly I notice an agreeable change in the environment under my observation. This change, caused by my very motion, in turn gives rise to a desire/interest that the object-process-movie-ride should last a long time, so that I could, in a way, possess it, and that I could derive some pleasure from its changing. This refers primarily to the changes associated with accelerating and stopping, and, consequently, to the facades alternating between being caught in an interval of a movie and re-entering again into the phase of rigidity, i.e. being re-composed into a stable form. The "movie experience" with the liquid architecture of the street, enabled by the interface of the bicycle, but indirectly—in "co-imagined" analogy—also enabled by the interfaces of the computer and the simulator, has been provoked by what Roman Ingarden termed "aesthetic original emotion" (Ger. aesthetische Ursprungsemotion; Ingarden 1969). By this, I intend to denote the stimulus which comes from the environment and manifests itself on a real object as its formal modification. The latter does not inspire indifference, but rather an interest in the particular superstructure that adorns the perception of the real ride through the exploration of an unreal tunnel. This impression, gained in the proximity of attractive qualities which arise from my perception in motion, is in fact only the beginning of the large-scale and complex process of aesthetic experience, which then accompanies my ride. In this experience I combine both modes: a real ride and a ride-supplement process in the world (tunnel) of images. What counts in all this is not only the pleasure derived from the changes which pave way to an ever more intense tunnel-movie (depending on the acceleration). What also counts here is the interest in changes resulting from stopping which causes opaque facades on both side of the street to reassemble back into clear architectural outlines.

I do not merely cycle through the city in terms of a simple corporeal activity, because in fact I cycle-click through it in terms of the network established both by spatial and temporal grammar. This means that I do not merely follow an urban street network, but I also draw my own loops between its threads and nodes: across courtyards, along poorly fenced building sites, through narrow passages. I make use of the bicycle to benefit from the quite special experience of the city's nearness: to encounter its underlying structures and configurations, to look across the river and into the canals which stimulates my proximate senses of touch and smell. With my bicycle, I stick to those parts of the city where, in a certain sense, the bicycle still belongs, where it is not thoroughly out of place. The bicycle is not like the scooter, the skateboard, or rollerskates, on which you can speed across the plazas of huge shopping malls, between skyscrapers, and all over wide platforms extending in front of contemporary cinemas which boast fourteen, twenty, or more theatres. The bicycle—to be frank—is actually an old device. It does not become any place (say, L. A. Downtown, especially if conceived as New Jerusalem handy for any sort of disaster movies), it does not suit anybody; not a few find the bicycle downright disturbing. However, the bicycle can still function as an interface, and by sustaining a particular framework (moderate speed, moderate detachment from the ground, pushing the pedals, the pedals offering sufficient resistance, the cyclist bending over the handlebar), it enables a quite particular kind of perception. Only the posture and the motion of the cyclist, associated with the pedal pushing-turning intervals, provide for the unique experience of a "co-imagined" projection tunnel and the experience of the city's buildings in it as the scenery of a digital cinema.

What kind of buildings are of interest to us and how do they outline the tunnel? At this point, I must be more accurate: buildings stand sideways to delimit the outer border. Buildings stand, buildings are there. As a cyclist I actually view whatever fills the area between the buildings and my eyes, and it is shaped as a tunnel network. The latter, in fact, contains not buildings but images: screens softened by motion, full of light and life, getting stuck on the nodes of the network. These, however, are not momentary stains extended to the degree of formlessness: we are not aboard a high-speed or bullet train (like the French TGV or Spanish AVA). The images in the tunnel therefore preserve the configurations of doors, windows, ornamental pillars and the like, which linger for an interval only to extend again at an accelerated pace.

Cycling on roads and paths and sandy trails: it is in this way that I watch-in-motion the images within the tunnel network. I perceive this network as a particular spatial configuration and the textscape, generated by my own activity. This is the space-time-event-textscape maintained and modified by my own cycling; it is one space-derivative out of an abundant set. The spatiality of such a ride does not presume the notion of a space that contains the cyclist but builds on notions of being-in-the-ridescape (as a kind of cityscape), full corporeal and mental engagement and orientation. It should be stressed here that "in" addressed in being-in-the-ridescape does not suggest rough containment; instead, its use should draw attention to involvement, and should thus be associated with being in love etc. More-over, thanks to its textual network-sequence structure, which presupposes the network of relations, not only can I see images and motion, i.e. I do not merely follow/read visualized nouns and verbs, but rather my gaze, en-abled by the interface of the resisting pedals, also touches—metaphorically speaking—the conjunctions and prepositions between them. As I cross a section of the cityscape as an artificial textwork of relations, I cycle into and I watch to, over, towards, in the direction of, from the direction of. Further-more, I cycle between and into, for, in a sense, I also dive. The space-time-action of cycling and/as clicking falls primarily under the domain of verbs, conjunctions and prepositions (there are also temporal before, not-yet and anymore).

RIDING/READING THE WOUNDED CITY

Is the virtual space of the tunnel constructed in relation to the perception of a cyclist the only feasible form by which imagination can enhance cycling through the city? Does the augmented gaze emerge only via the configura-tion of the tunnel? Can pedaling-as-clicking also be seen from a different perspective? It can be. There are areas and spots where the city exposes its bowels, or at least its wounds in terms of its uncanny, i.e. where it falls apart and where it is being built. Upon such areas I also cast—metaphorically speaking—the blanket of the satellite orbital gaze, which is needed for the readability of the cityscape. What do I mean by that? In this case, the whole thing looks as follows: I cycle and at the same time, by virtue of my perspec-tive modified with the optics of a satellite camera, I am—above. Cycling (say, around building sites, amid ruins), I look down as if from a space-craft slowly cruising over an unknown planet, stopping-clicking each time I push on the pedal, to catch a close-up image of some striking configuration on the planet's surface, say, a crater. My cycling-clicking corresponds to a point-by-point crossing of space, and it seems that the cycling also brings something "more" (e.g., aura) to the city's wounds.

The cyclist's drive in the cityscape can be discussed in terms of de Certeau's distinction between strategies and tactics, and with regard to his account of pedestrian (walking) experience in the city (de Certeau 1984). It is cyclists who will visit the city's wounds (e. g. sites of fire) and make them function as hidden spots of the urban uncanny, because the reading of the cityscape is enriched by reading and rereading of its dark voids and spots of indeterminacy. Cycling is riding and as such a kind of sophisticated narrative, which could be discussed even by the concepts applied in the phenomenology of literature (e.g., Ingarden's and Jauss's notions on spots of indeterminacy and voids). Each cyclists brings novel story to the urban narrative. A city is rendered worthless without pedestrians, cyclists, and car drivers. It cannot exist because it takes (moving) people to make a city on their own by turning cityspace into the network of places.

At this point we can refer to Jeffrey Shaw's The Legible City (1988-1991) as a striking example taken from the media art, which also demon-strates the very nature of cycling in terms both of full body (immersive) experience and the narrative. (This piece is described in the next chapter.)

This description of cycling is intended as an illustration of how a means of transport as traditional as the bicycle enables a quite particular kind of one's experience and perception, as of the moment we start using it as an interface in order to experience environment in a special way. Also the issue of (new) media in general is the issue of technologically modeled and accelerated perception, i.e. perception which is enabled via a particular matrix, or, better, enframing (Heidegger), and which—in the case of the bicycle—is fairly specific. It differs distinctly from perception pertaining to, say, the fashionable, re-actualized scooter. The defining feature of the latter—reiterating the mouse metaphor—is clicking by pushing against the ground in a vibrating ride into the image, which makes one the protagonist of quite specific pushing, and, subsequently, also the advantage of a long, economic use of the impetus in a fading ride without major intervals.

It is typical of state-of-the-art interfaces that they increasingly depart from separate, isolated functioning. On the contrary, they are being linked up and enhanced to form systems. Perception enabled by a particular interface, too, is intertwined, linked, combined with perception enabled by another interface. The city as a digital cinema in a cyclists's experience—as one of the topics of this text—is cycled-through and constructed—viewed through both interfaces, namely the bicycle and the screen and/or their peripheral devices, i.e. the pedals and the mouse. My cycling into the city as a digital cinema is also based on the everyday experience which had been shaped in front of the computer screen. Without any clicking, watching SF movies with special effects and those employing nowadays trendy 3-D technology (e.g. Avatar), and without racing in theme parks simulated rides, I would view things differently while I cycle, and I would see—in a certain sense—less. The cityscape would be poorer by that tunnel derivative of space which is shaped exactly by my ride and which exists in the time of this same ride.

The issue which needs to be raised is how to place this sort of hybrid experience and perception within phenomenological investigations. Could it be that my exploration of the city in the form of cycling-clicking experience (shaped with the cyclist attitude, which differs from the natural one) refers primarily to the mode of perception within the main stream interface culture—the mode which is foreign to the perception of situations which preoccupied Husserl and his successors? Does Husserl at all provides us with a phenomenological approach to the issues of this kind?

Our answer to the latter question is affirmative. Not only the texts gathered in the 23rd volume of Husserliana but also his analyses of space and time (say, temporal structures of kinesthetic sequences in the Ding und Raum) and perception remain of reasonable value as guidelines in such descriptions. Switching to the as-if mode and, consequently, the particular derealization of objects and processes, had been described also by Husserl himself, or better, they had been described in the form which calls for modifications, such modifications as I myself proposed describing a ride through an unreal tunnel. Husserl claims, "Reality can be observed as if it were an 'image.'" And, further, "In a way, any thing can be viewed as an 'image'" (Husserl 1980: 591, 593). In the context of phenomenology, seeing something as-if it were an image paves way to the procedure of derealization, and consequently to the as-if mode—which finally means that the given real becomes infected by the "as-if mode." Viewing the world as if it were an image, as Husserl explains in his Ideas, requires a neutrality-modification of consciousness that means, in the image we intend to see a certain reality within the mode of "quasi." Husserl is of great importance to this text also with his fundamental claim that every thing (and therefore not only a thing of artistic imagination) can be observed as an image, which means that every thing can be included among the objects of derealization. If I now return to the description of what I perceive cycling through my home city, I can note once again that I perceive the streets within some real (e. g. Husserlian natural) attitude, and at the same time I also see them as an image. Not only, however, as a static image in Husserl's sense, but rather as an movement-image (Deleuze), i.e. as in film. And, in a certain sense, not even only in that way, but also as a theme park simulator's screen.

The contemporary individual, confronted with the mediascapes of interface culture, is clearly urged to observe this reality's components and processes as-if they were images, movies, simulator rides, or computer games. Perceiving a mixed reality, she is urged to switch to the "as-if" mode.

LIQUID SWITCHING BETWEEN VARIOUS MODES OF PERCEPTION

The question raised at this point concerns the nature of this switching. What happens in the changing of attitudes, when the user of the reality mode that is characteristic for actions in everyday life switches to as-if world mode (and the environment in which it is included)? We have already mentioned Ingarden's notion of aesthetic emotion as a starting point for a process of experience leading to reality. Such a process is understood as something very demanding and sophisticated, as Ingarden wrote in The Cognition of Literary Work of Art:

> The appearance of original emotion in a person's stream of consciousness produces, above all, a certain check in the preceding "normal" course of experiences and modes of behavior in regard to the objects surrounding him in the real world (Ingarden 1973: 191,192).

But the rupture of the practical orientation with this "check" is very demanding in that it leads us far away from our normal conditions. The return to the normal conditions is demanding as well. Ingarden described this in the following way:

> The return to the concerns of earlier life is often accompanied by discomfort, by a feeling of the pressing weight of life, from which the original aesthetic emotion had, to a certain extent, freed us (ibid.,193).

Therefore, Ingarden's concluding thought about the nature of such switching is not surprising: "The transition from the practical to the aesthetic attitude is perhaps the most thoroughgoing change in man's psychological attitude" (ibid. 196).

At first glance Ingarden's notions can be perceived as extremely historical. They are bound to the time before new media-based interface culture became part of the mainstream, when only rare situations, connected to art environments (coming across works of art), made the switch off from everyday reality possible based on contact with original aesthetic emotion. On the contrary, the readiness to work in different generations of reality, different worlds and different times belongs to the present status of today's individual. Switching among them requires orientation toward very particular conscious acts, but it flows fluently, without extra difficulty for one's psychological life. It looks as if the horizon of expectations (it is Hans Robert Jauss' term from his aesthetics of reception) is used to the demands of participating in ontologically differently founded realities. Therefore the demands of entering the synthetic spaces and times do not cause additional problems to an individual. We are actually witnesses of a learned, routine readiness for such switching, for the contemporary individual spends more and more time in the as-if mode. It looks like Husserl's idea of the as-if mode infecting reality is being realized in the interface culture of mixed reality, as demonstrated by Barbrooke's notion in the final part of New Media Art as Research.

But is the change of attitudes, which today obviously does not cause major problems, and which completely coincides with the transition from the natural attitude to the aesthetic attitude, mean a specific profanation of phenomenological reduction? Does the cyclist on the streets of Ljubljana really function as some kind of "virtual phenomenologist"? Is the modern hybrid environment of mediatization and virtualization cleaned of the sharp edges of natural reality, as a kind of a "realm" of pure phenomena that follow the radical interruption with natural attitude that is bound to practical goals?

The answers to these questions are negative. Nevertheless, we have to be aware of differences between the current mediatization on one hand and derealization and neutralization in the context of phenomenology on the other. This trendy mediatization is not a "pure" derealization at all but is based on mixed experiences (Ger. Gemischte Erlebnisse), which Husserl addressed extensively in the texts collected in the XXIIIth volume of his Collected Works. The phenomenological device of changing attitudes is also useful in research on the specificity of media-based attitudes. However, the reality of the media is not the reality of accurately carried out phenomenological reduction but is the mediatized mixed and hybrid reality as a synthetic hyperreality—as argued in Jean Baudrillard's theory. It is characteristic of this new hybrid and artificial reality that often tries to be more real than the given reality. It passes for virtual reality in that is simulated in the context of reality, accelerated with artificial handling, and as convincing as possible.[10] Here we have a very typical example of the new interactive media that is formed polemically in opposition to the traditional mass media such as the press, radio, film and television with the promise that by using their devices (example web camera, logged on the Internet) they will get closer to the reality as-we-know-it in a more authentic way than the traditional media. The upgrade of the cyclist ride in the co-imagined tunnel described in this essay was also stimulated by the wish to upgrade the ride in the given

---

10 Virtual is not identical with the aesthetic mode of reality, it does not take a place within as-if mode, meaning that its chief concern is also a practical one like as in natural attitude. Virtual has a complex of the real, it even tends to be more real than the given real itself, and also the activities which take place within cyberspace are often directed to a very practical aims. The stress in VR applications is often laid on their striking real effects, VR is actually the reality upgraded to its most sophisticated high-tech form. Being active within VR does not simply presume taking their components within as-if mode. Virtual presupposed just a neutralization of the crude material features of the reality by replacing them with the data, i.e. digital features; on the other hand, the practical attitude is being preserved also in artificial and mixed realities. On the contrary, aesthetic attitude means something different, more subtle, and it could be applied also for the entities in cyberspace.

reality with the ride in a more complex form of simulated reality. The latter demanded the bracketing of the given reality, but this bracketing referred to the mode of this reality, to its "given" or natural and not to the characteristics of positing something real.

At the end we could say that the reality of phenomenology is one thing, the reality of the (new) media is something else. However, the phenomenological approach is the one that allows us to raise crucial questions in a moment that we are challenged with new media as well. In the case of life in mixed reality these issues are also associated with the investigations of attitude. In this essay we have seen that the plural mode of the forms of the real within mixed reality corresponds with the plural mode of perception and the latter requires the habituation of contemporary individuals to different attitudes and fluid switching between them. They need to customize the vertiginous experience of living in-between different and hybrid realities.

5 GAMING CULTURE: EVENT SPACE ON THE MOVE

Contemporary early 21st century cultures—post-industrial, software, information, spectacle, interface, breaking news-driven—are gaming cultures. Of course, games were also known to earlier cultures from distant times. It is difficult to state from the first that contemporary cultures are characterized precisely by games. Really there are many games, including playgrounds, theme parks, casinos, sport arenas, digital arcades, and especially games shaped by new technologies and media. In the present, it would also not be correct to consider games as the core of cultural mainstream since its main trends are linked to cultural changes that go hand in hand with the movements and streams of information, spectacle, and software society. Shifts concerning techno-science (a mechanical, electrical, and electronic approach being replaced by the paradigm "bio" and being integrated with the "info-sphere"), globalization, multiculturalism, empire, multitude, and the aftermath of The War on Terror can also be observed.

Games as entities with strict rules, process-like natures, competitiveness, and the ecstatic enthusiasm of gamers, are certainly not the main activities of the modern world. We witness another kind of shift. Contemporary cultures are not the cultures of games but the cultures where various components and activities are shaped and organized by the manner the attitude of games. With the manner of games we especially refer to playfulness, willingness, a sense of improvisation and lightness of playing with the possibilities, as well as simulations, experimentations, and working—all of which releases us from the "lead weight" of given-reality. With the attitude of games we refer to flexible and risky procedures, which often demand algorithmic (problem solving) activity presupposing an instant point of view on reality. Such an activity is based upon fluid switching among its different forms, which appear in some kind of reservoir (or, Heidegger's "standing reserve"). It can simply be said that they are at player's disposal. In relatively short intervals, the attitude of games enables us to operate in so called "given reality," which is defined by Newton physics and Euclid geometry. Next, we connect to devices to enter the world of cybernetics (and cyberspace, e.g., Second Life) that we observe both from fixed and mobile terminals.

Taking the gaming attitude means being aware of aspects of plurality and hybridization that are becoming universal in the present, in other words, going beyond the plurality of forms of reality mentioned before to also include a plurality of beings, actions, events. To the eye of an adherent to the gaming attitude, no thing is to be discarded beforehand for being utterly useless. In addition, this approach implies a creative ability to combine and test daring hypotheses, transforming every single phenomenon into an actual laboratory (i.e., an enclosed area behaving as a "wind tunnel" or dry run for testing different hypotheses, concepts, and actions). This phenomenology also arises from ontological plurality and has no complexes about entities characterized by very fragile and instant nature. This brings us to the following Herbert Spiegelberg's observation: "What is all-important in phenomenology is that we consider all the data, real or unreal or doubtful, as having equal rights, and investigate them without fear or favor" (Spiegelberg 1960: 892).

Why can we equate to a certain extent modern cultures with cultures that resemble a game in their manner and approach to reality? What are the changes that enable this expansion, and even the broadened reproduction of a manner of game? What is the reason for the turn that goes in the direction of playful design, which is connected with playful, sometimes even improvisational and experimental approaches towards reality? The main reason for this change is undoubtedly the cultural turn, which is based on the integration of modern technologies into the culture. These technologies, such as computers, robotics, and nanotechnologies, have become cultural tools and even the source of cultural innovations. They perform a representative and spectacular function. These technologies no longer play an important role in domination over the nature. In contrast, they are integrated into the processes of redefining a person, into new forms of presenting identity, spectacle, and processes of research and knowledge gathering. As such, the individual is not alienated from these technologies (as in the Marxian theory of alienation with its standard mode of industrial production as the frame of reference) but is connected to or integrated into them.

However, these new technologies are not the only thing of great importance. Changes in manners of thinking and perception also impact the field of cultural studies, techno-sciences, and new media art. Their aim is to overcome the difference between the cultures of scientists and literary intellectuals in terms of Snow's divide between two cultures (Snow 1963). Moreover, they want to integrate both realms. What is also important for the contemporary individual is the capability of algorithms, problem-solving, and new media literacies, which are directed toward an integrated and experimental approach to reality as a pluriversum of the given world and artificial realities. The game-like manner which stresses the importance of free experimenting and improvisation (games are also mind-shifters) is undoubtedly close to the techno-scientists, who are no longer fond of reading "the open book of nature" and assessing the hidden rules of nature, but are themselves part of the creative pole. They create new models of reality through the most striking ideas of genetics, nanotechnology, and artificial life. In a way they are artistically creative and their products are the source of cultural innovations. Their science is not a science-as-we-used-to-know it, but is instead "not-just-science" in terms of a more sophisticated activity that correspond with big shifts in contemporary, new media shaped art toward "not-just-art."

What is also crucial for understanding the key features of modern culture is the turn from a passive audience to active users. The passive audience was formed by traditional mass media (press, radio, broadcasting television) and was characterized by distant observation (seeing, watching). The reason for today's shift toward broader (inter)activity lies in the nature of new media and new interactive technologies, which are easy to get and enable media contents (for example, DVDs) with devices that are accessible for a broader group of consumers. Therefore, contemporary individuals do not only see photographs, videos, and movies, but also create them and are the part of the active pole that demonstrates the enormous production of moving images seen on YouTube and other Web 2.0 portals.

Janez Strehovec

PHILOSOPHY OF GAMES: THEORIES ON SUBTLE REALITY IN THE "AS-IF" MODE

"Follow me before the choices disappear" is a typical statement from Michael Joyce's hyperfiction Twelve Blue. When possibilities disappear, everything is over. Where there are a lot of possibilities, and everything is still open like at the beginning of life, the game begins. One of the key notions in Johann Huizinga's 1938 book Homo Ludens is that games are older than culture: even animals play. And a game—which connects Huizinga to the well-known claim of Friedrich Schiller on aesthetical education by means of a game—is more than a physiological phenomenon or a physiologically conditioned reaction. It exceeds the urge to confirm life, since a game is in itself an act of providing meaning. Homo Ludens claims that myth and language are also based on games (the game of words, the game of the spirit), emphasizing that a game is primarily an act of freedom since an enforced game is no longer a game; that is, a game is an activity of freedom, which is the characteristic separating the game from natural processes, physical enforcement, and duty. A game can normally stopped at any time, which means that the player can voluntarily give up and leave.

One of the key features of a game considered in terms of classical (as well as phenomenologically-influenced) game theory is its separation from everyday life, the extraction from its space and time, the transition to the playground as a particularly structured space of the game, and the transition to the intensive time of duration of the game. Games are not life, they are a simulation of life's possibilities in a condensed and programmed form, submitted to a special scenario that depends upon the genre of each individual game. What in life occurs rarely, exceptionally, completely coincidentally, or never even takes place in experience of most people (for example, radical enemy destruction), is arranged and compressed in a game. It seems that within a limited interval of time, a game establishes with an utmost intensity the availability of exceptional experience and impact. We can even understand it as a reservoir of options for accelerated rotation back and forth.

Separation of the game from everyday space and time—it must be stated from the first that today this separation is increasingly loosening, it is less distinctive, since a number of game characteristics are already inte-

110

grated into the labor of postindustrial society—implies the peculiar turning on and turning off, namely ecstasy as a radical transition to another state, and with this a consequent temporal delay. In a game, the landscape of time is maximally diverse, with a high frequency of powerful intervals, which—like life—flatten into a straight, uninterrupted line at the moment of the game's end. The game is over, although implying the end of a successful activity always hurts and shocks the gamer. Every time, it leaves the impression that the game continues and that it is just you being drastically removed from it. The feeling of being out is also tactile: the realization at the moment of game's end that the gamer pressing on devices for navigating and controlling the action is in vain—that there is no effect or response—shocks the whole body, inducing a feeling of complete helplessness. It is a feeling of isolation far worse than the one accompanying passionate viewing or participating at the moment when the curtain falls in a theater or when the gaze is deprived of a desired object in everyday perspective.

A game is a distinctively process-based activity with beginning, intermediate (gradation of the intensity of the game, entanglement in labyrinthine and maze situations, sporadic interruptions in intensity), and end levels, the latter being specific for each type of games. It is never a complete rejection, since the player can try or play the same game hundreds of times. Very few readers, listeners, and viewers return to the same text or work of art a number of times (unless the reception of such a text or piece of art serves their profession, meaning that they write a review or an essay; a single experience of the object usually suffices), while they can play the same game a hundred times or more, perhaps thousands of times in their life (card games, for example). The urge to continue, used and profaned by contemporary popular culture, is connected to the intoxicating effect of the "high-adrenaline" tension in the game, the programmed experience of uncertainty, risk, and accidents.

Uncertainty, risk, and accidents belong to culture, they are its essential part. Contemporary individuals in particular, need "packages of stimuli" of extraordinary uncertainty, risk, and compressed accidental situations, which are often delivered by contemporary art. The availability of constant repetition is therefore one of its more important features, which implies the recognition of the attractive atmosphere of games and the attractiveness of their goals (particularly true in gambling). Things that individuals/users consider as enforced or a burden are generally not repeated, whereas entering the game is always completely voluntary and cheerful (except in cases of professional players, in which case playing is their every-day job: a kind of craft).

Although ecstasy and enthusiasm are important features of a game, implying a Dionysian atmosphere of the chaotic and frivolous, games are in fact activities of unconditional order. A number of theoreticians—from Huizinga to Caillois—emphasize the latter. An utterly sophisticated order and discipline is perceived, co-existing side-by-side with extreme chaos and frivolity, often exceeding the order and discipline in other fields. This order is based upon the rules of the game. If these are omitted (usually omitting only one rule suffices), nobody takes the game seriously anymore. The rules of the game are unconditional, they provide the foundation for the normative traffic of the game's world and its time. Whomever breaks the rules is out, since his/her disrespect for rules undermines the illusive coherence of the world of games. "One who doesn't take the game seriously is a spoilsport" (Gadamer 1975: 92), Hans-Georg Gadamer described this particular feature of games. In his Wahrheit und Methode (Truth and Method), he provided a relevant insight into the philosophical particularities of games. According to Gadamer, a game has its own essence, which is independent from the consciousness of those who play it. The game exists even where there are no players, meaning that it transcends them as an autonomous entity. We also talk of phenomena such as the play of light, the play of waves, the play of colors, the play of forces, the play of hair, etc., which always imply "the to-and-fro movement which is not tied to any goal which would bring it to an end; rather it renews itself in constant repetition" (Gadamer 1975:99).

The emphasis in this notion is no doubt placed upon the "to-and-fro movement," the movement without stable destination, repeated and renewed. The game is played and replayed independently of those entering it, the repetition providing it with the characteristic of duration. Playing a game, we are in a repeating to-and-fro movement (that is often articulated as a loop, which is form of many new media shaped cultural contents), which is easy and effortless. It seems that persistent repetition (let us recall sport games, card games, and, of course, computer games) belongs to the gist of the game, precisely because of its easiness (the effort of players in a game is as a rule a high-adrenaline one, meaning that eventual pain and exhaustion are compensated with enthusiasm and ecstasy). Playful to-and-fro movement is not only aimless but also effortless: "it happens, as it were, by itself," as Gadamer (p. 94) described this specificity.

We have mentioned the high-adrenaline intoxication of the game, the zeal, and the entrancement, capturing and fascinating the players to the extent that they entirely submit to its flow, which in Gadamer's terms means that the to-and-fro movement takes control over them. It seems that the players are especially successful when they go with its flow. They must recognize at first glance the seemingly utterly nonsensical to-and-fro movement. Gadamer radicalized his view on the nature of the game in his statement "the real subject of the game [...] is not the player, but instead the game itself" (Gadamer 1975: 95.96).

Such approach is daily confirmed by the practice of playing computer games (also video games and games on computer-operated machines at the digital arcades). It is there where we encounter players completely immersed into the "to-and-fro" of the game; they take few things in life with quite the same amount of seriousness as the completely useless—to a disinterested observer—movement and destruction of (enemy) objects within the boundaries of a computer game scenario. It seems as if they are completely oblivious of time; the only temporal dimension is the enlarged, augmented present, gorging on the past and the future like a gigantic black hole. This is a present consisting of "nows," which the player perceives as physical entities, as if they are, in a way, objects with identities. Piled up in the flow of player's experience, they form a boundary, denying access to contents past and future. It seems that the player perceives the return to the time of every day—the time undefined by the enthusiasm of the game—as a stressful burden. It is the characteristics of the future that present the greatest disturbance and obstacle. Apart from "timescape," a special problem of all games is also their space in the sense of an area that needs to be explored, navigated through, and controlled. The player of computer games travels through space (in classical game Doom primarily through its corridors; in Myst, however, the movement is much freer), she conquers it and tries to navigate through it and control it to a much greater extent. Designers of (computer) games must therefore innovatively materialize complex environments consisting of conglomerates and spaces in different perspectives, the corridors and the arenas, suitable for fighting the "zombies."

GAME AS A SYMBOL OF THE WORLD

German phenomenologist Eugen Fink also devoted extensive analyses to the philosophical issues of games in his book Spiel als Weltsymbol (Game as the Symbol of the World, 1960), in which he—with introductions of metaphysical and mythological interpretations of games—also discussed the worldly nature of human games and the world as a game without the players. That means that he redirected the topic of games from the field of cultural and anthropological analyses to the field of ontology and even cosmology. A game with a cosmological feature is placed beyond the players: as a movement, it occurs independently from them, yet that movement is indefinable and evasive, the Gadamerian "to-and-fro" in the movement of the game confirms the thesis that the direction of this movement is not defined. Therefore, we can say, a game is a movement with no evident aim. With a game having movement and openness, only those partners are invited into the dialogue with it who are open and in movement themselves, which means they are on their way and approaching the game. In this respect, it is crucial that the openness to the world as "a game without players" does not belong to man but that the man belongs to the openness of the world, existing in the ecstasy of facing the infinite broadness of the world.

Fink writes about the world as play without the players and about playing as the ecstasy of man as world. The play of the world is directed to the groundlessness of the world, which anticipates the utter grounding of all its internal activities. Although itself is groundless and aimless, playing games provides the grounds to worldly activities, which have an aim and are bound to something that is not a to-and-fro movement but a movement directed either to or fro. A game— not an apparition, but a phenomenon—has very complex ontological specificity, which Fink, true to the phenomenological approach to the problem in question, summarizes in the following descriptions: individuals entering play take up a point of view that includes a very specific attitude to all the factors of playing. Everything taking part in play, both people (co-players) and things, and all have the character of toys, since they belong to the "unreal" world of playing.

> With man playing, a certain "unreal" sphere of meaning, which is here and is not, which is now and at the same time is not now, breaks into the whole actuality of real things and events. Using the term "unreal," we have not ultimately defined anything yet, we have just expressed that "the world of play" defies simple transition to the complex of the actual world, since its "seeming" character prevents their placing next to other things and complexes, and defined it as something "actual." (Fink 1960: 229)

A game therefore has an independent ontological status: phenomenologically, the status of the unreal. That means we encounter the field of "unreality," which despite its utter transitoriness and aimlessness—it is here and now and is not here and now—has the sui generis characteristics of the world with its own independent internal spaces and times when an imaginary scene is in question. Those spaces and times are just as non-definable, which directs us to the fact that the game happens in an independent field, constituted—as Fink emphasizes—with marking off, thus, as he writes, it is:

> Separated from other human activities and does not interweave with them in a joint striving for the aim. It "interrupts" the continuity of aim-directed activity, its aims are completely intrinsic to it in the manner that those intrinsic aims of gaming activity cannot be included to the general and common aims of life. The activity of play discerns itself from other activities, it isolates itself from them, having its own "closed area" in its own medium of appearance. (Fink 1960:234)

Sherry Turkle highlights this feature with respect to the video games, too: "Here is another world where everything is possible but where nothing is arbitrary" (Turkle, 2003: 508).

The crucial characteristic of this field is that it has no stable final destination, toward which it would be directed; it has no apparent foundation, although all things there are well founded. The game can therefore be understood as a metaphor of the cosmos within the media of appearance and thus within an independent modality, bearing the characteristics of the unreal, and existing under the "as-if" sign together with its spaces and times. The as-if mode infects the very activity of the game: the player "works-as-if-working," relieved of the weight of the world despite conforming to the rules of the field. To Fink, a game is a symbol of the world since the game reflects what is inherent in the world itself: lack of foundation, lack of aim, and the condition "beyond good and evil."

In his Letters Upon the Aesthetic Education of Man (1794-1795), F. Schiller pointed to the meaning of games in the sense of culturing and even humanization, which is what Huizinga and Caillois emphasize as well. The latter also anticipates an important emphasis on the consciousness of the game's reality, inherent in the worlds of games. The introductory chapter of Caillois' Les jeux et les homes (Men, Play and Games), entitled "Definition of Games," not only stresses the temporal and spatial elimination of the game and its unstable and—with respect to tangible, material aims—unproductive nature, but also emphasizes a key characteristic: its fictive nature in the sense that playing is accompanied by "special awareness of a second reality or of a free unreality" (Caillois 1967: 43) in relation to the given (everyday) reality. It is important that the author stresses the subtle consciousness of the independent, fictive nature of game reality in relation to the everyday, which no-doubt connects games with art. The player, like reader, listener, or viewer of works of art, completely surrenders to the game despite knowing that its reality is something special, that there are no equations between the game and the every day reality of his/her existence. The player cherishes the unreality of the game, developing a sense of working with fictive objects and events, forming the sense for the "as-if" and not for real. With all seriousness, the player indulges in things, which hardly count in regard to the principal trends governing the quotidian. The player's activity is accompanied by a consciousness of the co-existence of worlds within the augmented reality (as noted above, worlds considered as "pluriversum") and the need to fluidly switch between them. Entering the game mode demands a fluid abandonment of viewpoints and attitudes typical of everyday life and aesthetic enjoyment, and requires different modes of presentation (in video and film cultures).

The game therefore reveals itself as a maximally complex and distinctive cultural activity. This is also how Caillois sees it in his **Men, Play and Games**, an important part of which is a classification of games. He managed to actually embrace the broadness of the world of games by simultaneously leaving it open enough, allowing interconnections between the principal types of games: **agon, alea, mimicry, and ilinx.** The agon group are competitive games; alea games involve chance; mimicry contains games of deception, appearance, and assuming of roles; whereas ilinx comprises games of zealous enthusiasm and vertigo. However, in understanding computer games, it is important to bear in mind that these types are by no means ideal, isolated, or unchangeable. Caillois claims that we often encounter games in which two or three basic types of games combine.

Combinations of basic principles do not only imply the special nature of computer games but also a changed view of the world. Agon and alea anticipate an orderly world and discipline and strict rules, whereas the mimicry-ilinx combination produces an enthusiastic concept of the world of improvisations, imagination, and unrestricted inspiration. The space intended for a programmed experience of zeal, intoxication, vertigo, and panic is the amusement park, the genesis of which extends from fairs and fun fairs to theme parks. In his book, Caillois reveals the technological effects of fictive world creation, in a condensed form stimulating vertigo and panic. At one place and within relatively limited temporal intervals (from three to six minutes), the players can indulge in thoroughly exceptional situations completely different from the rhythm of everyday life. Caillois' theoretical views on the world of games are surprisingly up to date even today, regardless whether we direct our attention to contemporary theme parks (Disneyland, Gardaland, etc.) or consider them as a prism allowing observation of even such a recent genre of games as computer games. The typology of games, ranging from agon to ilinx, did by no means develop with computer games in mind, yet its very openness, in the sense of paying regard to combinations of main principles and types of games, speaks of the applicability of Caillois' approach.

The expression "computer games" is very broad, a term covering different types of games, which combine all the major Caillois' principles–from agon, alea, and mimicry to ilinx. Just as important for understanding particular features of computer games are Caillois' views of games at fun fairs, in which he emphasizes compression, programmed intensity, and limited duration of games and attractions. "By crossing the border, we find ourselves in a world, which is much more compressed than our everyday life" (Caillois 1967: 259). Everything is calculated, programmed to entice a powerful internal excitement, physiological fear, panic, sometimes acceleration, sometimes falling. The incredible intensity of game as a rich temporal event (shaped with special effects, concentrated exceptionality, the daring plot and the danger), is accompanied by precise rationing of time; that means that one of the attractive effects of the game is the very compression of extreme situations within a relatively short temporal interval and in a space, strictly separated from non-playing activities.

The question we are posing at the end of this survey of different philosophical views on games is to what an extent the thoughts represented still apply to our encounters with games in the context of contemporary new media-based cyberculture. At the beginning of the 21st century, can we still talk about separation of game from everyday life to the radical extent of Caillois and Fink? The answers to these questions are provided in the next sections of this chapter, which explores some aspects of computer games as well as the question of playfulness on the Internet. We would emphasize that the beginning of the 21st century is characterized by a greater intertwining of the gaming mode and reality in cyberspace manifestations as well as in the everyday reality of postindustrial societies, in which the importance of gaming activities constantly increases.

The game's authentic field still remains under the as-if sign. It is entered by switching to the game mode, which requires placing player's practical attitude to tangible and material reality in brackets. But the number of games is increasing, and switching into the game and immersion in it is no longer something difficult for today's players. It does not cause stagnation in player's mental life. No, today any movement among different view-points is as fluid as it can be. Games largely became an integral part of the present reality. Certain features of effortless manipulation of objects, which, in the paradigm of industrial societies was exclusively reserved for games, have already entered the production sphere in the context of activities, typical for the network-shaped new economy and the crucial mode of labor in augmented reality, which integrates the hybrid forms of labor in our everyday reality and cyberspace.

Following the mention of cyberspace with its rich range of online activities, it makes sense to direct the attention to the playfulness of cyberspace as shaped by its key software features. The backspace key, the paste and cut command, the mouse dragging and pointing the screen contents, and the absence of prohibition directly encourage as intensive and rampant playfulness in as possible. While simulating models by means of the state-of-the-art software, one works-as-if-one-does-not-work, even though one's intentions might be serious as can be and you are paid for your programming, which means that personal computer is a device, investing the as-if mode both on the level of activity and the level of reality form. In the as-if mode, actuality coincides with the already mentioned field of the unreal, with spaces that are here and are not, with times that are here and were not, and with to-and-fro loop-like movements.

Playfulness is also enabled by other ontological characteristics of cyberspace. Unlike moving in the real, physical world, where we need a lot of time and effort to move from one place to another, in cyberspace we can bounce with high speed from one point to the other, which means that we teleport ourselves. Cyberspace is data and the software-shaped space is without geographic distances (within cyberspace, distances are atrophied). In cyberspace, we are freed of direct influences of interactions between physical body and the environment, in which numerous obstacles can appear, which is why it functions as a playground. Thus, game as playful activity, both here and there, in the given space and in the cyberspace(s).

There is not a coincidence that such a playfulness was one of the key topics of the international conference The Internet as Playground and Factory (12-14 August 2009, New York), where the playbour—a word compound of play plus labor—came to the foreground as a crucial concepts. Playbour implies the core of the contemporary as smooth switching between various modes of reality and activities, which is demanded by one's everyday terminal activity:

> When they are on-line, people constantly pass from one form of social activity to another. For instance, in one session, a Net user

could first purchase some clothes from an e-commerce catalogue, then look for information about education services from the local council's site and then contribute some thoughts to an on-going discussion on a listserver for fiction-writers. Without even consciously having to think about it, this person would have successively been a consumer in a market, a citizen of a state and an anarcho-communist within a gift economy. (Barbrooke 2005)

TEMPORAL FEATURES OF GAMES

The general features of games are no doubt key moments in understanding contemporary computer games. Additional keys include: the playfulness generated by the activities in mixed and augmented reality, discussed in the previous section; and understanding of contemporary cyberculture, directed to the specificity of the new media, and emphasizing their interactive, digital, simulation based, and immersive nature. Yet the gist of computer games and their crucial characteristics can also be approached by a comparative discussion in the sense of comparing the medium to two popular mass media: film and the novel. A computer game is neither film nor novel. It is based upon a different form of representation, which no longer focuses on viewer and reader but on the gamer as user. The latter watches, listens and reads (e.g. instructions, or textual objects as parts of the game's scenario), and simultaneously plays. Activity is chiefly connected to the hand (sometimes both hands, depending on configuration of the interface), which means that the game also stimulates the sense of touch and demands great motor skills. Successful playing demands hand-eye coordination as well cooperation of hearing and touching. The computer game player is intensively immersed in the environment of the game, which requires unceasing interaction, rapid interventions, and immediate responses to the demands of the complex and live world of the game.

The gamer faces a starting point characterized by risky disorder, and as a rule accompanied by threats from different sources. This fundamental disorder is perceived as a task and a challenge to act and intervene. The gamer tries to restore order in a distinctively antagonistic world, which involves facing hundreds of tasks, connected with removing obstacles, with the original conflict, and with her enemy's counter-actions. The gamer does not have much time to hesitate and postpone the tasks to some later time. In fact, there are no "later" and "some other time" for the games—to know such times would make them unsuccessful as a player. Yet, on the other hand, they intensively exist in a time that is a very particular time of the game, its main characteristics a being weak past, a barely perceivable future, and a very "extensive" present. This is the present of interactions as intensive activity based upon feedback. The gamer plays in a present, which constantly implodes into the past and the future. This is a present composed of "nows" arranged in different directions (since it is space-time, which depends on the gamer's intensive activity).

A computer game is not a story, it is not an already painted painting, and it is not a finished film (i.e. the database logic considered in Lev Manovich's **The Language of New Media** is crucial for basic understanding of computer games). There is no "once upon a time," or at best such a narrative memento is just a subordinate component of the game's dominant structure, which does not exhaust itself in the narration of what happened but is based on forming a story in real time, that is, in its concurrent database composition. The course of the game does not rely on "once upon a time." What is important is the "now," the present reaction of the player. By destruction of obstacles and defeating of enemies in first person shooting game, the gamer destroys—metaphorically speaking—the past as well, wiping it away as non-essential, foregrounding the present. The question arises whether the game as a goal-directed activity is not, in fact, a very unique activity, in which the direction towards the goal demands a distinctive presence of the future? There actually is a demand for the future: solving conflicts in the game according to its scenarios is normally directed to a successful future as the initial task, yet the very dramaturgy of the game requires explicit activity in an enlarged/heightened present. Every "now" is arranged to be perceived as a task. Rather than being embedded in the cinematic world organized by the procedure of montage, the world of the computer game is an dynamic "gamescape," which is changed in real time by means of the gamer's activity as algorithmic and as problem-solving. Computer games presupposes code in two ways: playing a game and gaming a code are a part of the same process.

The future as a horizon of yet non-played units of the game and their "nows" is directed towards game's real time and implodes within it. Playing is not contemplation—not a distanced immersion in something that implies a lot of time or, metaphorically speaking, all times in the world (which a reader of traditional literature has at their disposal). There is little time in a game, often too little. The time that counts is the "now" as a moment filled with tasks. It is precisely because the player faces a lack of time that the time, metaphorically speaking, counts. They feel each individual "now." The player's attitude to the "nows" is tactile, and they perceive their comings and goings. For the player, every "now" is a digital unit as a possible "standing reserve" (Heidegger) for each particular situation. "Nows" filled with intensive action are expanded "nows" perceived individually.

Due to its byte coding, the digital environment of computer games implies knowledge on a peculiar atomicity, actualized as a reduction of complex components to their basic units. The description of the virtual "now" with a body, the "now" that can be counted, is, understandably, metaphorically approximate, figurative, based merely upon the experience of the author of this text in his encounters with the new media landscapes of games and digital textuality. The figurative sketch of "now" is important here only due to the emphasis that is placed on the experience of the complex present, in which a computer game runs, which, on the other hand, is observed through its temporal dimension, the environments of intervals and interruptions included.

Just as "textual landscapes" require spacing between words, letters, and punctuation marks (i.e. Maurice Blanchot's theory of "interruptions" and the practice of paying regard to the blanks between graphic signs as proposed by poet Edmond Jabes) in order to function or to be at all readable, so too the intervals are relevant in the landscapes of games. Intervals can be longer—when changing levels of the game, for example—or shorter, such as when connected to moments of decisions, or our possibility of choice in the unravelling of the game. They are also located within the "nows" and are distinctively felt while playing. Just as textual environments are not only filled with written or printed signs but also with blanks, so the game is not merely based upon the played "nows" but also the "nows of playing," the "nows" of selection, of transfer to a higher level of the game;

and of breaks, during which we feel the running away of time. It is during breaks that we count the played, the lost, and prepare for new challenges and decisions within the labyrinth of possibilities.

THE ACTIVE HAND AND THE COORDINATION OF MOVEMENT AND SIGHT

The computer (video) game is a medium demanding full engagement of all senses (and even their cooperation). The body participates in the game as well, via the maximally active hand, which needs to be properly trained in order to successfully manipulate complicated interfaces (joystick, console). In his book on reading paintings and watching texts Gandelman calls attention to the active, even tactile role of the eye and to different (historical) views of the relation between seeing and touching. In this regard, the author reaches back to the figurative interpretation of this relation in 16th century emblematics, drawing attention to Julius Wilhelm Zincgref's renaissance emblem Emblematicum Ethico—Politorum, depicting an eye placed in an open palm, seemingly observing the world from the palm. We are witnessing a deterritorialization of the eye through its nesting in the palm. The latter symbolizes the active and arbitrary role of the hand in the making of things, which Gandelman described as follows:

> In the emblem the eye is merely a pilot guiding the hand toward its objectives; in the Egyptian hieroglyph, on the contrary, the eye-sun rules over the hand in an absolute manner, just as the pharaoh ruled over Egypt. (Gandelman 1991: 3, 4)

I used this example to emphasize the historical tension between sight and touch, which in the ocularcentric paradigm of the Western world led to favoring of the role of looking and institution of sight in general. Within this paradigm, the true master is the one mastering the view (and his ideological interpretations). It is a tradition presently reaching its peak in the mechanism of video-control, in the computer war games with smart bombs and in using of satellite, orbital views (through the eye of the camera of weather satellites). In computer games—no doubt an excellent genre of visual culture, producing trendy iconography (influencing fashion, life-styles, movies)—we are still witnessing a peculiar affirmation of the hand, especially in its function of touching, holding and pressing of interfaces. It seems that the aforementioned emblem from Gandelman's book is symptomatic for the present condition: players' activities are successful only when the eye—metaphorically speaking—is in their hand, directing it as skillfully as possible. The eye must cooperate with the hand, they are "hand in hand," and optimum effect is achieved only through complete harmonization of both organs. A computer game is no doubt also an extremely tactile field, in which the tactile (haptic) vision, directed to the surfaces of objects, has the advantage over merely optic looking, directed to scanning of objects according to their contours.

At this point we can raise a question: "Who is the one with actual power in the world of computer games, who is the 'God' of these games or the monarch of the territory?" No doubt the one seizing both the player's sight and their hand, their "hand with eye", in short. In this case, mere "seiz-ing" of hand is not enough, since the game demands a number of kinaes-thetic and motor activities, boldly stimulating the integral perception. "The dimension of direct physical involvement or 'hands-on control', which the computer game grants to the spectator/player, is perhaps the central and defining characteristic of the genre" (Darley 2000:157). The author of this notion, Andrew Darley, compares the activity of a computer player to driv-ing a car, which is also based on complex interactivity and constant control, inducing a powerful impression of participation in the real time of pure present, in which something more or less controlled is constantly happen-ing. Driving a car (pre)requires certain skills, which is also the case in com-puter games with the user having to thoroughly adopt all the elements of steering and control.

The field of a computer game is arranged as to stimulate the feel-ing of distanced presence, the feeling of being there, in action, in which the player takes on roles, runs, rides, races, removes obstacles, jumps, and above all destroys the enemy with firearms. All this induces a regular blood-bath, as in the Quake game. To be there means to be within the screen, in its reactive environment of pure action, leading either to advancement in the game; transition to new, more demanding levels; or to failure, often resulting in very real frustrations. The unsuccessful player, intensively immersed in the world of action and thoroughly fascinated by it while playing, might perceive rejection in this activity more painfully, feeling more drastically excluded, than an unsuccessful reader or a bad film-viewer. We have mentioned the genre-symptomatic role of the—figuratively put—eye in the player's palm of hand, the function which is also not that of a passive observer of the activity or that of a reader of commands and commentaries. On the contrary, this is the eye, which must rapidly scan different aspects of the activity on screen. We can describe it as a bouncing eye, once directed to the top of the screen, then to its lower margin, and a moment later to its center, controlling the action, trying to perceive even more than is momentarily shown. It anticipates the action, looking behind the screen, seeing spaces around it, which are also important for establishing the field of vision of the game.

To be there, in the midst of activity on screen, in the world of action, where static locations constantly change into dynamic spaces, corresponds to the characteristic of "being in present," namely in the present composed of "nows" as described in the previous section. The game undoubtedly presupposes particular narrative structures, within it, stories come true and new ones emerge. Yet these stories run now and the player (players) is one of the main protagonists. It is not about "once upon a time" but about "it is now," which is connected to the nature of interactive representation in the sense of a shift, similar to the one from the accomplished to the unaccomplished, from outside of time to within it.

HACKER AND ARTIST MODS OF VIDEO GAMES

In all fields of new media shaped contemporary culture, stable works as closed artifacts are being replaced with structures and processes as open systems and interventions enabling numerous variants, transformations, and upgrades. Tendencies in contemporary art favor performativity, which often leads to an art without works in terms of stable products, meaning art without closed, material artifacts. The latter are replaced by instantaneous events, conceptualistic events, and works as programs. Creation of the new out of virtually nothing is decreasing, making way for objects or concepts composed of already existing models, i.e. ready-mades. Let us consider the changes the use of novel technologies caused in film. We are witnessing a development, which has changed film into data material, open to free user manipulation.

The film of yesterday, defined by strict authority and identity, linked to the director, actors, and a distinctive script, is changing into a reservoir of digital images (Manovich's concept of database), which users can slow down or speed up, scratch, remix, and change their score. Consider the variants of well-known movies, offering a different denouements from those in the original, sometimes completely opposed to the director's authorial intention. In a similar way, DJs' procedures in terms of mixes, cuts, and scratches are expanding from club music to film and other forms with new media shaped cultural contents.

Has this movement surpassed the genre of computer games? Not at all. In the field in question, there are numerous variants of well-known computer game: the so-called mods and patches. These variants usually do not bother the designers of games, who work for big companies. What is more, these designers sometimes even include the hackers' and web artists' transformations of their games in their new projects. In the case of **Tomb Raider**, for example, the main protagonist Lara Croft did not only appear in a film but also in a derivative form: the Nude Raider game. The field of net art can also offer computer games by net artists, which are usually not distributed in public in a form of artifacts (CD-ROMs, for example) but only exist in the authentic place of net art, i.e. on the Internet. In establishing the online artistic computer game genre, an important role was played by Anne-Marie Schleiner's 1999 on-line exhibition **Cracking the Maze**. The exhibition focused on variants of popular computer games, which retain the original settings (together with their graphic solutions, iconography and forms of interactivity), yet are subversive in dramaturgy and critical of the originals. As one of groundbreaking pieces in this movement we can consider Natalie Bookchin's video game "The Intruder" as a piece that demonstrates the blurring of the borders between two fields: elite, high art (e.g., Borges' literature) and popular culture genres (e.g., video and computer games). These fields were strictly separated within the modernist paradigm. The author was inspired by Borges's **Tale of Two Brothers in Love with the Same Girl** ("La intrusa," 1966) to create a multimedia story narrated through ten computer games, which makes references to some classic but now very outdated video games from the 1980s, such as **Pong, Kaboom, Laser Blast, Outlaw, Jungle Hunt,** and **Gal's Panic.** The crucial point in this piece is the feminist approach of the author, where the hero of Borges' text is understood as an intruder and a disturbing element in a world controlled by men. In the last unit of the game, she even takes the role of a moving target at which shots are fired from a circling helicopter.

Although suspicious of the expression "feminist variant," Schleiner's statement accompanying the exhibition mentions that a number of patches replace the male hero (and macho organization of action, also typical for the most popular variants of the shot-them-up computer games) with female protagonists and androgynous animals, or, alternatively, the patches transform female protagonists in official variants of commercial games such as **Tomb Raider, Resident Evil,** and **Final Fantasy VII.** We are witnessing the birth of a new subculture and also a new net-based artistic practice, boldly interfering with commercial products of big companies and ironically enforcing a new ideology upon them, transforming their heroes and also providing a new audience (new users). Such parasite-critical-subversive practices can undermine the dominant ideology of "official," commercial computer games and introduce new, more subtle configurations of (main) characters, spaces of the game, as well as manners of playing and modes of interactivity. The established semiotic and iconographic structures of games are adjusted to new tactics and strategies, which demonstrates the most recent genre of tactical games, designed by artists-activists. As striking examples of such a game we can mention:

1. Gonzalo Frasca's "September 12," which shows the inevitability of collateral damage in the war on terror,

2. "Raid Gaza," which criticizes Israel's military strategy,

3. and "Gulf War 2," released six months before the invasion of Iraq, and anticipating the terrible consequences of confused politics in approaching the Middle East issues.

Such artistic mods and patches are involved in the contemporary hactivism movement, which is close to tactical media. This movement was described in Galloway's book **Gaming: Essays On Algorithmic Culture** (2006), as "countergaming," in terms of the subversive strategies of net artists who generated projects and programmes that try to subvert and critique the formal structures and political implications of mainstream games. Galloway even draws parallels between the work of Jodi and other "countergaming" net art artists to the "countercinema" of Godard and others in the 1960s.

Today, the patches are primarily enabled by hacker interventions into commercial games and their artistic upgrading in terms of activism and hactivism. Yet it will soon be possible to arrange the official variants of popular mainstream games for a broader group of consumers, in order to allow different courses of action, different heroes, more types of iconography, more spaces of the game, and different plots and endings. By this, the entertainment (and art) industry would accomplish what the so-called new economy is based upon, namely offering product in the form of a flexible service and not as a closed artifact. After the postmodern destabilization of subject (its deconstruction into the fractal subject or the multiple "I" within computer culture), today we can observe the destabilization of object, especially the one with an accomplished material form, and a transition to open, unstable structures. Sharp-edged (material) objects are being replaced by processes, the emphasis is placed on a service rather than the artifact, and instead of experiencing pleasure in a closed, thoroughly perfected work, we encounter experience. In this sense, with regard to the question of the work of art today, Marc Napier explained as follows: "The artwork is not a thing, it is a process, an interface, an invitation to participate in a creative act" (Napier 2002). The striking forms of such an experience are no doubt also provided by video and computer games, their key component being an original form of experiencing, their nature characterized as a service and a process. When purchasing a video game, the consumer does not buy a traditionally conceived artifact but a scheme for a certain activity, for an arrangement of certain actions, and a package of scenarios for different experiences and sensations.

Gaming culture, as well as video game mods, impacts post-hypertext e-literature. Textual instruments and text-based literary patches contribute to the broadening of the field of e-literary investigation. E-literary patches (mods) invite the gamer to behave in a way that, to a certain extent, diverges from her ordinary attitude to gaming reality within the mainstream gaming.

The moment that interests me could be seen as "emergent" game-play, in the sense of an unplanned and unexpected use of the game. The result is not a new behavior, however, in the sense of "game currency trading" and other complex emergent gaming. It is closer to a glitch like the famous "M" Pokémon glitch that introduces an alternative being from within the game's coding. (Baldwin, p. 7)

Janez Strehovec

6 E-LITERARY TEXT AS A RIDE

"So, like earlier generations of English intellectuals who taught themselves Italian in order to read Dante in the original, I learned to drive in order to read Los Angeles in the original" (Banham, 2009: 23). Why begin this chapter with a quotation which directs us toward Los Angeles and driving as the ultimate skill needed for reading this big city? Answering this question is not too difficult, because our basic approach to e-literature is not shaped only by academic literary theory: in addition, we try to deploy and combine several disciplines that originate from non-academic fields. E-literature is not the continuation of literature as-we-know-it. In it, the literary as such is at stake. We consider this practice as a field bringing together the e-literary, new media art, popular culture, and club cultures. To read e-literary texts in the original one needs to deploy various skills, i.e. reading as decoding is not enough. Furthermore, the criterion "born digital" does not suffice in explaining today's e-literary endeavors: this criterion needs to be deployed hand in hand with the "born corporeal" and "born social."

Pieces of post-hypertextual electronic literature are emerging in proximity to new media art and to its genres such as (techno)performance, (multi)media installations, virtual architecture, locative media, and software art. A number of innovations applied by new media artists are also useful in the field of electronic literature. Here we must point to net art, whose notable representatives intervened in the field of new media textuality, and thereby realized projects that are also significant for digital literature (e.g., the work of Vuk Čosić and Olia Lialina). In fact, the Slovenian e-literature authors Jaka Železnikar and Teo Spiller emerged from net art and today work at the intersections of digital literature (Železnikar), digital textuality (Spiller), and new media art. Slovenian artist Srečo Dragan, who is also primarily engaged in the video, has likewise delved into the domain of digital textuality (e.g. in E-Book Nomad).

The concept of the specificity of new media art with regard to the social (Domenico Quaranta's notion on the new media art world) is no stranger to the field of e-literature, where we can also speak of a very specific world that is essential for its works. Participation in it is crucial for its authors, since outside this world, which involves highly specific apparatuses of its sense-making and interpretation, they have little chance of surviving. Today, the shift in theory has been associated with the shift from one type of content (linguistic, discursive, and cultural) to another (material, biological, and expressly political), which also has an impact on digital literature as an emerging field. Since the bio paradigm is becoming a source and generator of contemporary social and cultural creativity (Negri, 2011), the material, the biological, and the political also concern the field of textuality in new media, as is demonstrated in writings by Alan Sondheim and in Sandy Baldwin's computer game patch New Word Order: Basra (2008).

Likewise, the new generation of electronic literature embodies a practice that enters into a dialogue with the tendencies and forms present in today's technoculture, cyberculture, algorithmic culture, and even club culture, for which practices such as VJ-ing and processes such as mash-ups are essential. E-literature's nature is encapsulated in the broader context of contemporary algorithmic culture, which also affects the creation of an expanded concept of the digital literary text, which we can define as a "ride," in order to emphasize its new media nature and proximity to trendy forms of contemporary popular culture.[11] What do we mean by this?

First, we try to enter the issue of the ride by addressing its philosophical feature. The ride is an intensive, rich, event-based, corporeal experience, which takes place in compressed time, presupposing ascents and descents, heavy rhythm, suspense and dissolves, emotional ups and downs, and even daring feelings of uncertainty when the rider suddenly realizes that she is not in charge. Switching to the riding mode also means one's readiness to enter unstable conditions filled with many non-trivial tasks that deploy algorithmic (e. g. problem-solving) thinking and decision-making. There are various kinds of rides. One striking and thrilling mode is the roller coaster ride, which turns the negative condition of fear into fun and leisure.

The ride presupposes a tension between its Apollonian mode (in the Nietzschean terminology of rational decision-making and control activities) and its irrational and euphoric Dyonisian mode (tendency or

---

11   The metaphor of a ride is also useful when considering several works of print literature, as well as theatre and film. For example: Homer's Odyssey and its cinematic derivatives, Poe's A Descent into the Maelstrom, and Butor's novel Modification.

principle), which might be explained even in terms of the concept ilinx, as discussed in Caillois's book Man, Play and Games. First (e.g. the Apollonian), refers to a very efficient fashion of one's hands on control activities and rational procedures of riding. The second refers to conditions when the user is not in charge and is faced with dazzling sensations. The encounter between both principles is what makes the recent rides so attractive (e.g. game-influenced rides in digital arcades and theme parks).

The perceptual features of the ride provoke a desire directed toward beholding the particular qualities of the ride, and enjoying its striking and extraordinary atmospheres in its pure, crystal form. Such a desire is driven by a hunger to have exciting and rich experience, which often demands a check in our normal attitude toward reality shaped by everyday goals. Many technical devices have been invented to arrange pure driving experiences as a basic experience (from a carousel and roller coasters to race simulators), which are specific to particular places (e. g. theme parks, and digital arcades). Today similar riding experiences have been generated in other fields of entertainment industry (e.g., 3-D films and computer games). Watching Cameron's Avatar movie is also a kind of ride for its spectators. However some of these particular experiences can also be found in the new media shaped art and literature.

Rather than being about transportation of passengers and freight from point A to point B, to be carried or conveyed (as in a private or public vehicle or on horseback), and moving activity in general, in terms of pushing the pedals or simply rolling on two or four wheels, the ride is in its very core a narrative and the organization of travel. It consists in moving intervals, situated in short temporal units that enter in the viewing field of the rider, which is narrowed and limited with her very movement and navigational activities shaped with her proprioceptive and kinetic arrangements. The ride which counts today is often the ride for pleasure or excitement. Such a ride doesn't take place only in the amusement park; it is often the general form of crucial recent cultural contents. The ride also challenges contemporary cinema, and in this field we are witnessing the birth of hybrid genre of movie-ride based on the convergence between films (primarily science fiction) and theme park rides.

The ride is not unfamiliar to traditional arts and literature. Consider Edgar Allan Poe's A Descent into Maelstrom, Michel Butor's novel Modification, and Erich Wonder/Heiner Goebbels/Heiner Müller's Maelstromsüdpol, performed at Ars Electronica festival in Linz (Austria), 1988.

IN THE WORLD OF TO AND FRO MOVEMENT

The ride often presupposes the activity of returning, going back to the point of departure; and secondly, the movement, which is juxtaposed and broken in a way that it suddenly replaces the final point (let us say B, in a case of A toward B movement) with a novel one (e.g. the C or D). As a loop-designed ride, the form of many theme parks rides is circular, as are plays, cultural and artistic contents, and sport games. By linking the loop, play, game, and the ride, we are challenged to consider the issue of ride also in the context of Hans-Georg Gadamer's play philosophy, which addresses the issue of play within a very subtle fashion by referring to those playing (and gaming) features that foreground its autonomy and specificity. In Truth and Method (1975), Gadamer argues that the play has its own essence, which is independent from the consciousness of those who play it. Play exists even where there are no players, meaning that it transcends them as an autonomous entity, since we also talk of phenomena such as the play of light, the play of waves, the play of colors, the play of forces, the play of hair etc., which always imply "the to-and-fro movement which is not tied to any goal which would bring it to an end; rather it renews itself in constant repetition" (p. 99).

The emphasis in this notion is no doubt placed upon the "to-and-fro movement," the movement without stable destination, repeated and renewed. The game is played and replayed independently of those entering it, the repetition providing it with the characteristic of duration. Playing a game, we are in a repeating to-and-fro movement (that is often articulated as a loop, which is the form of many new media shaped cultural contents), which is easy and effortless. It seems that persistent repetition (let us recall sport games, card games, and, of course, computer games) belongs to the gist of the game precisely because of its easiness (the effort of players in a game is as a rule a high-adrenalin one, meaning that eventual pain and exhaustion are compensated with enthusiasm and ecstasy). Playful to-and-fro movement is not only aimless but also effortless: "It happens, as it were, by itself' (94), as Gadamer described this specificity.

We have mentioned the high-adrenaline intoxication of the game, the zeal and the entrancement, capturing and fascinating the players to the extent that they entirely submit to its flow, which in Gadamer's terms means that the to-and-fro movement takes control over them. It seems that the players are especially successful when they go with its flow. It means that they recognize at first glance utterly nonsensical to-and-fro movement. Gadamer radicalized his view on the nature of the game in his statement, "the real subject of the game(...)is not the player, but instead the game itself." (p. 95-96). Such approach is daily confirmed by the practice of playing computer games (also video games and games on computer-operated machines at digital arcades).

The key topic of this book relates to e-literature and new media art. This leads to the following questions: Can draw parallels between Gadamer's account of games and digital literary texts understood and explained as a ride? Is there any point in digital literary text which corresponds with the notion of to-and-fro movement? It is self-evident that Gadamer's notion of play devoted to philosophical observation did not take into account electronic literature, however we will try, to a certain extent, to apply Gadamer's game/play paradigms to our discussion on digital text as a ride.

The to-and-fro movement is an ever circular movement of a loop, and the loop in a form of a feed-back loop is the basic form of cybernetic systems; there are various loops (between the code and the displayed text, between the text and the reader-user and in the displayed text itself). The to-and-fro movement is basic for all responsive environments as event-shaped structures, and implies a desire to be part of it or to control it. Even a ride itself is caught in such a circular form, which is familiar to many sport games (from football and basketball to tennis, car racing, and boxing).

Digital text is in-between, traveling to-and-fro between the screen and the reader/user, between the underlying code and displayed text, between one screen and another, between one author and others, and between one node and others. It is like a ball, a nervous, movable entity, which behaves unpredictably. And the digital text also seems to be also a nervous gaming device, which enables counter-play in various directions, sophisticated chains of responses that challenge the user/reader to react, enact, and choose one or another possibility. The to-and-fro movement is a crucial paradigm for signifying the sophisticated relations between reader/user's activity and displayed text in responsive environment. The reader/rider steadily manipulates the text, clicks on the single word or the cluster of words, and gets real time responses of her activity that provokes her novel set of clicking, dragging, scrolling, or even grasping the text by means of data glove, mouse, joystick, and other navigating devices.

One example of playful to-and-fro movement in the field of electronic literature is The Screen by Wardrip-Fruin et al., which is accessed by the user/reader in the 3D Cave virtual reality platform. This piece stimulates user/reader in daring search for unusual textual combination that are at her disposal by means of reaching the 3-D virtual words on the sides of an open cube shaped Cave and manipulate them. The to-and-fro movement is also common to e-literature gaming patches (e.g., Bookchin's The Intruder) as well as e-literature projects shaped by textual instruments (Wardrip Fruin, Eskelinen)

Text as a ride presupposes the very act of reading in terms of riding as a kind of integral excitement, which is not only a mental issue of meaning, decoding, and task-solving activity, but also a corporeal one provoked by the nature of digital text as a kind of bodily structure based on the richness of relations among the textual components. Digital text can be unpredictable, and sometimes one just has to ride and roll with it. Digital texts with literary features challenge the hybrid reader-viewer-listener (as user) to approach the textual environment in a way that demand several cognitive and even bodily, kinesthetic procedures. Such texts based on words-images-bodies intersect the literary avant-garde, visual culture (e.g., video and computer games, digital cinema, the Web 2.0 visual contents), and even tactile culture, meaning that they address the entire user's perceptual apparatus. Due to the very nature of digital textuality the user is not safe; they are faced with several non-trivial efforts and procedures that shift from the ordinary reading of print-based textuality. Their problem-solving, algorithmic activity often demands the preparation of a plan of several tasks for approaching a text as a not self-evident item. The user writes down the notices of their current steps in exploring text, and experiences an alternative way of textual decoding.

Mark Amerika's FILMTEXT (2002) is a striking example of a novel hybrid genre at the intersection of avant-garde, hypertext, film, computer games, and hactivism based on the mixing and (re)mixing, interfacing, and sampling. It demonstrates that text-making in terms of the new media paradigm is surf-sample-manipulate research practice. Rather than being an artist or author (written with capital letter), the textscape producer could be defined as a (new media) investigator. This artist's transformation fits well with our already mentioned claim for the investigative value of digital literary creation, which comes to the fore within new media shaped art-making.

RIDING A DIGITAL TEXT

Digital text as a ride presupposes the intensification of the role of the user/reader in terms of their extremely rich experience, which is not in play through (print) textuality as-we-know-it. Such a text (experienced even as an adventure, crowded with stimuli of various origins and intensified to the thrill, when the user/reader is not in charge) is, as much as possible, rich in visual, motor, and kinesthetic features that accompany the new media textuality. It is about the text displayed within the economical pace of time (the elevator pitch effect[12]), and about the performance of text. When performed live, it attracts the user/reader with various special effects and devices such as loops, tunnels, roller coaster curves, tornado eyes or volcano eruptions designed and prepared by means of computer graphics. Such effects take the role of experience enhancer. Text as a ride presupposes the user/reader's

---

12 In today's mixed reality of change everything is under the sign of the elevator pitch as the key strategy in approaching the present consumer within a sophisticated and as much as possible persuasive fashion. An elevator pitch is a concise, carefully planned, and well-practiced overview of an idea for a product, service, or project, which can be delivered in the time span of an elevator ride (e. g. thirty seconds or 100-150 words) with the purpose of hooking the audience into a positive response to the offering product. What is crucial here is the first impression in terms of getting the investor's attention with a certain hook expressed in a statement that piques their interest to want to hear more about the aiming product or service. To get the consumer excited, involved, and thinking about, one needs to adopt her (cultural) contents and products to the novel reality of a shorter attention span.

involvement in textual experience, and the act of reading ceases to be just reading or hybrid veading (reading plus viewing), and is instead getting transformed in reading-riding as a kind of sophisticated adventure, which deploys both the demanding mental activity and corporeal, bodily (kinesthetic, motor and proprioceptive) procedures and skills.

When we are talking about a digital text as a ride, it makes sense to reach for historical examples of (text-based) electronic installation art. One predecessor in this field is Jeffrey Shaw's piece The Legible City (1988-1991). What does this responsive environment look like? The user in a role of cyclist/reader rides a stationary bicycle through a simulated representation of a city (it uses the ground plans of actual cities: Manhattan, Amsterdam, and Karlsruhe) that is constituted by computer-generated three-dimensional letters, forming words and sentences along the sides of the streets. The existing architecture of real cities is completely replaced by textual formations written and compiled by Dirk Groeneveld. Daring and curious (even nervous) cycling/riding along the streets of words represents a journey of reading. The choice of path one takes is a choice of texts as well as the spontaneous juxtapositions and conjunctions of meaning that is constituted by computer-generated three-dimensional letters, forming words and sentences (as artificial buildings) along the sides of the streets. The handlebar and pedals of the interface bicycle provide the cyclist an interactive control over the direction and speed of the ride. The physical effort of cycling in the real world is transposed into the virtual environment, affirming the cyclist's activity within the mixed reality (of the given reality and the world of virtual architecture).

As an example of digital literary piece prepared and designed in the riding way, fashioning by this Shaw's piece, consider Jason Nelson's Dreamphage (Version 1, 2003), where the drag and drop on the screen causes a tunnel graphics effect. Bold readable text appears just on certain screens during the user's fast immersion into an attractive visual environment saved on the simulator drive. Rather than being a safe ride, such a piece demonstrates that riding of the digital text is often a risky adventure, because the author's special effects are even designed in a manner which disables the very act of reading. We face the issue of unreadable text, which is one of the topics of experimental e-literature (e.g., Jim Rosenberg's Diffractions Through, 1995). Such a process in destabilizing the perception by provoking (and organizing) one's vertiginous experience (the ilinx in Roger Caillois's play theory) could be understood even as an attempt to enhance the ostranenie effect in terms that are not just about the making strange solely of the object of one's observation, but it also estranging the pure act of observation/experience/perception. The destabilizing of one's everyday perception (within the framework of the present technoculture) is also one of the key devices deployed in new media influenced literature.

FROM READING TO RIDING OF DIGITAL LITERARY TEXT

Three basic steps:

- Jumpy reading in terms of nervous jumps from one hyperlink to another (e. g. in hyperfiction) accompanied with techno-suspense and techno-surprise.

- Not-just-reading as hybrid and composite activity of reading, listening and viewing (and also clicking, dragging and scrolling) of multimedia shaped digital text (e. g. on the web site displayed text).

- Reading/Riding a digital literary text in terms of complex corporeal activity, which demands the active palm and even hand(s) or the whole body (e. g. at text-based VR-shaped installation). The reader/rider is set in the virtual cockpit position, their reading/riding presupposes hands-on controls activity

Riding also represents the user's procedures in Mary Flanagan's [domestic] (2003), which functions as a virtual, interactive installation and a flexible means of storytelling, where the navigator is free to explore and ride. There is a subtle anxiety between traditional 3D game conventions and discovery in the highly stylized nature of the [domestic] experience. The "house" as a basic environment of this piece is less a physical space than a psychic one: it refers in each step to memory, with texts lining and extruding from walls. The reference to the memory labyrinth and to immersion with movable environments, which refers to the computer games' architecture, demonstrates that the riding experience of this piece is first and foremost a kind of narrative. While [domestic] works first and foremost as a new media art installation with textual components play an important role, *The House*, another Flanagan piece, might be considered as an example of expanded concept of e-literature. This piece places the movable digital text within the 3-D environment of virtual architecture, made of blocks with ever changing, nervous, hardly readable text displayed on them.

Text in *The House* is written upon "rooms," and these rooms emerge as floating cubes to create "houses" next to and among the intermingling text. This work is approached, perceived, and read through user interaction and navigation, by clicking and dragging. There are no stable points with regard to up and down, side and center, left and right. Everything is defined just by nearness and remoteness. The reader/viewer/rider is on the move. She tries to catch the meaning of floating chunks of textual components. In fact, she surfs with them and by them.

RIDING A CUBE

The House is significant because through it we approach the digital literary text as an entity which can be animated and displayed as 3-D object, e.g., a virtual body consisted of 3-D displayed words on its sides. Such an arrangement of digital text on the cube or within it, means that the cube seems to be the proper place for displaying 3-D through special effects enhanced digital texts. What is the nature of a cube? It is a component by which the whole is composed. It is a brick, and is not only a brick. It is also the house, room, gallery as a "white cube," a Heideggerian "Gestell" and shelter. Unlike the sphere as an extremely movable, nervous body, the cube is, to a certain extent, a stable one, and such temporary stability is needed to be a shelter or a home of digital text displayed on its inner or outer sides.

The cube is a self-contained, compact body, which closes down everything that enters it. In a moment of entering text, the cube is opened up for novel ways of reading. Rather than being a book, which enables the turning of pages, the cube opens up novel ways of interacting and enacting. Text from one side interacts with the text on another. The cube is suitable to form a cluster of cubes. It can move or float around as is demonstrated in Flanagan's *The House*. Digital text in a 3D environment addresses the virtual reader. The reader gets to use an invisible avatar as a chance to enter a textual body or to possess textual components as tangible objects. Not just to write down a word but to touch it, to possess it, and to manipulate it tangibly—these are the demands of the contemporary individual who is used to being fully immersed in their own various everyday activities. Rather than just read and watch a word, line, or sentence, the user is interested in grasping a word physically. Having the digital word in their palm seems to present them with the full experience of the digital "text" and invites them into the enjoyment of it. Such a condition even implies a tactile feature of digital literature, simulating bodily interactions between the textual body and its reader-user: "The ability to rotate the whole poem gives the impression that it is an object, something one could hold between one's hands and gaze into" (Karpinska, The arrival of the beeBox).

Another digital literary piece that enables the reader to experience the digital poem as a (virtual) body is Aya Karpinska's and Daniel C. Howe's open ended. This text-based installation is designed to reveal itself through continually shifting geometric surfaces. Verses appear on the faces of two separate, translucent cubes situated within one another. In order to experience this textual work the reader/rider manipulates a joystick or touchscreen to rotate the cubes, bringing lines on various surfaces into view. As cubes and faces and layers are manipulated by the reader, dynamically updated lines move in and out of focus. The structure of the poem allows it to be read in any number of ways, from single verses on cube faces to sequential verses across faces, to juxtapositions of verses across multiple cubes. We face a novel manner of reading/riding a digital literary text as a non-trivial task, which is driven by the anxious uncertainty about what's going next. Such uncertainty is the very core of all significant digital literary projects shaped as a ride.

The common denominator in these examples of new generations of e-literature is that the reader-user is less and less engaged in understanding the symbolic nature of works and decoding of meaning, while their interest becomes focused on a new series of (rich sensory) experiences by which they expect to be addressed as directly as possible. The reader-user demands from the digital text that it strikes them even with its visual and tactile effects, and that it arouses their motor stimuli. The reader-user, who is more and more a rider, expects even literary and artistic content to be organized in the kind of form ("package") that they encounter in attractive products of the entertainment industry, that is to say, the reader-user expects that they will also strike and intoxicate themselves as if they were a roller-coaster ride or a movie (e.g., Cameron's *Avatar*, 2009).

The "more" in the sense of tactile and motor arrangements in the practice of reading/riding is accompanied by a sort of "less" on the level of the reader/user's focus on semantic and symbolic features of post-hypertextual literary projects. We encounter jumpy reading in the sense of a progressive scanning of textual components on-screen, which means that this type of reading is extremely vulnerable to distractions and interruptions. The reader-user keeps herself busy with a number of tactile and motor tasks. These have already been characteristic of reading hyperfiction with the aid of a mouse or touch-pad. In the moment when "our urge to click" (Mangen, p. 410) is upgraded by the "urge to ride," the reader-user comes across even more sophisticated corporeal procedures which challenge the reader-user's attention span and destabilize their concentration. The reader-user is placed into a **jetz-zeit**, an operational realtime where their experience is continuously provoked by expectations directed toward what is yet to come, where they will react to the current state with the aid of an interface. The reader-user is continuously distracted by both expectations on the level of mental activity and by the physical activity required for her participation in the event of such a text. When discussing the specificity of holopoetry, Eduardo Kac wrote that

> Freed from the page and freed from another palpable materials, the word invades the reader's space and forces him or her to read it in a dynamic way; the reader must move around the text and find meanings and connections the words establish with each other in empty space. Thus a holopoem must be read in a broken fashion, in an irregular and discontinuous movement, and it will change as it is viewed from different perspectives. (p. 131)

Here the emphasis is placed on "move around the text," which undoubtedly directs us toward the concept of reading as riding, which foregrounds even the topological feature (at the expense of the pure semantic one). "Move around" is actually the basic way one approaches the new media content(s). It implies the tactile arrangements and an approach, which demonstrates that the user is often not in charge, and that this unstable condition generates the readiness for being "in search."

In contact with digital literary texts on new media platforms, reading as a multi-sensory and riding activity also mutated in the field of wholly intellectual processes, that is to say, the challenge for the reader-user is not only with regard to motor and kinaesthetic arrangements but also on the level of very specific apprehension intended for the software bases of digital literary texts. What do we mean by this? Works of digital literature are essentially defined by the programming (and scripting) languages by which they are generated. The basic information about the sort of software (as a cultural tool) they are supported by is crucial. More than a decade ago, the Australian author of digital literature Komninos Zervos even titled individual cycles of his digital poems "Shockwave Poems" and "Java Poems" with the intention of pointing out the essential link between his texts and the given software. Later, even Flash poetry became popular, as did digital poetry generated by other tools (for example, Perl).

This fact is also fundamental for reading those types of works, since the reader-user who is familiar with their software base will necessarily see "more" in them than the reader-user who is not. Likewise, the reader who is perhaps herself a programmer will not "fall" for the special effects which sometimes populate these works with the intention of realizing a certain breakthrough, since she will be able to delineate the ordinary use of a given programming language (which also includes its spectacular applications) from its creative upgrade.

What sort of text articulates itself as a ride? It is post-literary, as-if-literary, or hyperfictional, but certainly a text with which emphasizes materiality and eventfulness whose arrangements address embodiment and thus intervene in the world of the biological. We live in a time when all the decks are being re-shuffled, and so the authors of e-literature also find that their work becomes a problem, a riddle, an activity at stake. Before every text they begin, they find themselves in a state of uncertainty. And it is also the reader-users who encounter the world of (post-hypertextual) electronic literature with non-trivial effort as they participate in an augmented experience of such a literature, articulated as a series of events and rides on them.

Janez Strehovec

7 DIGITAL POETRY AND THE WORLD OF CYBER-LANGUAGE

Digital poetry is an umbrella term, which for the flexible purpose of identification often encompasses various multi-media projects at the intersection of digital textuality, hyperpoetry, experimental writing in digital media, net art, software-controlled electronic text-based installation art, text generators, textual software art (code poetry), and text-based computer games with elements generated by the author's very individual approach to the textual material. Some pieces of digital poetry allow the reader to enjoy so-called lyrical atmospheres and qualities; others are even counter-lyrical or post-lyrical. On closer inspection, digital poetry turns out to involve several experimental projects, which are articulated as hybrid entities devoted to in-between cultural, literary, and artistic spaces. Attending some of the important events of digital poetry (e.g., E-Poetry festivals and conferences) enables one to experience the richness and diversity of today's experimental writing in digital media, which is often about the research in a specific field of cyber "language"[13] shaped by the author's individual attitude regarding writing in digital media. The common ground of digital poetry performances refers to a variety of forms and genres, spanning from net art and software art (e.g., Eugenio Tisselli's degenerative website project) to pieces devoted to an author's live performance of reading and interacting with visual displays (e.g., Aya Karpinska's and Jörg Piringer's performances).[14] Rather than being a continuation of poetry-as-we-know-it, it is a novel textual and meta-textual, linguistic and not-just-linguistic practice, which has moved away from the printed page and is shaped with the key paradigms of contemporary art and culture. Digital poetry projects (from hyperpoetry and animated poetry to text-based installation and textual VJ-ing) challenge literary theory to redefine and adjust its methodological approach

---

13 The neologism cyberlanguage' refers to the language generated and shaped in online communications, in programming and scripting languages, and in cyberculture.

14 Cf. their performances at the E-Poetry festival in Paris 2007. A video of Karpinska's Lala is available at http://technekai.com/lala/index.html (18 Mar. 2009); information on Piringer's piece can be found at http://www.epoetry2007.net/artists/oeuvres/piringer/piringer.html (18 Mar. 2009).

Janez Strehovec

by applying the concepts and theoretical devices taken from other fields, e.g., from Internet studies, studies in techno culture, new media theory and (socio)linguistics. Rather than regarding digital poetry as a purely linguistic phenomenon, our research in this chapter foregrounds its broader interactions with the key fields of contemporary technoculture and new media art.[15]

CALLING INTO QUESTION THE DIGITAL VERBAL

Poetry's traditional role of creating lyric atmospheres by imparting intimate feelings and sensations of a so-called lyrical subject and as a place of "a projective saying" (Heidegger) is fundamentally challenged by information technologies that are able to create their own particular cultural condition, new ways of user-related text organization, and new generations of hybrid and artificial languages. Today we are witnessing how digital media generates very specific modes of experiencing mixed or hybrid realities, and we can see the particular ways of perceiving, knowing, and making culture in a reality of heightened complexity that involves both the given (physical) as well as virtual worlds. In a way, digital media also makes language perform differently from the language of traditional print culture, as demonstrated by both the artistic examples of text-based computer and video game mods, and—in terms of popular media—bullets on websites written by means of online journalism. Novel textual practices are emerging in which presentation, linear construction of narrative, depths, and meaning give way to the liquid textscape, blog-based remixability, the multi-sensory textscape experience, and special effects (e.g., Amy Alexander's VJ show CyberSpace-Land featuring text visuals generated live from search engine queries). Text is undergoing radical shifts in addressing both the author and the reader: within a new media paradigm, we face the linguistic realm articulated in

---

15 Since 1997 the author of this essay has been dealing with the theoretical paradigms of very experimental forms of digital literature that intersect the literary avant-garde, text-based installation art and various forms and genres of digital arts. In his paper Text as Virtual Reality, presented at the first Digital Arts and Culture conference in Bergen (1998), he had introduced the term second order digital literature in order to refer to digital writing, which is beyond hypertext that, in the 1990s, was regarded as a basic and the most talked about genre of digital literature.

a digital medium with new properties which allow people to write, read, communicate, learn, explore, and create in novel ways.

How do we imagine the very nature of digital poetry placed within a broader field of interactive new media art and culture? How do we approach its poetic specificity? Let us say first that digital poetry, as a very experimental field of approaching the realm of cyber language in an extremely intimate manner, belongs to digital literature more broadly, which can be considered as a part of new media. That is, digital poetry is characterized by new media features such as digitality, interactivity, hypertextuality, dispersal, and virtuality (Lister et al. 13). Apart from those features there are a number of others associated with the textual specificity of a new medium. Yet—and this is crucial—digital poetry generated by programming and scripting languages and made possible by a very specific interface (the computer screen or a navigation device such as the mouse or scroll-bar) is by no means merely about technical innovations. It enables us to face textual practice occurring inside the text and in the context of the present cultural production as defined by globalization, multiculturalism, and new economy; by new forms of experiencing identity; by the issues of gender, community and embodiment; by new forms and new modes of representing the world and its objects; by a new audience which is sometimes closer to the club (DJ- and VJ-) culture than to the elite culture; by the Internet; by aesthetics of special effects and of mosaic; and—and this is of crucial importance—by the contemporary linguistic practices of on-line communication.

In terms of the audience interested in digital poetry, we can encounter individuals who rarely read books but are more familiar with software, PCs, palms, and mobiles. They even participate in club culture events. While mentioning club culture, one may also say that digital poetry can be performed in clubs as well and not necessarily in spaces assigned to the elite culture (libraries, university classrooms, cultural centers, etc.). Blurring the difference between the elite and the popular arts also motivates the authors of this poetry, among which we often encounter net artists and programmers who have not undertaken traditional training in the humanities.

By considering the various streams and forms in digital poetry (e.g., its performances within E-Poetry biannual festivals, and pieces in the ELO

Collection, Volume 1 and 2), we can discover that many of them belong more to the world of new media art than to the world of the book-based literary culture. Due to its new media art features, this practice is also placed beyond the traditional boundaries between two cultures, as they are discussed in Snow's lecture on the divide between scientific and literary intellectuals (Snow 1959). It seems that Manovich, in the Language of New Media, does not pay enough attention to digital textuality and digital literary projects, since events also take place in the medium of "linguistic works," which in a striking way demonstrate key features of new media. Digital poetry's fundamental connection to new media art is essential, since such art has today established a supportive function for all art in terms of a broader activity including: artistic software; a service devoted to solving a particular (cultural and non-cultural) problem; a research; an interface which demands from its user the ability for associative selection; algorithmic (logical) thinking; and procedures pertaining to DJ and VJ culture, such as mixing, cutting, sampling, re-purposing, and recombination.

In any case we can find out that the links between digital poetry and net art, software art, browser art, and text-based electronic installations, are often stronger than their connection to poetry printed in a book and aiming at traditional literary culture. Interestingly, the authors of this kind of creativity do not foreground the question of genre: some of them declare themselves to be creators of digital poetry, others do not. Some pieces (e.g., Giselle Beiguelman's Poetrica and Eugenio Tisselli's Degenerative) also function in the context of net art, while others (e.g., Camille Utterback's Text Rain and Simon Biggs's Rewrite) function in the context of text-based electronic installations.

Digital poetry as a precarious and therefore threatening field is based on a text considered an experimental artistic environment for establishing new relations between textual components as well as for striking and challenging experiences of unusual meanings. The readers of such pieces are facing the author's very intimate attitude and her strong emphasis on the language used; in digital poetry, the author tries to establish a relationship with the word-material that is as individualized as possible. We even find cases of the creation of a new language (for example the "text-wurks" of the Australian author Mez).

On the other hand, Maria Mencia's Cityscapes: Social Poetics/Public Textualities project is basically aimed at extracting a visual text from the city environment, and then deconstructing, re-purposing, and re-mapping it into a different context. The readers/viewers/listeners of this piece are challenged by the author's interesting research on how to integrate digital poetry into the realm of social and urban poetics, i.e. into the calligram of the city itself.

> In western culture, the realm of media and advertising has absorbed the language of Visual Poetry, and calligrams have become another official way to engage people in the selling of their products. Reciprocally, poetry has also been influenced by this exchange and has moved to other domains away from the page and into the public display. Therefore, my interest was to use the language of advertising to create poetic/artistic public work in urban spaces, and in so doing to explore the new calligram, that of social poetics, of the neon lights, flickering letters, moving messages, and public textualities of city environments (Mencia).

Rather than deal with the very intimate contents of modern lyrical poetry, this poetry foregrounds an attitude of social poetics, which is based on the interplay between the language of poetry and the language of commercials arranged within the cityscape's flickering imagery.

What is lacking in digital poetry are the formal demands of the medium of the printed page; in digital poetry the text is displayed on computer screens and stored for further applications in computer storage units, and the demand of alignment as well as the striving for rhymes, assonance, and other features of (traditional) poetry forms are often pushed aside. The very lyrical nature of print-based poetry in terms of a very emotional response to an event or occasion, even in a very passionate moment of the lyrical subject, is also often left behind; on the other hand, the demands of the conceptual, the purely linguistic, and the not-just-linguistic experimentation are gaining importance. Such a poetic work is sometimes more about the questioning of the very nature of the medium itself (e.g., software poetry, poetry generators) and about analyzing how the word behaves within the new media paradigm. The state-of-the-art software special effects in terms of attractive 3D visualization[16] are often privileged at the expense of a more innovative use of ordinary language itself.

Although defined as an umbrella and technical term, digital poetry implies poetic and literary referencea. Therefore, the question needs to be raised: what precisely is the specific literary nature of this kind of poetry? Can it still be considered poetry or has it already developed into something else?

We have seen (in the chapter on algorithmic culture) that digital (poetic) text defamiliarizes our expectations of what digital "language" looks like, of how a special feeling of a digital word is shaped, and of what the crucial features of the literary genre are within the paradigm of cyberculture (e.g., feedback loops, customization, new media-shaped materiality—and even physicality—of the text displayed on screen, as well as the user's textual control and navigation). Inside the digital medium, the word loses its authority and solidity—which characterized its role in printed texts—and appears as a raw material for numerous transformations and interventions (made and controlled by software). Text is a textual "moving reserve," a new media-shaped textscape, which challenges both the author and the reader in terms of navigation, orientation, and decision-making. Noah Wardrip-Fruin described these features by referring to Screen, his textual Cave Installation:

> The experience of Screen, we hope, is one of oscillation. The words are at times objects, and act like graphical objects, and we concentrate on playing them that way. But sometimes the words are words, and we read them as clusters of text—seeing them overlap, hearing them spoken. And sometimes the words are part of a memory, a fiction, and we remember the context in which we heard a word before, we see how the texts are deforming through the play process, deforming more the better we are as players. (Wardrip-Fruin, Interview)

---

16 In Jason Nelson's Dreamphage (Version 1, 2003), drag and drop on the screen causes a tunnel graphics effect; bold readable text appears just on certain screens during the user's fast immersion into an attractive visual environment saved on the simulator drive.

Underlining the sophisticated nature of new media-shaped textual experience, we can also mention Komninos Zervos's digital poem Beer based on the animation of nouns (beer, beef, heel, hell, etc.) by means of digital morphing that changes letters within words over time, making an instant word that is constantly changing into another word-compound. We can also take into account the role of software with the digital morph, which often replaces the metaphor in print-based modern poetry, and the use of devices such as parataxis, which establish within a single word an actual "stage of tensions" among new meanings, issued from units made of the primary word, now cut to pieces.

Digital poetry also often enables the reader, in the role of the user, to have a very creative and intensive contact with the text. Deena Larsen's Carving in Possibilities expressed this characteristic with the final call to the reader to "sculpt again" and not to "read again." In the already-mentioned VR text-based installation Screen, the text comes to life in relation to the reader's body demanding bodily interaction with the data-words-bodies. Even devices such as the scroll-bar, mouse, and stylus (when using a PDA), enable the reader to handle the written text in a very specific, intimate way and to interfere with the text through an interface (e.g., by means of a mouseover event). In Larsen's Carving in Possibilities, words are hidden behind the surface, similar to the objects temporarily wrapped by the visual artist Christo in his pioneering Land Art projects. The reader is asked to find—by means of the "mouse event" procedure—the covered/wrapped words and make them appear on the screen. By touching various points on the screen, an image of shapeless stone is transformed into Michelangelo's David. The user's action is individualized; the sequence of textual components adapts to her interventions (this is "customization" which, as a procedure, is well-known in the networked economy) and it always produces or sculpts different sequences of the written, that is to say, accomplishes a different textual event. Larsen's opening line—"I saw precisely what the stone was meant to be"—is a starting point for various textual continuations/derivatives caused by random repositioning of the mouse-touch on the screen.

I have used the word "event" (in Flash vector-based graphics, the term is the "mouse event"), because digital poetry really is about events:

it is about creating text with temporal features emphasized, based on two levels—on the internal "unwrapping" of the textual hidden layers as well as on the reader's/user's reading in the form of her interactive intervention into the texts (which is often the case). Beyond the temporal "richness" of the text in terms of its event nature, such a text even demonstrates a very sophisticated structure, based on the relationships between the words and on the special atmospheres connected with these relationships. The author's role lies not merely in projecting the poetry's words, it lies above all in arranging the stage of relationships among words and even within one single word (e.g., in Komninos Zervos's and Mez's texts). Therefore, the digital poetry text (designed as an object, browser, textual ambient, text-based computer game, web installation, piece of software, textual instrument, etc.) innovatively challenges to our traditional approach to language in the context of new media.

TOWARD TOTAL KINETIC TEXTWORK

In The Language of New Media, Lev Manovich argued that:

> the printed word tradition that initially dominated the language of cultural interfaces is becoming less important, while the part played by cinematic elements is becoming progressively stronger. This is consistent with a general trend in modern society toward presenting more and more information in the form of time-based audiovisual moving image sequences, rather than as text. (78)

Such a trend is even foregrounded within important parts of digital textual production, which is organized today in the form of time-based audiovisual moving sequences. In other words, it is based on words in motion that appear as a film of words. Texts themselves have passed into the filmic mode as crucial for the cultural and extra-cultural contents of the 21st century, transformed into a kinetic textscape with emphasis on the visual, whose main purpose is to attract the hybrid reader-listener-viewer of today as a voyeur, i.e., the staring one. The moving textscape is, metaphorically speaking, designed as a seductive physical entity. In order to fulfill the demands of such an attractive representation, the textscape must be organized and arranged as sophisticatedly as possible. Cave-based projects such as Wardrip-Fruin's et al. Screen and Cayley's Torus can serve as a paradigmatic examples.

Furthermore, it must be possible to satisfactorily perform this textscape exclusively through computer tools, i.e., in order to present the textscape as a seductive entity, it must become a digital text generated specifically by means of different types of software.

The high-tech solution of searching for textual arrangement beyond the printed page is also represented by Simon Biggs' Tower (2011), an interactive installation where the computer listens to and anticipates what is to be said by those interacting with it. It is a self-learning system: as the interactor speaks the computer displays the next words, in the order of frequency in its database. The speaker may or may not use a displayed word. All new word conjunctions are accumulated and added to the corpus. The initial corpus can be formed from any source. For its premiere exhibition as part of "Poetry Beyond Text," the corpus was formed as a mash-up of Joyce's Ulysses and Homer's Odyssey.

The idea of text-film is not coined exclusively by digital culture. It is already found in the historical avant-garde, especially in Marinetti's Futurism, which was based, as far as the poetical practice is concerned, on free, nomadic words, i.e., on the "parole-in-libertà" ('words-in-freedom'). In the manifesto The Futurist Cinema, we encounter the idea that

> the most varied elements will enter into the Futurist film as expressive means: from the slice of life to the streak of color, from the conventional line to words-in-freedom, from chromatic and plastic music to the music of objects. (Marinetti 131)

We can see the actual realization of this idea in certain films. For example, in A Clockwork Orange (1971) by Stanley Kubrick, where textual components made of different symbols and formulae move over the screen. In 2001: A Space Odyssey (Kubrick) textual design insertions also represent an important component.

Moving text is also an essential component of many electronic installations. For example, writings flowing vertically over light emitting diodes (LED) are the trademark of Jenny Holzer's visual art projects. Moving text, based on word-objects designed by computer graphics, is also a characteristic of Jeffrey Shaw's electronic installations mentioned above (for example The Legible City and The Virtual Museum). The Canadian media artist Michael Snow was also among the pioneers in this field, with the 1982 experimental film So is this (16mm, b&w, silent, 45 minutes), a text-film in which each shot is a single word.

The noticeable swing of the text in motion (which, as a rule, emphasizes visual features because it has to fulfill the imperative of being organized and arranged in an attractive fashion) can be encountered in particular within the digital visual culture and within the culture of informing and communicating in the society of information, spectacle, and new media—all of which are also tied to the demands of new media aesthetics, as well as to the contemporary individual's need to receive information in a form arranged as multimedia, presupposing the coexistence of language, sound, visual, kinetic, and tactile effects. By entering the new mediascape, we find out that the most talked about cultural contents are arranged in a mosaic and hybrid format based on the coexistence of different forms, i.e., that "the logic of replacement, characteristic of cinema, gives way to the logic of addition and coexistence. Time becomes spatialized, distributed over the surface of the screen" (Manovich, 2002: 325).

Text—by no means as something disappearing, but rather as something adapting itself to the aesthetics of new media—has an important place in the midst of new media. We come across it in the "balloons" of comics and in short information bits about pop stars in some music videos, and it also appears in the design of television news based on a mosaic format. "What is evident in current television is that the screen is no longer a 'sacred space' dedicated to a single image. Television has diverged from film in this way—its screen is divided in its presentation of information." (Burnett and Marshall 89). On CNN we thus encounter moving text flowing underneath visual contents (the so-called bizbar, newsbar, sportbar) which means it is not enough to merely watch and listen: the user must constantly receive a package of information organized in a mosaic fashion, represented in scriptural, aural, and visual forms. The mosaic design is also the constant companion of websites, which still contain a lot of entirely linguistic features, arranged in a language characteristic of the web media (the so-called "netspeak") and in the form of bullets with striking visual features. The "linguistic" element in the textscape (which is often the medium in which digital poetry is generated) is not based solely on kinetic text—i.e., where understanding sequential syntax as well as knowing the syntax of film language are essential to its understanding—it is also based on highlighted visual features, which implies some consideration to the spatial syntax. Within a digital textuality, the spatialization of textual components comes to the forefront. In fact, before digital media, the aspirations of Visual and Concrete Poetry for "total textwork" have not been completely fulfilled. In many ways these aspirations have been surpassed and complemented by new elements deriving from the aesthetics of the digital.

In any case, it is important that the words inside the textscape are "words-images-virtual bodies," and that they are self-contained signifiers which must be perceived not only in their semantic function but also by considering their visual appearance and their position and motion in space. A user of digital textuality needs to focus on the visual aspect of the text, on the digital word-image itself, i.e. not purely using it as a point of departure for mental "travel" towards something entirely different, to literary worlds with "meaning." Unlike this print-based state, in digital textuality the emphasis is not only on the decoding of a meaning. A hybrid reader-viewer-listener of digital text is also interested in the visual features of a signifier, meaning that the spatial syntax organization of the text units come to the forefront.

When we are talking on "words-images-virtual bodies," we need to stress that the representation of the digital, through software-controlled (and accelerated) words, is bodily and corporeal is its perception. Text-based electronic installations such as Jeffrey Shaw's The Legible City, Camille Utterback's Text Rain and Simon Biggs' Bodytext, all demonstrate that digital words appear as 3-D objects one can reach toward, lift, and manipulate within a playable mode. However, the bodily nature of today's objects is not enough: they need to be put in motion. "To speak about bodies is first and foremost to explore the ways in which bodies move," argued Erin Manning in her book Politics of Touch: Sense, Movement, Sovereignty. One can get more information about the body when it moves rather than from its static appearance. This is demonstrated even through the proximal sense of touch, which gains more information when it circles around the investigated body than when it is simply reduced to the laying of hands. What Manning wrote on the body and the touch is also pertinent to the digital word-body that turns to the filmic mode to enables it reach toward new spaces and gain new temporal features. As a moving one, it doesn't leave only the printed page or the screen: by leaving the lightness of screenic text it enters the darkness of outer space that one also needs to consider in order to read the entire ride of textscape (and textbody).

Animated digital poetry is one of the new media-based textualities with literary features deploying a moving textscape and virtual bodyscape. It is situated at the intersections of Avant-garde and Neo-avant-garde Poetry, Film, Special Effects, Text-Based Electronic Installation Art, Concept Art, Net Art and Computer Graphics. It includes kinetic and animated poetry, kinetic digital sound poetry, poetry generators, as well as kinetic digital textscapes and installations with poetry characteristics. How can we approach such poetry? What are its main features?

One of the crucial features of the poetry-as-we-know-it (e.g., print-based poetry) is connected with the whiteness of the printed page, the absent, the untold (e.g., Edmond Jabès' account of the issue of words in his Le Parcours). Hidden text units, i.e., units not yet displayed on the screen, usually keep the readers in suspense. In the case of animated poetry based on moving letters and words, only a small part of the text is in a screen focus, and there is no telling whether or not all the letters and words will appear in the foreground. This means that the reader is faced with the non-trivial effort of having to catch the point of such a work. Interesting examples of such texts are Brian Kim Stefans's piece The Dreamlife of Letters and Mary Flanagan's project [theHouse]. The latter, as a digital poetry piece which takes the form of a computer-based flowing and spatialized organism, is based on the interplay of moving words and unstable geometric structures (designing the rooms). In her statement, Flanagan suggests that through the process of enacting texts within, alongside, and outside of the text of the computational code, this autobiographical work is regulated by the computational process of the sine wave. Here, the text is written upon "rooms," and these rooms emerge to create "houses" next to and among the intermingling text. This piece, which is about language and embodiment in terms of moving, very unstable—even nervous and hard-to-catch—structures, is only realized through the user's interaction and navigation. The spatialization of the piece intersects with both digital poetry and embodiment, in terms of virtual architecture arranged by means of special effects. Relatively weak and less innovative language of the author's impressions and commentaries give way to attractive spatial visualization; i.e. the linguistic element in such a textscape is to a certain extent deprivileged at the expense of the state-of-the art technical (e.g. software) solutions.

Reading/watching such digital poetry pieces that are articulated in a language owing much to cinema and music video syntax, e.g. to suspense, short and fast cuts, (re)mixing, recombination, and surprise, implicates some essential changes on the level of their perception. Instead of the traditional reader, the digital text user (in terms of hybrid reader/viewer/listener) is being recreated: she abandons merely linear readings and becomes as capable as possible of complex and non-trivial perceptions and cognitions of such texts. This is also connected to the navigational skills that the user needs in her approach to such pieces. The linear reading gives way to an instable, jumpy perception demanded by the textscape as a sophisticated multimedia-shaped phenomenon that challenges the user to approach it with novel, as a rule hybrid, perceptual acts (e.g., tactile seeing.)[17]

Early in the third millennium, it appears that the demands that the viewer was faced with by Nam June Paik's video installations in 1980s and '90s became generalized (these installations often involved dozens of video screens). The viewers had to follow all the screens simultaneously. Their gaze had to make an effort to encompass the entirety and through "jumping" they also had to scan and "sail" a landscape of divergent video tapes. They often could not pause and "fall" or immerse just into one visual field (screen). Rather, they had to cope with the divergence of images (and also these images' temporal divergence) in the entirety of their idiosyncratic appearances. In the daily life of the contemporary net surfer, such an encoun-

---

17 The seeing within the interface culture has ceased to be a pure act of contemplative vision of a distanced viewer; on the contrary, it interacts with one's tactile activities enabling a dynamic oscillation between visual and tactile feedback. Vision is activated by the movement of a hand, seeing (and reading) become tactile, and the new generations of words-images-bodies called onto the screen by means of navigational devices generate a new circle of tactile and kinesthetic activity.

ter is a familiar one. The posture at issue is by all means a tough one: it requires adjustable observation of and complex identification with the units of the website which the surfer navigates either with the cursor or with the scroll bar and, secondly, it requires imaginative surfing of a surface which is now highly heterogeneous and complex and no longer homogenous. The latter is by no means a coincidence; rather, it is a requirement posed by the fundamental cultural paradigm of our day: simultaneous coexistence of divergent cultural contents and formats.

The very principle of plurality and non-conflicting coexistence of heterogeneous elements is characteristically demonstrated by the website. Within the mass culture of the last decade, the website has played a similar paradigmatic role as did the music video in the 1980s, shaped by a daring digital morph which provided for swift transition of images one into another. What gave rise to this morph was the demand that within a few minutes a genuine world of images should be shaped in an extremely compact fashion, with the purpose of defining the locus of the music tape.

Crucial to the understanding of the "philosophy" of the website is its mosaic structure where documents of divergent origin are uploaded and piled, where they coexist and are placed side by side. Each has its own particular identity and exists in its own particular time, yet it easily coexists with other, equally complex documents taken from divergent contexts. Ours is an age of the simultaneity (in Michael Foucault's claim) of images, metaphors, discourses, concepts and scripts, and its symptomatic manifestation is the computer screen with the graphic user interface providing for the coexistence of windows and even the simultaneity of various application operations.

Watching several images at the same time, writing/reading divergent documents written within divergent datascapes, switching smoothly between various approaches: these are the requirements faced by the present-day adjustable user of the "pluriverse" of cultural contents. Digital poetry pieces also belong among them demanding such a sophisticated reading-viewing of a textscape divided on multiple screens with moving texts (e.g., Maria Mencia's Cityscapes).

Contemporary animated digital poetry, as a field with its own specificity, provides us with a new, provocative, and challenging form of experiencing digital text in terms of the word-image-movement that also is testing our senses. However, beyond the efforts of organizing words in the form of moving images, cyberlanguage also challenges special effects in a basic form, i.e. how the words look like. Referring to the research done regarding the visual features of digital poetic words, one can mention texts by Mary Anne Breeze (Mez), who invented her "mezangelle"-language which combines English letters (English being her native language) with symbols taken from the programming languages and with ASCII symbols and punctuation marks, making traditional, linear and out loud reading procedure rather impossible. Mez uses a broad spectrum of various procedures and textual devices based on investigations of meanings under the condition of artificial juxtapositions, syllable and letter parataxis, and interjections of the words. By using interjected words set off in square brackets, she also tries to demonstrate a wealth of new and daring associations. By parenthetically splitting words, Mez changes the dynamics of reading and creates new polysemantic structures within one word, as in this part of her T.ex][e][ts:

Th[es]is Mes.sage was[h my space with text, drench my wonnetonne-wurdz in silken static and blend yr boundariez] un[der yr thumb, yr noze yr ovariez]liver[N kidneyz N prostrate[tingz]]sendable due to the follow[inge the stuporic superhighwaze]ing reas. on[N off, flik off N on]

Although the applied signs borrowed from the language of code do not work on the level of computing procedures, they grab one's attention through very sophisticated metamorphosis of language within the new media paradigm, and via the fact that they blur the inflexible borders between various linguistic and textual practices. The silent reader is curious about the compound of letters that are fenced in within the square brackets (Mez's trademark), implying the feeling of being threatened when they are set within non-bracketing clear spaces of the digital textuality.

By encountering this piece—which challenges, among others, both aestheticians and programmers—we come across a sort of textuality that stimulates feelings of the uncanny and can even be located near those streams of net art that deal with the malfunctioning of modern technology. Mez "netwurker's texts" can even be understood as a striking and sophisticated practice of an expanded concept of textuality using netspeak (in terms of David Crystal's analysis from his book Language and the Internet), i.e. the underlying programming and scripting languages and web visual culture devices. Text as a naked body? How can we understand this metaphor? Challenged by the phenomena of contemporary mainstream visual culture, Fredric Jameson has argued that

> pornographic films are thus only the potentiation of films in general, which ask us to stare at the world as though it were a naked body. On the other hand, we know this today more clearly because our society has begun to offer us the world—now mostly a collection of products of our own making—as just such a body, that you can possess visually, and collect the images of. (1)

The main two emphases of this claim refer to the naked body and seeing in the form of staring. In other words, they draw upon two moments that challenge the thing (and those who produce it) as well as the perception of the viewer to pass into an intensified and enforced state. According to Jameson, it seems that a certain thing can enter the field of the mainstream visual culture precisely when it becomes as interesting, attractive and seductive as a naked, undressed body. The transformation also concerns the very nature of perceiving a certain thing as if it were a naked body, which means that seeing is not enough: what is required is staring, in other words, a sophisticated process of seeing combined with additional affects and emotions connected with astonishment at various things, as though they were naked bodies.

It seems that in today's culture a great number of things strive to be presented as naked bodies. It goes without saying that naked bodies (understood in the context of Jameson's aforementioned statement) can also be (fashionably) dressed bodies, as well as landscapes including lakes, mountains and deer, things and images of politics, of economy and the jet set, scenes from sporting events, etc. What is shown or staged can also be (well) dressed, "buttoned up," but it nevertheless functions as a naked body—meaning it possesses the function of attractiveness and seduction and, to put it simply, is for that reason worth staring at.

The demand of the text as a naked body, meant to be stared at, is by no means unknown to digital poetry as a linguistic art within the digital medium, attracting both the process of reading as well as a process of seeing, as is demonstrated by Brian Kim Stefans' "Thanks For Watching" at the end of his animated piece The Dreamlife of Letters. In searching within this paradigm, authors are engaged with the challenge of a poem designed as a 3D object; that is—in terms of the reader's attention—a seductive body inviting the user's full immersion into such a virtual bodily environment. As a poetry project that enables the reader to experience the sensation of a poem as a (virtual) body, we have already mentioned open.ended by Aya Karpinska and Daniel C. Howe. This text-based installation is designed to reveal itself through continually shifting geometric surfaces. Verses appear on the faces of two separate, translucent cubes situated within one another. To experience this piece, the reader manipulates a joystick or touch-screen to rotate the cubes, bringing lines on various surfaces into view. As cubes and faces and layers are manipulated by the reader, dynamically updated lines move in and out of focus. The structure of the poem allows it to be read in any number of ways: from single verses on cube faces to sequential verses across faces, to juxtapositions of verses across multiple cubes. We are facing a novel reading procedure that can be taken as a point of departure for our further investigation in the field of perception and cognition of digital poetry texts.

Researching digital poetry within a broader context of new media art means taking into consideration all its crucial paradigms as well as cultural turns in today's new media-shaped culture. One of the distinctive features of the present phenomenology of new cultural contents is the striking role of the body within the interface culture, in which the issues of materiality and even physicality come more and more into the foreground. Rather than being pushed aside or left behind as it was within the cyberpunk ideology of the 1980s and '90s, the body of the present nomadic individual armed with the nomadic screenic devices is becoming more and more crucially significant, even in terms of reinventing its novel tasks and functions. The body as "our basic organ of having the world" (Merleau-Ponty, Phenomenology of Perception 146) enters the novel ontological condition of the present mixed reality, determined by hybridization and merging of in-between spaces and times, which challenge our ways of perception in terms of linking and amalgamating different perceptive acts and procedures. This paradigm, which implies a greater stress on corporeal, motoric, and tactile perception, is crucial also for the present new media art and digital poetry. It seems correct that the perception of new media contents is a dry run for detecting the consequences of this reinvention of the bodily activities within the new media arts and culture.

Drawing on the poem designed as a cube by Aya Karpinska, we touch upon the contemporary trend towards designing cultural contents in 3D, e.g., physical approaches, which stimulate the tactile and haptic as well as motoric perception. Rather than consider contemporary culture just in terms of its striking visual features, we draw upon tactility in terms of mainstream endeavors striving to (re)present cultural contents within 3D fashion (e.g., as virtual bodies).

Reading, looking, and listening are learned skills. Their conventions and procedures are particular to any mass and new medium. Viewers are expected to look at paintings in a white cube in one way, and listen to the symphonic orchestra in Philharmonic Hall in a different way. Also, the new technologies of organizing and processing a text emerge with their own conventions and demands of reading. Along with the hybrid, complex, and heterogeneous nature of digital literary pieces, one can discover a similar complexity and the hybrid nature of procedures devoted to perception and cognition in this area. Reading in terms of decoding symbols for the purpose of deriving meaning gives way to not-just-reading[18] as an essentially more complex activity, including both mental and corporeal arrangements. The not-just-reading directs attention to a broader scope of the user's activity in terms that we face without the finished product, i.e., after reading is terminated, when nothing in terms of materiality and physicality is left behind. Aya Karpinska has described this new reading experience with the following words: "Instead of forcing the reader to go from left to right, I suggest that she reads front to back, as I am curious about when the transi-

---

18 I presented my paper "Not-Just-Seeing, Not-Just-Reading (On the perception and cognition of digital literature)", referring to the very sophisticated manner that the reading of digital pieces can look like, at CHArt 2008 24th annual conference at Birkbeck College, University of London.

tion from surface to depth occurs" ("The arrival of the beeBox"). The digital poem in a 3D environment addresses the virtual reader, the one who can as an invisible avatar get a chance to enter the textual body of the poem or to possess a poem as a tangible object. Not just to write down a word, but to touch it, to possess it, to manipulate it tangibly. All these are demands on the contemporary individual who is accustomed to being fully immersed in her various everyday tasks. Rather than just read and watch a word, line or sentence, she is interested in grasping a word physically. Having the digital word in her palm seems to present her with the full experience of the digital "text" and invites her into the enjoyment of it. Such a condition implies a tactile feature of digital poetry, simulating bodily interactions between the poem's body and its reader-user: "The ability to rotate the whole poem gives the impression that it is an object, something one could hold between ones hands and gaze into" (Karpinska, "The arrival of the beeBox").

Rita Raley introduces a fourth type of reading, with reference to Wardrip-Fruin's claim for the three levels of reading enabled by the screen: reading along the z-axis

> That is, the user does not simply read the words as they circle around them but they also read through and behind them to the text on the walls. In other words, it is deep reading in this other sense: reading volumetrically, reading surface to depth and back again. (2)

However, the reader's experience in a Cave is not just about reading. Digital text in a virtual environment is an experience that shapes the reader's more complex behavior: it hits a body and strikingly stimulates its activity. The traditional perspective places the observer outside the event space and excludes the bodily perception, reducing it to an "observation only" event. The 3D immersive text-based environments draw the reader-user into the object of vision/reading, within and among the words, and stimulate its tactile perception:

> The things of the world are not simply neutral objects which stand before us for our contemplation. Each one of them symbolizes or recalls a particular way of behaving, provoking in us reactions which are either favorable or unfavorable. Our relationship with things is

not a distant one: each speaks to our body and to the way we live. (Merleau-Ponty, The World of Perception 63)

In the moment the words come loose in a 3D virtual environment, they are the things Merleau-Ponty refers to. Each of them speaks to our body, hits it, and challenges its complex behavior. The reader-user of Screen is a reader with a body, and her behavior is physical par excellence. And her reading is not-just-reading, it is a corporeal experiencing of words-in-motion, which includes kinesthetic and motoric activities, navigation, pushing, lifting and sending back the words—the hand with the data glove controlling the activities. Such an experience of a digital poem or a digital textscape is in the first place novel. It is enabled only by new media technologies (e.g., VR), which transform the reader into the user of an immersive environment and puts her into a kind of cockpit position. And, on the other hand, when the virtual words-images-bodies break loose and become extremely flexible, they are transformed into interactive and impressionable things that enable the new manner in which we approach and interact with them. Such things themselves become actors, affecting change through their observations and reading. They challenge the reader-user to become curious about what happens next, even as an aftermath of her experienced bodily activity in immersive textual environments.

ERASED, SELF-DESTROYING, AND VANISHING TEXT

What lies in a core of a text which strives to be considered e-poetical? Why do we use the term digital or e-poetry, if these are textual instruments—often formed by poetry generators, and controlled by software—are without lines, strophes, rimes, assonances, and as a rule do not generate lyrical atmosphere? At first glance, are there any common denominator at all between these strictly separated fields of print and electronic poetry?

We try to consider and compare both fields due to the investigation into language at the core of both of them. Poets research into the very nature of language. They call into question its common use, they approach the word as broken down into letters, and they even depict linguistic failures. They see the "wordness" of the word as if the word would suddenly happen anew in front of their eyes. Modern poets like Stéphane Mallarmé,

e. e. cummings, Paul Celan, and Edmond Jabès were important innovators in the realm of language by broadening its material presence with the blanks, void, silence, intervals, interruptions, loss of capitals, and unstable margins. They called into question the entire field of poetry and destabilize the meaning, the power of sayable, and the link between the things and the words. One can say that they had struggled with language and the outcome of this struggle was quite uncertain. In the background of their writing emerged the following question: why letter, word, line, lyric and not just a silence, void, whiteness and blanks? Sometimes it appears that the nonverbal signifiers, as in a case of blanks and isolated, dead, crossed-out letters, are as important in their poetry as the verbal ones. The unsayable as the hidden (and metaphysical) part of all literary language is deployed in modern poetry through a poetical textuality which brings the silence and the desert of meaning to the fore. In addition, the blanks and intervals of modern poems convey meaning.

E-poetry engages in similar research questioning the very nature of language and textuality. E-poets break all languages down into their elements including html and other programming and scripting characters. They try to move fluently between the code and its screenic output, where it is devoted to human reading. In fact, it sometimes appears that the e-poets place themselves in the non-space between the code and the displayed word. They make sense not just of a material (visual and temporal) appearance of the word but also of the punctuation, square brackets (e.g. in Mez's poetry), struck-out letters, interruptions, blanks, erased words, and voids. Some procedures in Mez's poetry (the use of punctuation, brackets and interruptions as well as the innovative approach to typography) resemble the e. e. cummings poetics (e.g. in poem I Will Be). However, the use of software advances enable e-poets a new approach to the issue of textual voids, unsayability, absence, erasure, and vanishing. We can even see in the erased, unreadable, and vanishing text one of the most particular feature of digital poetry. Here the use of the software as well, the materiality of the screen, and the use of controlling/navigating devices brings advantages to the fore as compared to print:

In print literature, actual erasure is difficult to attain. Print writers can allude to a segment of text that might not be present, they can make a part of the text less readable (type size, strike-out, etc.), or they can leave a space to indicate what has been omitted. Sometimes this faux-obscure text is part of a deconstructive practice. Usually translated as "under erasure'" it involves the crossing out of a word within a text, but allowing it to remain legible and in place.

One predecessor of recent accounts with the erased and vanishing text in e-literature is Agrippa (1992) by cyberpunk writer William Gibson, with artist Dennis Ashbaugh, and publisher Kevin Begos Jr. The project consists of Gibson's electronic poem, embedded in an artist's book by Ashbaugh. This poem was stored on a 3.5" floppy disk, and it was programmed to encrypt itself after a single use. An artist's book was prepared with photosensitive chemicals, causing a fading of the words and images as the pages of the book were opened up to light. In recent, post-hypertext e-literature, several projects deal with erasing, vanishing, and self-destroying text, as well as with text on the limits of legibility (see Luesebrink, 2014).

There are also many examples of new media art and e-literature projects associated with the procedure of destroying the text. One example discussed earlier is Tisselli's "Degenerative" project (2005), where a web site slowly becomes corrupted. each time it is visited, one of its characters either destroyed or replaced. Another example is Thomson and Craighead's video game mod "Trigger Happy" (1998), in which users are challenged to shoot the moving target consisted of sentences taken from Foucault's essay What is an author. "Trigger Happy" is a first person shooter mod of the seminal video game "Space Invaders." The gamer destroys the letters and words of Foucault's text, but more is involved than merely this procedure: she must critically consider her activity as not directed to the hostile objects but to the institution of the word and the text, which lies in the core of Western cultural tradition. On the other hand, we can explain such gamers' activity as the metaphor for the fate of the word and the text in the contemporary moment, in a copy/paste culture of googlezation, where the institution of author, text and word loses its authority and autonomy and are endangered by visual popular culture. A further explanation of this projects is that the point of gaming is the will to kill the "death of the author" text before it gets you.

Agrippa opened up the added possibility of temporary textual projects brought to life within a very short temporal interval. Temporary text is where existence is restricted to a very limited time. It demonstrates the author's struggle not just with the text but also with its communication possibilities. The question is raised whether the text needs to be the an entity that persists? In 2003, I published an essay Verses for seven weeks which related to my project of writing poems for a very short temporal interval (seven weeks or less). After this period, I burned the poems, and what remained was just an essay (as documentation of this endeavor) which informs the readers forever onward of the flames of vanishing poems. In this experimental event the issue of communicative function of poetry was addressed: Does a poem exist solely under the condition that it is presented for human readings?

Verses for seven weeks was a project based on print literature deploying the materiality of paper, which burns in fire. The technological basis and the (non)reading procedures of Slippingglimpse (2008), by Stephanie Strickland, Cynthia Lawson Jaramillo and Paul Ryan, is quite different. This visual and textual project is arranged in regenerate, scroll text, and full text mode. It is a 10-part regenerative Flash project based on algorithmically generated text following the movement of chaotic water patterns (chreods). It challenges the established concept of reading as meaning decoding by considering reading as a broader cognitive activity in which machines also participate in (water reads text, text reads technology, technology reads water). This means that several reading events enter into the life of this project, including the machinic event, which is not fulfilled in the human readable output. In fact, the human reading is enabled just in the Scroll text mode where one window appears in which the stable text included in moving pattern suddenly appears. This piece demonstrates that the reading is not a self-evident issue: text appears or not, and there must be a very particular conditions fulfilled whether the word may enter the human readable mode. In fact, such a mode is sometimes just conditionally readable. Big efforts are needed by the user is needed to identify the word interacting with the water chreods. Lines of this project are sometimes presented within inhuman outcome: not evident enough to be read. Legibility goes hand in hand with the illegibility.

What is in the background of this will to erase textual signifiers, to strike-out them, to stage the absence and the void, and make the text unreadable? What is the philosophical point of such procedures that link e-authors with those modern poets who are engaged in struggle with the language. Whereas some authors as well as critics try to explain such endeavors with one's mental states, I see in them an attempt to answer the question relating to the desert of the meaning, the weakness of language, and the triviality of the present McDonaldized language. While today there are too many words mediated and distributed by Google, there is a lack of words that stage their uncertainty, their crossing-out, erasure, and acceleration toward the illegibility. The words entering the silence, magic, and abyss of void, and the relationship with the absent God.

8 NEW MEDIA ART AND THE SOCIAL

The concepts of "artistic autonomy," i.e. in that the sphere of art and literature cannot be simply deduced from the basic principles of a given social reality and it cannot be explained by them, impacted the understanding of European modernist art and literature in the twentieth century. Art is one thing, but social reality with its historical variables is something entirely different—this was the standpoint of the most of aestheticians and other theorists of modernist art that was also acceptable to the artists and theorists of art in the countries of European socialism, who appealed to artistic autonomy especially when they defended their different, dissident views, which departed from the dominant interpretations and expectations as regards the content and the functioning of art.

When we encounter such a view today, we can understand it as markedly historical and volatile. The historical avant-gardes and neo-avant-gardes of the twentieth century already presupposed the implosion of the artistic in the social sphere. American pop artists did not find it difficult to say "yes" to the iconography of popular culture of that time—just think of Andy Warhol and his Red Elvis—the concept of artistic autonomy was also alien to some artistic traditions in the Far East, which today display an orientation towards "device art" (as mentioned above), which hinges upon connecting aesthetic, exhibition, and use value. And finally, the concept of artistic autonomy is far from being close to the understanding of the field that occupies the centre of our attention, namely, new media art, which is increasingly defined through the use of new media and technologies, while at the same time—and this is one of the key points of our account—it is also increasingly and ever more explicitly situated in the world of new social paradigms and contemporary modes of production.

The questions concerning the relationship between art and social reality were also involved in aesthetic debates referring to the notion of realism as a complex and multifaceted structure (theoretical as well as ideological), split between "the great European literary realism" and the simplifications and biases of socialist realism, which were framed by the dominant (mainly Soviet) ideology. When today some theorists (perhaps nostalgically) recall the debates about realism, we can see that, in social theories, realism in the form of mimetic artistic practices—which presuppose the so-called objective reality as the basis of artistic (mainly literary) activities of reflecting and mirroring (György Lukács)—has been increasingly displaced by links between art and social reality that are much more direct. These links are characterized by their abandoning of claims about artistic autonomy, as well for mimesis (imitation, mirroring), as key functions of so called realistic art. These social theories, which establish knowledge about new social paradigms and cultural turns, are also fundamentally related to the challenges that derive from contemporary cognitive capitalism as a social machine that leaves nothing outside and from an understanding of immaterial and precarious labour, which encroaches upon the individual's 24-hour rhythm of life. Therefore, a number of fairly recent and contemporary social theories consider artistic practices as fields that do not refer mimetically to the world of capitalism; rather, they are fundamentally embedded in it. Their products are less and less aesthetic in an isolated sense. Instead, they confront us with images and stories that prefigure and construct the essential moments of reality.

At this point, we should mention the Situationist Guy Debord, who wrote that "the spectacle is not a collection of images; rather, it is a social relationship between people that is mediated by images" (Debord 1997:12). Or even more straightforwardly: "The spectacle is capital accumulated to the point where it becomes image" (14). The view that images are not only caught in the postmodern play of signifiers but are also significant for understanding contemporary production of commodities, as Naomi Klein discussed in No Logo, is radicalized by Maurizio Lazzarato: "Contemporary capitalism does not arrive first with the factories: these follow later, if at all. It first arrives with words, signs and images" (Lazzarato, 2003). Spectacles, images, logotypes, and performances are less and less something that is essential only to art. Additionally, they are less and less determined by the boundaries of artistic autonomy and the world of aesthetic values. At the same time, their significance in the world of immaterial labour and the post-Fordist mode of production is increasing.

In order to come closer to the problem of new media art and the social, we need mention two theoretical interventions: Jonathan Beller's discussion of the cinematic mode of production and Antonio Negri's analysis of art and immaterial labour. Both explore the above-mentioned relationship between art and social reality precisely in the sense that the sphere of art is certainly not about replaying (merely) the froth of special (aesthetic, spectacular) effects, and it is even less about artistic imitation or mirroring of reality. The sphere of art involves things that concern not only the narrower field of art theory, but also contemporary social life in general. They serve as crucial guidance to and an explanation of the key paradigms of contemporary social life. Debord's view of capital accumulated in images is incorporated in Beller's thinking about cinematic moving images, whose understanding is key to an analytical approach to new social paradigms and therefore also to the basic principles of cognitive capitalism, whose main characteristics are 1) the fact that accumulation in cognitive capitalism focuses on immaterial contents, and 2) its objects transform the subject.

THE MONTAGE OF MOVING IMAGES AND THE SEQUENCING OF THE WORKER'S MOVEMENT

Jonathan Beller, the author of The Cinematic Mode of Production (2006), is interested in the history and the aesthetics of cinema (he dedicates some attention to Dziga Vertov and Hollywood). He situates the art of moving images and their perception within the context of industrial labor, Taylorism, psychosocial management (Pavlov's theory), and psychoanalysis, which means that the aesthetics of cinema gives way to a theory that establishes a fundamental embeddedness of cinema in industrial production, particularly in that segment of industrial production which is defined as a Fordist and Taylorist mode of organizing industrial labour (by means of assembly-line).

> Early cinematic montage extended the logic of the assembly-line (the sequencing of discreet, programmatic machine-orchestrated human operations) to the sensorium and brought the industrial revolution to the eye. Cinema welds human sensual activity, what Marx called "sensual labor," in the context of commodity production, to celluloid. (Beller 2006:9)

This quote articulates a significant understanding of cinema in the context of the industrial revolution. Namely, it is a specific understanding of cinema, which does not presuppose any reference to or imitation (or recording) of what transpires in industrial settings. Rather, cinema itself is an abstraction of working process on the assembly line, which, like cinema, presupposes a montage of sorts and cuts, an intervention into the worker's movement, and a strictly rationalization of the work process.

Beller's interpretation of the activity of viewing is also far-reaching: viewing has become productive labor in the paradigm of capital. For the viewers, like workers in the Taylorist organization of industrial production, perform sequential visual operations on the elements that form moving images. The function of the latter, however, is no longer to represent capital; rather, according to Beller, moving images are themselves capital. Images as capital are conceivable within the frame of contemporary social turns, which lead us to the world of immaterial labour, the new role of circulation as essential to the processes of evaluation, and also the new dispositif, in which commodities are now constituted, organized, and distributed. As Naomi Klein and Maurizio Lazzarato have both argued, commodities seek the status of images.

According to Beller, cinema is not only the art form that fundamentally defined the last century (even in the sense of Jameson's cultural dominant), but also the dominant mode of production. It concerns the industrial revolution and the industrial organization of labour on the assembly line as well as capitalism itself, which is increasingly structured like cinema, so we can even observe a continuation of the industrial mode of production in film production:

> Cinema as a process, a complex of movement, bodies, and consciousness, which I will refer to as "cinematic process," becomes the dominant mode of production itself. Not all production passes through cinema in the institutional sense, but global production is organized as cinema is. Consciousness is dominated by the organization of movement – the organization of materials produces affect. In the cinematic organization of global production and reproduction, this logic will be interiorized in, and as, the postmodern—to the extent that for the postmodern sensorium the world is a world of images. Cinema provides the architectonics of the logistics of

perception for capital. Indeed, it represents their fusion. Hence, the cinematic has been machining the postmodern for nearly a century. In this sense, we can say that during the twentieth century, much of the world is literally in cinema, much in the way that the futurists intended to put the spectator inside the painting. (p. 109)

Beller emphasizes the duality of cinema, that is, cinema as cinema and cinema as capital, which can be seen as a theoretical tool that can be used in other fields as well. Of course, it is not difficult to establish that Debord already observed the duality of image as image and image as commodity, the spectacle as the ecstasy of aesthetic effects and the spectacle as a social relation.

IMMATERIAL LABOR IN MATERIAL NETWORKS WITH MATERIAL EFFECTS

The shift away from the understanding of art in its representational function and towards interpretations on the basis of its position within a given general mode of production is a concern shared by Antonio Negri, who has co-authored (with Michael Hardt) theoretical blockbusters such as Empire, Multitude, and Commonwealth. His 2011 book Art and Multitude raises the question of art in the context of the so-called immaterial labour and cognitive capitalism.

> My point is simply that artistic activity always exists within a specific mode of production, and that it reproduces it—or, more exactly, that it produces it and contests it, that it suffers it and destroys it. Artistic activity is a mode—a singular form—of labour power. It is no accident that all the products of artistic activity can so easily turn into commodities. (Negri 2011: 108)

When we speak of art as commodity, we are thus dealing with a special kind of production, exchange, market and capitalism, for Negri believes that as follows:

> one can in fact trace a correspondence (rough, of course, but nonetheless real) between the various periods of artistic activity (what

173

one might call the "style" and the "poetics" of art) on the one hand, and the forms of capitalist production and organization of labour on the other. (p. 102)

The challenge facing contemporary art theory is thus to understand art on the basis of a specific mode of production (as far as contemporary art is concerned, particularly the capitalist or, in Beller's words, the cinematic mode of production), whereas contemporary social theory is also faced with a challenge: the challenge of analyzing and reflecting upon what happens to a specific historical mode of production once it is interiorized by art (which, however, also defies it, evades it, and departs from it).

Namely, to understand art on the basis of a specific mode of production and the processes of commodification certainly does not produce a "lack" of sorts, which would automatically subsume this field, the actual activity, under the dominant mode of production. If we consider Debord's as well as Beller's and Negri's theoretical insights, we can see that what, at first sight, might seem like a "lack" is in fact a "surplus" of sorts, namely, the distinctiveness of artistic activity, which can also be paradigmatic of a general mode of production in a given period. When explaining the specificities of immaterial labor, Paolo Virno used the example of the so-called reproductive artist in a role of performer whose activity does not objectify itself in the finished product (see quotation on p. 57).

Nowadays, we can observe a noticeable increase in activities that leave nothing material behind, especially no so-called material products. On the contrary, everything essential, everything that defines them, is determined by the process of activity embedded in the event, which, however, must be public (to put it simply, it requires the presence of others who see and hear it). A number of such activities are taking place in new media art with its would-be-works of art, which is emphatically post-objective and immaterial. The key things in new media art happen at the level of performance, action, and software

The arguments, such as those that go that labor is becoming more and more abstract, and so is capitalism, or that immaterial labour produces only immaterial products, have become truisms by now, which is why the important contribution of Negri's text lies in the recognition of a certain contradiction, which now accompanies immaterial labour as well as the general processes of abstraction and dematerialization. Despite the fact that immaterial processes are increasingly a part of our reality and that our lives are progressively more determined by numerous abstractions, intellectual services and immaterial data—just think about financial markets and abstract evaluations of derivatives, that is, expert financial instruments, which dictate the "economy of artefacts"—there is a growing correlation between these processes on the one hand and very material processes and contents on the other. Such material processes and contents are forcefully surfacing in contemporary productions and they question the self-evident purity of the immaterial sphere.

> [T]o speak today of "immaterial labour" no longer means speaking of abstraction, but, on the contrary, of a real plunge into the concrete, into matter. So what we are dealing with here is no longer spirituality and vision from afar, but an immersion amidst bodies, in other words an expression of flesh. Immaterial labour makes material products, commodities and communication. It is socially organized through linguistic, cooperative, electronic and digital networks, which are all extremely material, and it takes place through types of association—and movements—which are multitudinarian. Therefore we are dealing here with an immateriality which is very full of flesh, very mobile and very flexible: an ensemble of bodies. (Negri 2011: 107)

This view can be polemically situated in the context of digital culture, which was hailed in cyberpunk literature and cinema as emphatically anti-corporeal and platonic, while some of its prospects were even accepted and affirmed in the early theory of cybernetic worlds. However, today's view of digital culture (which enters augmented reality as a complex intertwining of the actual and the virtual) shows that the opposite process is more apposite as regards derealization directed towards the digital image, namely, the process of realization in newly discovered bodies, which form relations to new generations of technological devices, particularly interfaces. If we consider the technology of virtual reality, for instance, we can see that its popular interface, the so-called "data glove", has aroused interest in the human hand, the fingers and the palm and the tactile feedback, which is related precisely to the materiality and the anatomy of the hand and its components. And if we consider contemporary art, we see that it has long been exposing, questioning and wondering about precisely the investment of bodies—often naked and vulnerable bodies in extreme situations—in the art of performance.

Capitalism equals abstraction and dematerialization, a shift towards images, logotypes, the cinematic mode of production, spectacle, and skillfully constructed worlds. However, art has found its role in it in that sense that

> artistic development has transformed into corporeal figures the abstraction of the social relations in which we exist; and it has given importance to the vitality of flesh—through images which move and flow, in a process of continuous transformation. From Bacon to Warhol or Park Yong, the artist imagines, within a thick space, an indistinct magma; and they fearlessly considers the prospect of a world freed of its internal architecture. Henceforth, artistic development takes place in biopolitical terms as much as in immaterial terms. (Ibid., pp. 107-108)

Since the paradigm shift from mimesis to poiesis, that is, from the imitative to the constructive and creative function of art, we have witnessed the entry of art into the biosphere. The key streams in this field are explicit bioart as well as contemporary performance art, which increasingly explores the body brutally exposed in barely imaginable situations. In particular, we should consider performance projects by feminist performers in the tradition ranging from Marina Abramović, Carolee Schneemann and Valie Export to contemporary artists, such as Ann Liv Young.

> We are no longer going towards postmodernity. Or rather, we have gone beyond all the "post," we are in contemporaneity, and contemporaneity has further deepened the transformation of labour. Labour—which, as we have seen, was immaterial, cognitive and affective—is in the process of transforming itself into bios, into biopolitical labour, into activity which reproduces forms of life. From now

on it has new properties. It is with these properties that I would like to conclude. (Ibid. p. 115)

This view entails a revision of and a supplement to the almost oversimplified view in common parlance that immaterial labor produces immaterial products; but it is important that this view was articulated (and expounded upon) on the basis of the author's reflection on art. It seems that art is not some kind of froth or a second-rate field. Rather, it can serve as a laboratory for experiencing the key contents that concern our understanding of the present (including the individual and his or her work). Beller's and Negri's texts prove that contemporary social theory can benefit from a more detailed analysis of what transpires in contemporary art. A part of global production and even of the economy of the operations of perception, according to Beller's theory, is in cinema, that is, it participates in the cinematic mode of production; however, the whole "package" of immaterial labour, immaterial products and services was already anticipated in the artistic dematerialization of the object in various avant-garde practices (particularly those associated with Marcel Duchamp). A glance at contemporary art (first and foremost in the field of activism and hactivism) can even be challenging and productive for contemporary political theory, while contemporary artists including the new media ones can gain a lot from a dialogue between their practices and contemporary social theories.

ABSTRACT ORNAMENTAL MOVEMENTS IN STRAIGHT LINES AND LOOPS

Contemporary art, and particularly new media art that manifests itself in the globalized world of new social and cultural paradigms, is at play with other social fields. One of new media artists that tries to consider their artistic practice as embedded in the present world of post-Fordist labor and social networking is Natalie Bookchin, with her piece The Mass Ornament. In conversation with Rhizome.org, she very precisely located the theoretical underpinnings of that art project in the world of immaterial and post-Fordist labour, and thus also defined her relationship to Kracauer's text on mass ornament as a crucial reference for her "YouTube" project.

> As the Tiller Girls dance embodied characteristics of Fordism and Taylorism, the YouTube dance, with its emphasis on the individual, the home, and individuated and internalized production, embodies key characteristics of our economic situation of post-Fordism. (Kane 2009)

Both the spectacular dance of the Tiller Girls in the stadium (which Kracauer refers to in his seminal text) and the private dance of the YouTube dancers in front of web cams internalize foundational paradigms of contemporary society. The former deals with references to mega-events, large-scale serial factory production, the logic of machines, and the conveyor belt, while the latter confronts us with a much more flexible and individualized action, which frequently takes place in the home and whose machinery is no longer mechanical but increasingly digital. "The YouTube dancer alone in her room, performing a dance routine that is both extremely private and extraordinarily public is, in its own way, a perfect expression of our age" (ibid.). The video included in this project has lost its autonomy and only appears as part of a social and cultural context that overdetermines the choreography of bodies and their media-proliferated practices. Her installation also hinges on the technological basis of the YouTube portal, which offers links from one video to a different, similar video (these appear off to the right) and thus addresses the culture of video distribution where one video can trigger a veritable chain reaction of numerous manipulations (mixes, remixes, copies, variations, modifications, etc). Bookchin's project is embedded in a culture of social networks and their media, and try to critically illuminate the numerous variations and antagonisms that accompany the "post-Fordist" mass ornament.

Her piece is without a doubt a manipulation that can be located in the core of today's media-proliferated mass culture of remixes, machinima and mash-ups.

> Our perception of intentional disparity derives from the fact that Bookchin has clearly taken all of these solo performances and turned them into a collective dance, transforming individual, isolated performers into a dance troupe. (Baron 2011: 34)

We are faced with a situation similar to that of the Tiller Girls, where dancers lack a view of the whole. The dancers who entered Bookchin's Mass Ornament from this or that place did not know that their dances would contribute to a whole. Baron also points to the duality and conflict that permeate the dancers of today, caught and manipulated in Bookchin's video. On the one hand, they express anonymity and privacy, voices and choreography from below, while on the other, their private dance has already been mediated and influenced by popular culture, the stars and trends dictated by the market.

We have mentioned Bookchin, but it is time to turn our attention to Kracauer's classic essay from the field of critical cultural theory. "The hands in the factory correspond to the legs of the Tiller Girls" (Kracauer 1995: 79). This theoretical point is central, as the dancers involved in the ornamental, desexualized and highly abstract dance of the mass spectacle (ranging from the rituals of the Third Reich to more contemporary versions such as Yugoslav Tito's Youth Relay and North Korean Kim Il Sung's ceremonies) do not reflect anything but rather work hand in hand with the workers behind factory conveyor belts whose movements are Tayloristically trained and adapted to machines. There is a smooth transition between dancers and workers, similar to that of the organization of moving cinematic images (as is claimed by Jonathan Beller). Thus, there is not only a correspondence between cinema and industrial production behind the conveyor belt, but also between industrial production and dance, as the latter is staged at events of the mass spectacle. The Tiller Girls' movements form geometric shapes characterized by their abstractness (that is, de-realized embodiment and sexuality) and the fact that they play out in ornaments, which are also present in the circular capitalist movements of loops that characteristically demonstrate this type of drive. The Tiller Girls dance with parts of bodies that seem emphatically isolated; their choreography is a symptom of capitalism itself. The dance ornament demands the subjugation of body parts to more complex patterns, such as a row of lines, which no one dancer can perceive. The dance movements of each individual dancer were thus interpreted only as functional parts of a system, just as a worker's hand in Taylorist organized labour behind the conveyor belt.

"The ornament is an end in itself" (p. 76) writes Kracauer, and thus directs our attention to the vacuum-like expanse of ornamental forms that empty all substance of its contents. "The ornament resembles aerial photographs of landscapes and cities" (p. 77), since the matter at hand can only be truly perceived from the air. When dealing with ornamental patterns, we can only make them out in images "from above," for example, the images that were transmitted by the top-most video cameras at the JLA Stadium in Belgrade during the spectacles of the Youth Relay ceremony devoted to former Yugoslav president Tito. This "above" is indeed fitting when speaking of those things produced by global capitalism, the war machine and mass culture. The lens of the "smart bomb eye" of guided missiles, relayed during the first Gulf War to television screens during CNN's breaking news, has become acceptable for such arrangements.

We are hereby dealing with abstraction (of straight lines, loops, repeating forms, the reduction of contents to highly economical and palatable signifiers), which is inherent to both capitalism and post-Fordist production (especially to Taylorist production). The latter has undergone certain changes in the post-Fordist paradigm, yet much of its cultural contents is still overdetermined by the social and ideological system. Abstraction could also become a legitimate yardstick for numerous critical approaches to new media art and e-literature, whose contents are frequently markedly abstract in the sense that they are preoccupied with forms, media and smart technologies. Faced with today's production in this field, we often find that it revolves around artists' explanations and statements, and even theoretical texts from this field are more often than not mere explanations of art works rather than critiques comparing and evaluating them in relation to other similar art or e-literature projects.

Both traditional mass media and the new media linked particularly to the Internet boom generate various forms of media and new media art, where theoretical approaches have begun to replace "media-specific analysis" (as introduced by N. K. Hayles) with socio-critical frameworks that emphasise the embeddedness of this art and literature within contemporary social paradigms, so that Nicolas Bourriad writes about relational art "taking as its theoretical horizon the realm of human interactions and its social context" (p. 14).

Text as Ride

9 DERIVATIVE WRITING: E-LITERATURE IN THE WORLD OF NEW SOCIAL AND ECONOMIC PARADIGMS

In this chapter we seek to broaden the conceptual field of e-literary studies by exploring the social and economic context that shapes e-literature as an emerging field of textual practice in new media. Our research is driven by the idea that e-literature and its institutions might also be explained by applying some key concepts taken from the social sciences (including economics) as we have presented them in previous chapter. E-literary text is viewed as a social event: it needs the presence of the audience, and the process of its making is embedded in its social context.

The contemporary is defined by capitalism, which does not leave anything outside of its influence, and it would be inappropriate if the e-literary text were left outside, i.e. without any references to "the social" and to theories which deal with "the social." We are aware that the decision for such an approach may be a subject of critical rejection, as if to say that e-literature exists outside of its own world, which is defined first and foremost by new media features, especially software. It is also clear to us that many authors who work in this field, as a rule do not show larger interest in modern social-theoretical concepts: they write and program e-literary pieces, irrespective of their social grounds, and the specificity of their pieces is defined particularly by new media features (software, protocols, interactivity, immersion, ludic features, connectivity). We should not forget that the language itself (both natural and programming) is a historical and social category either. However, the challenge of the broader social theory application in this field remains the current topic of interest. Emphasizing the specificity of an e-literary piece (as a performance, event, procedure, programme, ride, textual instrument) directs us to its materiality, which is a very historical, variable category. Requirements for full autonomy of this field as excluded from the social, have passed, after all. Software is also a cultural and social tool, therefore we direct attention a striking impact of some key theoretical notions on the issues of "the social" in the contemporary and to their application in the field of e-literature.

When e-literary text is integrated into a broader social context by means of recent social networks, globalization, and software culture, we may also begin to understand (and explain) its specificity by concepts, which are not strictly related to e-literary theory and e-criticism, but also extend into other fields, especially the economic, new media theoretical, sociological, and political. Such a turn towards the life, body, politics, and gender has also not been alien to some authors of e-literature and their pieces, e. g. Alan Sondheim's practice of "wryting", Francesca da Rimini's Dollspace, Natalie Bookchin's The Intruder, and Sandy Baldwin's New Word Order: Basra (to list only some historical examples).

In the first section we address the e-literary world as a field comprised of various institutions that make up an framework for e-literary production. The second section relates to the present state of global financial markets, demonstrating some procedures that are common with e-literature.

THE E-LITERARY WORLD AS A REFERENTIAL FRAMEWORK FOR E-LITERATURE

Social theories provide basic understanding of e-literature as embedded in broader social context. First and foremost are theories that address cultural implications of contemporary capitalism. Along with Naomi Klein's No Logo, which deals with issues relating to the corporations and their brands, this claim by Maurizio Lazzarato needs to be considered:

> Language, signs, and images do not represent something, but rather contribute to making it happen. Images, languages and signs are constitutive of reality and not of its representation [...] The corporation does not generate the object (the commodity), but rather the world in which the object exists. Nor does it generate the subject (worker and consumer), but rather the world in which the subject exists. (Lazzarato, 2003)

Signs are those which construct the "event-like." They actually have an advantage over material contents. Factories, in terms of (heavy) industrial units, become secondary; they appear, if at all, later, after the corporations have already established the path to corporate marketing by attacks with sign contents; they migrate, or already have, to the Third World. The former is therefore concerned only with symbolic operations and marketing strategies and with constructing a world in which the products are incorporated. When we talk about such an artificial world, we may ask ourselves whether this concept is also useful in the field, which is the topic of interest in this essay, and that is e-literature and "the social." The answer is affirmative. Lazzarato's account is also of import in understanding the developments in the field of current creative communities of e-literature, as they are directed towards the shaping of this field, which, rather than focus on finished e-literary pieces, focuses more on where these pieces are staged: symposia, presentations, conferences, readings, seminars, workshops and performance .

> I show that the term New Media Art is not used to describe a practice, but the art cultivated by a particular community, or better by a whole art world […] A work of art—whether based on technology or not—is usually classed as New Media Art when it is produced, exhibited and discussed in a specific 'art world', the world of New Media Art. (Quaranta, 2011).

Writing about Dierk Eijsbouts's Interface #4/ TFT tennis V180, presented at the Ars electronica festival in 2005, Quaranta argued that this piece "is a typical artifact [sic] of the world of New Media Art. Outside of that world, it would not have much of a chance: the contemporary art world would disparage it as a vacuous celebration of technology, while the video games industry would file it away under unsustainable ideas." What is essential here is that such a new media art piece doesn't fit the demands of either established art (e.g., the contemporary art world) or the trends of popular culture (e.g., the video games industry).

Is a developed concept of new media art, with its distinctions to both contemporary art and popular culture, also significant in defining the social condition of e-literature? Is e-literature also a field which cannot be adequately evaluated and classified, either by the institutions of modern literature and criticism or by the other institutions of recent technoculture? When talking about e-literature, we need to emphasise that this is an emerging field, which is in search of institutions for reproduction and dissemination, theory and criticism, so by drawing on Quaranta's concept of the new media art world, we can introduce the technical term of an e-literary "world." Such a world might be understood on the basis of Lazzarato's account of the construction of "the world in which products are incorporated," in that it is not only about production (of e-literary pieces, projects, performances), which would be situated in an abstract environment and randomly seek theorists and critics who are active in the field of traditional and modern printed literature, but it has its own frame of reference: a very special world in which the e-literary contents exist.

In this particular world it is essential to be present at events such as Electronic Literature Organization conferences, E-Poetry Festivals and relevant conferences, in specific publications (e.g.: Dichtung Digital, Cybertext Yearbook, etc), and national and international research projects that deal with e-literature and are visible to scholars dealing with e-literary theory and criticism (e.g. the ELMCIP Knowledge Base). Collaboration in the e-literary world, in the economy of events, and performances and experiences is essential for every participant in this field. For them, this is the basic environment from which they get the feedback that allows them to be noticed. The e-literary world gives them an autonomous context in which their works can be produced, performed and discussed. E-literature authors do not create their pieces blindly, for the sake of history, for some future abstract readers/users who will come or not, but for a community composed of individuals within institutions. Just to create an e-literary piece is not enough: it is also necessary to present it in the community, find an audience for it and critics and theorists who will refer to it. Outside of the e-literary world, many e-literary pieces do not have much of a chance.

TOWARD THE SPECTACULAR ECONOMY OF FINANCIAL MARKETS

In the 1980s and '90s, in China and developing countries as well as USA and Western Europe, we witnessed a boom in the financial markets, which were "flooded" by capital from all economic sectors. Indeed, it became clear that said markets—particularly in the short-term—allowed significantly higher yields than markets of material goods. The growth in this field can undoubtedly be attributed to technical progress, particularly in the field of software and global networking, which allow today's spectacular events in financial markets worldwide: soon after Wall Street closes the Far East financial markets start to open (the Tokyo stock exchange opens at 2 am CET) and the staged spectacle indexed in the Dow Jones and composite NASDAQ, as well as in the European equivalents (such as the DAX and FTSE), continues with events measured by the Hang Seng, Shanghai Composite index, the Japanese Nikkei and other Asian indices.

In terms of content, we are the contemporaries of a visible transformation of an (industrial) economy focused on material production into an economy based on services and finances. To put it simply: the latter is a far more abstract economy, where the exchange of commodities is being replaced by a series of new financial instruments, including derivatives. Rather than deal with stable artifacts, we deal with unstable concepts, ideas and, of course, code. In drawing attention to this paradigm shift toward the abstract, let us point out that those involved in analyses of contemporary culture and art are no strangers to the above. If there is any field that is constantly subject to destabilization, volatility, introduction of news, hybridization, mixing and remixing, the promotion of (exchange) value and the rapid decline of particular trends (and value), it is contemporary art (including e-literature), in which the object's dematerialization plays a similar role to that played in the field of economy by the transition from the (material) production economy to an economy of (far more abstract) financial products and services.

However, contemporary art did not just passively follow the changes generated by social and economic shifts, but accomplished pioneering work in itself. Just think of Marcel Duchamp and his ready-mades, which drew attention to the relevance of the author-brand (as a potential logo) in the field of modern art, as well as the broader effects of the institution of art as the mechanism promoting the exchange value of certain products and pushing others to the margins. Duchamp's message with his urinal project, "Fountain" from 1917, was precisely this: that artistic context, and its formation through branding, allows an ordinary object manufactured for a specific use to enter a completely new and different life. As to theory, Boris Groys' work Über das Neue (1992) is one of the rare ones that followed the economy of art in the sense that this field is constantly subject to valuations and devaluations as well as dynamic transitions between profanity and valuable (cultural) archives.

Flexibility in the field of contemporary art and e-literature finds it easy to follow the network-supported economy of financial markets, where new financial products bring dynamics into the spectacle of the global, 24-hour market mentioned earlier. Due to the fact that—at least in the short-term—financial markets allow significantly faster and larger profits, they generate new products that attract buyers and speculators. Additionally, hedge funds and derivatives (options, futures contracts) have a special place and bring a new quality to these markets. This is particularly true for trading in derivatives as financial instruments, the price of which depends on the underlying asset (commodities, currencies, and securities), reference rate or index they refer to. There are situations when hedge brokers try to reduce the risk whilst speculators increase it in order to maximise their profits. In short, it is a situation where we have an indisputable value basis that we use to increase our assets in the future (or secure them).

With some works of contemporary art, and in particular new media art, one notices that artists in the field also focus on the "artistic underlying asset" and refer to it in order to secure their interests and even make a profit. They produce derivatives in the sense that they refer to the indisputable value of the underlying reference work (taken from the high-valued artistic and literary tradition), which indirectly—through its "branding value"—also guarantees the branding of their derivatives. Indeed, "a question about the value of a work is a question about its relation to traditional examples and not to extracultural profanities" (Groys). Let us mention the Slovenian new media artist Marko Peljhan, who, in collaboration with Carsten Nikolai and Canon Artlab, designed the Polar project (2000) and has entered in creative dialogue with Lem's novel Solaris (1961). Despite being rooted in a significantly transformed world of the information society and new stories, Polar strives to establish contacts with the unquestionably recognised Solaris, which is already included in the artistic pantheon.

The hedgers (brokers of so-called hedge funds) speculate (in order to secure their investments) and so do artists; they keep counting on the spectator, reader or listener who is not here yet but who will add surplus value to their product in the future. They bet on the future, they live by and in their insecurity, they speculate and bet on it. They are convinced that the course of events will add surplus value to their work. Their option contract refers to some point in the future. They reckon the situation in the market or art scene will change toward their interest. They design works oriented to the new and at the same time their value basis refers to the institution of art, to its "approved" works (quote, remake, remix), which gives them a certain amount of security. For example, Natalie Bookchin's art project The Intruder, produced in the ddynamic and insecure media of artistic video games, establishes a reference to Borges' novel La Intrusa in order to provide added value to an uncertain, new media work (a so-called "mod," i.e., artistic derivative of a commercial video game).

Bookchin's work can be understood as a contribution to a broader concept of e-literature, which extends beyond hyperfiction towards different genres (from video games to performance) positioned at the intersections of e-literature and new media art. In this domain we are contemporaries of different e-writers' strategies for drawing attention to their work and inventing their own economies. Many of them decide, for example, for derivative writing and programming in the sense that they themselves also refer to the indisputable value of the underlying reference work of well-known artists and authors. Here we can mention several authors, from Simon Biggs and Neil Hennessy to Alison Clifford and JR Carpenter, whose e-literary pieces relate to predecessors' texts taken from the world of literature-as-we-know it. Simon Biggs' The Great Wall of China not only borrows Kafka's title, but appropriates the whole body of his text, taking the multiple individual building blocks that make up the story and feeding each word into a generative computer program that randomly re-assembles them into new sentences. Hennessey's Jabber produces nonsense words that sound like English words, in the way that the portmanteau words from Lewis Carroll's "Jabberwocky" sound like English words. The key reference of Jabberwocky is Carroll's nonsense verse poem from his 1871 novel Through the Looking-Glass, and What Alice Found There, while Alison Clifford in her The Sweet Old Etcetera relates the work to e. e. cummings' poetry, which has poetry procedures (e.g., use of parentheses, capitalization, and spacing on the page) that impacted several authors of e-poetry (e.g., Komninos Zervos,

Mez, et al). In JR Carpenter's Along the Briny Beach some quotations from Elizabeth Bishop, Joseph Conrad, Lewis Carroll, and Charles Darwin are employed, as well as the code of another e-poetry generator (Nick Montfort's Taroko Gorge). Such an intrinsic link to Montfort's poetry generator contributes to an understanding of the e-literature world in terms of the field that is becoming self-referential and autopoeitical.

The decision of e-literature writers to write texts that can be considered as roughly analogous with derivatives on financial markets and thus to some speculative and abstract activity, is certainly not pejorative. Rather than being considered imitation, such an activity reflects the nature of an e-literary area that is full of uncertainty, in the sense that authors, once they begin creating such works, always find themselves facing the unknown and searching for ways to highlight in it something that will attract readers and critics. The practice of connecting to other works, in the form of "derivative writing," allows them to add value to their works, which often also implies an entry into the valuable archives of literature and art, whose common denominator is a surplus in the field of creativity and innovation. Thus, derivative writing presupposes writing, which deploys such an underlying asset (and which has a big part in the attention economy) to help the author to enter the valorized archives of the e-literary world.

10 THE NOMADIC COCKPIT

New mobile technologies shape the way people communicate and perceive reality. Our basic position is the nomadic cockpit i.e. where one is armed with many navigating and controlling mobile screenic devices (from cell phones and tablets to consoles, cameras, and various players). When we move around in our surroundings armed with such devices we steadily perceive the data shown on the screen of such a device, which means that both the visual and aural interfaces are integrated in our experience of walking or riding through the environment. Virtual data approaching from the remote context on the screen are related to and coordinated with our basic, non-mediated perception from the physical here and now. Such a digital technology, provoking one's hands on controls, leads activity to become incorporated in the experience and understanding of our being on the move.

The nomadic cockpit's focus on mobility and corporeality is close to the cultural shift in contemporary philosophy, where the linguistic, discursive and textual give way to the material, biological, life, event-driven, and post-political (Negri; Agamben; Virno; Thacker). The shift to focus on life, bio-politics and the body, highlights political issues that concern movement, feelings, affects, and broader perceptual issues, particularly with regard to art and new media (Hansen; Massumi).[19]

It is characteristic of recent communication with mobile screenic devices that the latter introduce users into situations based on the virtualization of space, for they smoothly incorporate remote data into the user's current position and the "text" connected with it. Such devices, which presuppose the disappearance of hard and fast boundaries between physical reality and virtual worlds, are changing the way we perceive geographical space and encouraging new forms, not only of communication, but also of behavior, movement, and participation. Mobile screenic devices are strikingly applied also in locative art as one of the significant movements in the most recent new media art. In 2012, the Jodi group, which has been pioneering the Internet art since the 1990, launched project ZYX, which is

---

19 When addressing philosophical issues of mobility, de Certeau's observations on pedestrian's tactics should also be taken into account.

designed as an iPhone and iPod Touch application. It guides users through a series of gestures from jumping with it, pushing it, turning it, and shaking it. The user of this app is transformed into the performer, who is situated in mixed reality co-formed with her choreography. ZYX can be considered as a striking example of ubiquitous and persuasive computing as a new paradigm in the contemporary culture (Ekman, 2014). It demonstrates that cyberspace and VR data enter the given, physical reality and modify it, causing the smooth co-existence of both modes of reality. Such a computing shaped by very novel and mobile interfaces impacts the individual's nature, modifies it, and profiles her real time gestures.

The contemporary individual placed in the nomadic cockpit performs by interface shaped gestures that are differentiated from those triggered by stimuli originating in "given" reality. On the contrary, the interfaces are not neutral tools but are non-transparent and demonstrate their own materiality and functionality. The interface is not just a message but modifies movement: it is a shifter of one's behavior. The metaphor of window is not a good fit for the most recent generation of interfaces. Rather than enabling the entrance into artificial (data) worlds, these interfaces react to the given reality and the space of one's bodily actions. The body equipped with the interfaces (e.g. the body in nomadic cockpit mode) performs very particular gestures that differ from those formed by the non-equipped, bare body, which means that the body is spread out between the constraints emanating from physical space and the real time cyberspace instructions one receives from the interfaces. Once again, Jodi's ZYX is an example: it deploys virtual and physical components in creating a new form of public performance that implies a birth of a very sophisticated choreography shaped by the app's instructions entered on the iPhone.

Today we are witnessing more and more new media shaped contents enter and modify the given, physical reality. Video games (e.g. played on the Wii console) stimulate one's physical activity, which is influenced by stimuli originating in physical reality, as well as by cyberspace data mediated by state-of-the-art interfaces. One's gestures are modified as well, through such profane activities as using the touch screen (e.g. touch and drag the page with one or two fingers, pinch-to-zoom), which have rarely been executed before in everyday practice. A very particular case is also one's behavior during calling on the phone, when it is not based on hands-free calling devices. In this case, the body is stimulated to behave in a special way, one required for mobile phone conversations, which would come off as artificial and unnatural when compared with its ordinary posture and movements. We encounter a series of specific responses of the body to the mobile screenic device. Taking a call often requires that we stop, move away from the chosen path, and start walking in a new direction. Similarly specific is the way individuals turn away from their physical interlocutors in such moments, the way they cover their mouths and search for, let's say, a closed-off privacy, as is needed for a calm conversation with a distant caller.

In the present, it can be seen that an individual's path is a function of data being received in real time via mobile screenic devices, including the individual's nomadic cockpit. On the path from point A to point B the individual has an incoming call, which she directs to point C. When she reaches that point there is no guarantee that she will then direct herself to the original destination of point B, but might keep going towards point D, based on a received call or other crucial information, for instance, about the road and weather conditions, which she looked up on the mobile screenic device. The individual's path is a journey, constantly interrupted and modified by different pieces of information and feedback loops. Such a trajectory is non-linear, contingent, and speeded-up by means of technological advances that occur in networks, in which the flow of data is too fast for the cause-and-effect manner of behavior and thought.

FROM PHYSICAL MOBILITY TO E-TEXT ON THE MOVE

Similar uncertainty arising from mobility and stopping in intermediary positions, defined by before and after, not-yet and not-anymore, also accompanies electronic literary text (as one of the topics of this essay), which is a variable, uncertain entity that seems very nervous to a static observer. Let's call it a textscape on the move. It is displayed on desktops and laptops and is even more conspicuous on tablets and mobile phones, on which digital literary texts are also starting to be placed. This places increasing importance on new media specificity and integration into an algorithmic culture as the principal culture of the present (Strehovec).

191

This direction is not held by e-writers alone. In the present we are contemporaries to a number of projects in new media art that likewise use such devices, especially in connection with mobile, locative, and tactical media. Along with this practice there are also attempts to generate projects on locative literature, which is in fact disseminated by locative media. Such a practice should not be strictly speaking considered as electronic literature. In describing one such project, Anders Sundnes Løvlie writes:

> The most important outcome of the flâneur game, then, is not in the literary texts as they appear on screen, but in the exploration of a new way of perceiving and interacting with the urban environment. Thereby, the texts take on a certain documentary quality—in that they are produced from raw materials that are found in the urban environment. (2013)

In contrary to such movements in locative literature, which is first and foremost born mobile and locative, electronic locative literature is bound to the screen and deploys the new media specificity as well as mobility and speed issues (say, it is born digital as well as mobile and locative).

When discussing e-literature on mobile screenic devices, we must also draw a line between projects that merely use such a device as a medium for e-literary projects that could also be viewed on stationary computer screens and between projects made exclusively for mobile screenic devices, which are adapted to the experience of new modes of mobility. One of the projects that make good use of the advantages of mobility and locative networks is AndOrDada by Bauer and Suter, which is based on an application for the Android operating system.

This piece (subtitled "the road poem"), which also has a significant audio feature (the live changeable text is read aloud), is created with the intention of generating text depending on the user's passage through locations. The application produces text-under-transformation, depending on the user's path (walking, driving), when the input captured by wide local area network communications at a certain location influences the flow of the text and modifies it. In short, this project expands the area of e-literature by opening itself up to direct influences from the environment. In the case of AndOrDada, rather than being a means through which urban spatiality is formed, mobility as bodily-situated practice generates a textual event shaped by new media technologies.

Such an event based on mobile and locative experience occurs in a world whose main quality is speed, which implies a special constellation defined more or less by speed, acceleration, riding, and racing. Without being familiar with the hardware and software that generates contemporary textuality, William S. Burroughs wrote in The Invisible Generation:

> Take any text speed it up slow it down run it backwards inch it and you will hear words that were not in the original recording new words made by the machine different people will scan out different words of course but some of the words are quite clearly there and anyone can hear them words which were not in the original tape but which are in many cases relevant to the original text as if the words themselves had been interrogated and forced to reveal their hidden meanings. (218)

Burroughs was fascinated with the capabilities of the tape recorder, whose functions he applied to textual material. His essay, from which this quote was taken, dates from 1962 and everything in it focuses on the technical manipulability of text, which experienced an actual bloom only with the new generation of technologies, namely those that are based on computers and digitization. In any case, Burroughs's reference to speed and the acceleration as a generator of new modes by which the modern textuality operates is important even with regard to e-literature as a practice based on placing textual components into a "dry run" situation.

Speed brings things to clarity, to an experimental and accelerated state, which puts them in motion in the sense of an intensive riding (e.g. as in popular culture, attractions, etc.) often through experience shaped by loops. Such a mobility implies even the condition of being endangered, which the German expression Erfahrung used by Walter Benjamin alludes to etymologically: the expression contains both Fahrt (ride) and Gefahr (danger). In a certain way both of these components are also involved in the English term "experience," since when one experiences something, one moves around it and if one goes too far, one becomes endangered. Speed is also experienced in e-literary texts, for example in electronic animated poetry and poetry generators, when one "rides" the tapes of words-images-in-motion, yet at the same time the text/film tries to capture and perceive that which has not yet been included in the ride, is not accelerated and is outside the field of vision, but is also important for the understanding of such a screenic text (Strehovec, 2010).

AndOrDada as a piece of locative textual art presupposes both motion and Erfahrung, because "in locative media, representation becomes secondary in comparison to the sensorial experience" (San Cornelio, Ardevol), which relates in a same time to textual and physical ride. What is still essential for, let's say, the philosophy of AndOrDada and other pieces of locative e-literature, such as Strange Rain by Erik Loyer (which is designed for iPhone, iPod-touch and iPad)? First of all, it concerns an application accessible to a broad circle of users of mobile phones with this OS. The reader/user of the application is by no means the only one familiar with e-literature (and with mobile and locative media): this application can address an ordinary user as well, for whom this project presents the first, perhaps completely accidental encounter with e-literature, which means that such practice has a highly democratic nature. What is crucial for the understanding of e-literary projects for mobile and locative media is primarily that which comes from the new phenomenology of mobility and location crossing, which means that we are no longer dealing with static forms of reading, but with, for instance, two readings/riding. Namely, one that defines the very journey into artificial e-literary worlds and one that derives from the various physical movements of the reader, i.e. reading/riding in a physical space.

Suddenly, both rides are important, as well as their interactions (including intervals between them in terms of in-between). This creates a new experience of e-literary space, one that is more complex than interactivity, and in opposition to immersive effects. Now the text comes to life during a ride in physical space, because the user is constantly stimulated by the adventure of the ride, as several crossings (and feedback loops between both rides, the textual and the user's) provide richer perception and experience of e-literary text, which is the case of AndOrDada.

In relating to this "road poem," we can talk about expanded textuality as a result of a stable textual scheme overlaid with mobile informational texts considered as a derivative of writing on the move. Such an expanded textuality is flexible and nervous to a greater extent as a result of our ability to "move physically/spatially and virtually/informationally at the same time" (Lemos 404-405). We are facing a new mode of textual experience in terms of relational text, which is increasingly experienced as shifting, variable and contingent. Such a text is an outcome of our traversing of the relational space generated at the intersection of various practices, discourses, tactics and (bio)politics. AndOrDada also demonstrates that it is no longer point in addressing the e-literary text as being only generated by the author. On the contrary, such a textuality merges into a hybrid one, where one meets both the author's text and the platform text that are shaped by the networks and transmitted by GSM, GPS, CCTV, UMTS, WIFI, and RFID. We live in a mixed and augmented reality, which is also the text consisting of the author's text and by components of algorithmic culture, i.e. by generated and contextualized textual components.

FROM E-LITERATURE TO NEW MEDIA ART

In such e-literary projects, it is the very integration of mobility (ride) in the physical world that distinguishes the perception and reading of these projects from the reading of traditional texts on mobile phones and e-book readers (e.g. Kindle). The philosophy of the latter manner of reading characteristically employs new technology to continue the reading-as-we-know-it, the only change being that it takes place in new locations with the use of new devices. Its aim is the transfer (or the mental ride) of the reader into fictitious worlds, which is adapted to new locations only. For example, the project Shadows Never Sleep by Aya Karpinska, is a special example of e-literary work for mobile phones, which inventively uses the specificity of Apple multi-touch displays (on iPhone, iPod touch and iPad), and which the author expressed with the syntagms "zoom narrative" and "read by zooming." However, this app does not make use of the effects of pedestrian mobility and mobile networks.

On the other hand, e-literature in projects such as AndOrDada takes into account the context (including the new media paratexts and other non-verbal metadata), the materiality of the non-transparent interface, and the specificity of the location and the networking junctures, and in doing so introduce this experience into the very concept of e-literary work, which lives off the contents and stimuli received in real time in a specific location, to which it directs the algorithm that is integrated into such a piece.

Through the emphasis on relationality found in such projects, an understanding of context as something open and constantly shifting rather than static emerges, an understanding similarly suggested by socially-oriented locative media projects where what is at stake is not just placing data or locating objects but a dynamic relationality that occurs through the overlapping of different kinds of mapping—geographical, social network, etc.—within social interfaces to places (e.g. locative.org; see Hemment).

Also characteristic of the philosophy of such a piece is that in the age of new media we encounter an expanded concept of authorship, defined as an art platform (Goriunova). The contemporary pluriverse of texts contains both authorial texts written in natural and artificial languages and texts that are machine generated, or a hybrid of the two (as in the case of poetry generators).

In the case of AndOrDada we encounter an expanded concept of reading/riding, which denotes corporeal experiencing of texts beyond traditional reading in the sense of meaning decoding and linguistic comprehension (Hoover and Gouch). The reader is a flâneur, who integrates into her mobile experience the perception of location in a real standpoint as well as the data she receives from various networks via smart screenic devices that are included in her nomadic cockpit. The reader gains "more" from the ride or walk by completing her experience of the real location with the data contents that are being generated in that location and distributed via networks. If the reader enters into the dispositif of reading an e-text such as AndOrDada, it makes sense for her to open up to such multi-modal textuality and follow the moving road poem on the screen. The algorithm for this poem enables the entry of new textual units into the basic poem structure. The reader must also possess prior knowledge in order to experience and read such an e-text. She must start by obtaining as much data as possible on the piece (e. g. reviews, documentation, metadata and statements considered as new forms of paratexts), and become acquainted with the new media art of mobile and locative media, with e-literature, and with similar projects in particular. In order to read, understand and experience such a piece properly one must also possess new media literacy (as an ability to navigate the new media contents) and abandon the established horizon of expectations on textual specificity (Jauss's term) as defined within print-based literature.

Today we are witnessing the closeness of the newer generation of e-literature to new media art, so now let us devote our attention to a typical new media work of art in the field of mobile and locative media. The project **The Transborder Immigrant Tool**, created by the Electronic Disturbance Theater 2.0, aims to re-appropriate widely available technologies to be used as a form of humanitarian aid. Such an artistic tool consists of an inexpensive GPS cell phone and custom software. The software directs the user of the phone toward the nearest aid site, be that water, first aid, or law enforcement, along with other contextual navigational information. This is accomplished by a Java based application, written by Brett Stallbaum, which accesses the phone's ability to receive GPS information without needing to send out data that locates the user or network connectivity. **The Transborder Immigrant Tool** can be seen as part of a larger shift from tactical media to tactical bio-politics. The EDT seeks to engage the political potential opened up by technologies which can serve to improve people's lives directly, including medical technologies and systems such as GPS.

On the other hand, if we take a look at e-literature, we can find out that this field in its extreme forms, primarily revolutionizes language itself, redefining narrative in terms of replacing its linear forms with the more abbreviated and multi-medial storytelling, establishing a laboratory for the experiencing of the letter and the word under new media conditions (for example, the practice of e-poetry generators and John Cayley's "Writing to be found" with Google). E-literature also challenges reading by focusing on arrangements of words in a mode of illegibility (e.g. Jim Rosenberg's "Diagrams" series). However, it is less radical than new media art in regard to experiencing new forms of social engagement, .

Furthermore, e-literature and new media art are faced with the challenge of significant shifts in their functionality, as both are expanding their area of activities and aims far away from the canon and the functions of traditional art and literature. E-literary projects are becoming increasingly post-literary in the sense that they are abandoning literariness, narrative, metaphysical qualities (Roman Ingarden's term), and evoking lyrical atmospheres, and instead are placing other qualities and tasks to the fore, including those that e-literature has in common with new media art. What is essential for the latter is that it is post-aesthetic and post-artistic, meaning that it no longer places aesthetic and artistic values in the foreground, nor the aspirations to exhibit in the traditional places (and institutions) of art that are connected with them.

Since the origins of new media art we have been contemporaries of a strong tendency towards a spectacle, produced with high-tech, towards the surface and the play of attractive signifiers, stimulating the senses (at the beginning of the 1990s, the Ars Electronica festivals promoted such pieces first and foremost). Yet today it seems that an artistic performance of a pure event and of "intensities of direct sensual stimulation" no longer suffices (Darley 3). It is expected from this practice to contribute some surpluses in outlining an alternative politics (hactivism), alternative approaches to scientific research, as well as alternatives on the level of the social organization of life itself and ethics (i.e. helping people in need, spreading literacy). E-literature has a strong presence in this, especially when it concerns education for new media (e. g. digital) literacy and the critique of metaphysics, connected with the traditionalist literary pedagogy and with the role of the author-genius-brand.

TOWARD THE SUBTLE EXPERIENCE OF THE DIGITAL TANGIBLE

New media shaped texts are intended for screenic presentation, which is why we always read them on a very specific technological platform that (over)determines the accessibility of the text, its manipulability, and its ways of reading. The crossing over from the text's physical presence to its digital expanse on the screen presents theories of reading with certain problems.

> The reading process and experience of a digital text are greatly affected by the fact that we click and scroll, in contrast to tactilely richer experience when flipping through the pages of a print book. When reading digital texts, our haptic interaction with the text is experienced as taking place at an indeterminate distance from the

actual text, whereas when reading print text we are physically and phenomenologically (and literally) in touch with the material substrate of the text itself. (Mangen 405)

In fact, in the process of reading we are not in direct physical relation with the e-literary text (we do not touch the pages of printed text, nor turn them), yet this is by no means a drawback. On the contrary, e-text is there in a very subtle interface-shaped dispositif, so that we are in a certain sense closer to it than we are on the printed textual platform, which presupposes merely a sort of rudimentary turning of the pages. Let us note here that turning the pages, touching the paper, and even sensing its scent, undoubtedly signals the presence of a text in the reader's physical proximity; however these activities are accompanied by the reader's powerlessness to simply reach into the text and manipulate it. On the other hand, with an e-text, we encounter the subtle, interface-based presence of the reader/user in the text itself in terms of her identification with the cursor as a moving avatar, which marks the reader's position in the textscape.

In the digital text the reader is in fact where the cursor is, while the latter is in near proximity to the word itself and to its atomic units, i.e. letters. Furthermore, the cursor is not there as a coincidental ornament but is an active factor that can erase a letter, add a new one, or insert a punctuation mark, that is to say, alter the text from the inside in such a way that its operations can be concealed (it is impossible to do this with a printed text). Rather than being a simple opposition (e.g. the material tangible vs. intangible information), the digital and the tangible are linked by new media technologies that enable subtle forms of, let us say, the digital tangible. Such a tangibility is not something concrete: we are not dealing with visible effects and operations, but with very subtle ones. The sense of touch at work with the digital tangible is a "sense theoretician," since it is a sense that does not grab in a rough physical relation but functions precisely through its avatar in the textscape. The term "sense theoretician" was coined by Karl Marx in the following context:

The forming of the five senses is a labour of the entire history of the world down to the present. The sense caught up in crude practical need has only a restricted sense. For the starving man, it is not the human form of food that exists, but only its abstract existence as food [...] The care-burdened, poverty-stricken man has no sense for the finest play; the dealer in minerals sees only the commercial value but not the beauty and the specific character of the mineral: he has no mineralogical sense [...] The eye has become a human eye, just as its object has become a social, human object—an object made by man for man. The senses have therefore become directly in their practice theoreticians. They relate themselves to the thing for the sake of the thing, but the thing itself is an objective human relation to itself and to man. (Marx)

What is crucial in Marx's notion of the human senses is the very historical (e.g. changeable) attitude to them. They are mutated across history, and this point is of also significance in a moment when we draw upon the senses engaged in the present interface culture and their deployment in the cognition of digital literature.

We have seen in the previous sections of this book that mobile and locative media presuppose one's mobility and feedback with regard to the current location in which the user enters the network. For art and e-literary projects in locative media are significant that they also deploy the sense of touch, which is stimulated by the very nature of tactile interfaces (e.g. touch screens). The touch that contributes to storytelling itself is not a vernacular one, because it causes the event to happen. Therefore, it could be named a touch theoretician even in terms of the aforementioned Marxian theory of sense theoreticians. The touch theoretician is a self-learning touch, which makes progress over the ages of its experiencing.

One of the significant works in the field of e-literature, which stages the material/immaterial problem as well as the subtle issue of touching within the interface culture is Serge Bouchardon's Toucher. Touching means exploring, i.e. there is a certain curiosity that generates touch as a sense of proximity and of movement (the touching hand gets more information, when it moves around the object). In Toucher the shift from immediate touching to the interface mediated and driven one is thoroughly demonstrated. The touching in this piece requires an interface mediation by the mouse, microphone, and webcam. Such a subtle touching experience reveals a lot about the way we touch multimedia content on screen, as well as the reading of e-literary contents. We enter them by interfaces, reading mutated to interface reading (e. g. the mouse reading, the term coined by the author of this essay). The reader of this piece is actually the user, provoked to access the text by means of sophisticated interface-shaped procedures that include various modalities of touching. This piece demonstrates that its reading is first and foremost through an interface-shaped, sophisticated experience, which stimulates various senses and puts the reader-user into the riding adventure as an event that stimulates several senses and provokes reader/user's corporeal and kinesthetic participation.

New generations of digital devices and interfaces most assuredly provoke new forms of perception and action. Their user is expected to enter into a novel generation of objects and events in a way which basically differs from her pre-technological relation to reality. With a stylus or touch screen we can come into very direct, although virtual contact with the word, contact that is much more immediate and intimate than using a typewriter, which means that these devices once again establish an immediate relation between the body (in fact, the hand) and the word. This is why they are not subject to Heidegger's critique intended for the fate of the word in a time of the typewriter.

> The hand is, together with the word, the essential distinction of man [...] Man does not "have" hands, but the hand holds the essence of man, because the word as the essential realm of the hand is the ground of the essence of man [...] The typewriter tears writing from the essential realm of the hand, i.e. the realm of the word. The word itself turns into something "typed." (Heidegger 80)

Heidegger was unsettled by the fact that the typist uses a keyboard set in front of her, that she touches only the keys while the text that is created is over "there," and is separated from direct contact with the hand so that the individual letters that constitute it are not physically touched. The directness between the hand and the text may be lost with the typewriter, but my opinion, mobile digital screenic devices once again enable the proximity of the hand and the text. This proximity now takes place in more subtle and virtual, often simply tele-forms, for example in touching the virtual keyboard on tablets (e.g. iPad), digital phones and PDAs (deploying the stylus), or in the touch of an individual letter through a word processor with the use of a cursor. Physical tangibility has been replaced with the digital, and with mixes of both. Real and digital modes have become intertwined in contemporary reality, shaped by the ubiquitous computing. Tele-labor and long-distance sensations enrich our activities as we know them.

11 E-LITERATURE AND NEW MEDIA ART

R ather than being a continuation of print-based literature, this chapter considers electronic literature as a novel practice of digital textuality that foregrounds new media specificity, digital literacy, and new approaches to the issue of writing in programmable media. This practice is also embedded in contemporary society, which means that along with the new media specificity the authors and theoreticians need to take into account the new social paradigms. I address the very nature of e-literature with regard to the new media art as a striking field of contemporary creativity, which contributes to the basic understanding of new media literacy and strikingly demonstrate the links between e-writing and its social basis (see Paul, "New Media in White Cube," and Quaranta "The Postmedia Perspective").

In mentioning new media art, we need to highlight the following features as essential for this practice: database logic (the components of new media artworks considered as a list of non-hierarchically structured items, ordered beyond the cause-and-effect trajectory); process-like nature; software, algorithms, interactivity; playful effects; the use of interfaces (according to Manovich, creating a narrative work in new media can be understood as "the construction of an interface to a database"); and customization. Along with new media specificity (i.e. e-literary text is displayed on the screen, stored in digital storage devices, and controlled by software), e-literary texts are embedded in the social in a way, which demonstrates some of the key features of the contemporary social paradigms. E-literature and new media art also challenge one's perception and deepen the experience of cultural contents.

ON THE SHRINKING ATTENTION SPAN

The new ontological picture of the world implies novel forms of perception and cognition that are shaped and augmented by several technological and social tools. When we are talking about new movements in e-literature, we need to be aware that such a textual and post-textual practice is embedded in contemporary culture which is shaped by software (as a mind- and perception shifter), by ubiquitous computing (Ekman, 2013), by Internet language (Crystal, 2001), by Web 2.0 remixability, and by the repurposing of various cultural platforms and contents. The user of contemporary cultural contents is faced with changes, shifts and turns steadily increasing in pace and degree. Her basic condition could be defined in terms that she finds on a deceptive axis between invisible up and down, front and behind, left and right. Stable view points are at stake, and hard and fast lines between different fields are being pushed aside. In terms of perception we face an individual, who lacks the ability to concentrate needed for the reading of longer textual passages; and is instead used to very short, direct and functional messages, bulleted web site organization, music videos, YouTube video formats, elevator pitches, sms, and breaking news. She has lost the taste for more sophisticated language, ambiguity, and imagination. Our ability to perceive the things in a distance is at stake as we have got used to various tasks, which we need to execute within a very short temporal interval, with a profound impact on the way we form and create within the realm of the "cyberlanguage".

Due to the pace of life in such an instant culture of speed of light and breaking news, based on augmented and mixed reality, our attention span is getting shorter and shorter, which has been significantly expressed in the following post to iDC mailing list: "I really think hyperlinking has changed the way I read and my concentration span. I'd like to be able to stick to one thing, but I seemed to be easily distracted, so each email has about 1-3 seconds to grab my attention" (O'Donnell 2007). The crucial point in this statement is the mention of a very short temporal interval, in which the e-mail recipient is in position to accept or reject the message, meaning that her attention is limited by the very reality she is exposed to in her real time activity. "Our observational skills have suffered as we have mastered multitasking. We now commonly send messages while we are in the act of receiving information (Sherman 2008). Such an alert (and nervous) condition impacts several aspects of the present social life, meaning that the most common communicational and cultural contents need to be adapted to the demands of shorter attention span of today's individual (as a user, consumer).

The shrinking attention span even implies a profound turn in the language of contemporary marketing strategies, which is often shaped by the demand of bullet points list statements. It seems that in today's mixed reality of change everything is under the sign of the elevator pitch as the key strategy in approaching the present consumer within a sophisticated and as much as possible persuasive fashion. An elevator pitch is a concise, carefully planned, and well-practiced overview of an idea for a product, service, or project, which can be delivered in the time span of an elevator ride (e. g. thirty seconds or 100-150 words), with the purpose of hooking the audience into a positive response to the product offered. What is crucial here is the first impression, in terms of getting the investor's attention with a certain hook expressed in a statement that piques their interest to want to hear more about the intended product or service. To get the consumer excited, involved, and thinking about, one needs to adopt her (cultural) contents and products to the novel reality of a shorter attention span.

Walter Benjamin was a theoreticians who saw the danger to one's attention as well as for language in the age of information. In his **The Story-teller**, he writes:

> Less and less frequently do we encounter people with the ability to tell a tale properly. More and more often there is embarrassment all around when the wish to hear a story is expressed. It is as if something that seemed inalienable to us, the securest among our possessions, were taken from us: the ability to exchange experiences. One reason for this phenomenon is obvious: experience has fallen in value. (p. 77)

The richness of one's experience is endangered by information arranged by a pace of breaking news and stock exchange indices that diminish the lengthy temporal interval needed for storytelling and storyhearing.

BEYOND THE AUTONOMY OF E-LITERATURE: CONSIDERING NEW MEDIA ART ACTIVISM

In this book, e-literature (as a technical expression) is considered as a textual and new media practice placed in the midst of profound shifts of paradigms that impact upon how people approach the cultural contents. Therefore, the shifts in the contemporary individual's perception discussed in previous section are crucial for the way media shaped language art is formed and structured. It is self-evident that the e-literature author needs to take into account how cyberlanguage behaves within the elevator pitch paradigm. The author finds their task through designing their piece in a way, which hooks the reader/user within a very short temporal unit. They need to be aware that in terms of aesthetics (considered in Baumgarten's original meaning, as cognitio sensitiva), the attention of such an individual is opened up just to striking qualities and characteristics—of objects, events, situations, relations—that possibly hit or grab them within a very economical temporal interval. The author is in search of qualities which put the reader into a condition of unrest and even a condition of a hunger, striving for the possession of the particular quality of the object or to part in an event, which has suddenly struck them attention with a very subtle manner and made them abandon the ordinary everyday practices which shape their attitude to reality.

The author is striving not just for the qualities but for the novel and sophisticated procedures, which are crucial for the functioning of the most advanced cultural devices and tools. The growth both in quantity and diversity of online activities across recent social networking, along with an array of new technologies that enhance both social interaction and content design, enables the condition that stimulates its participants to be involved in various practices. The participants submit videos and photographs, write blogs and profiles, design web sites, prepare presentations, and create sophisticated cultural contents. Surfing the Web gives way to more creative role of the Internet user who gets more and more interested in how the things they deal with work, what the language of the code looks like, and how the technologies that enable the users on-line activities behave. The user is curious about the invisible, underlying structures (algorithms) that enable the displayed textscape. They try to get acquainted with the web and mobile applications in terms of their actors.

New media art is certainly a field that helps in the understanding of some novel directions in e-literature, particularly those that are expanding hypertext to new areas of textuality, shaped by new media. Discussions of fundamental paradigms of new media art demonstrate that we are functioning within it as contemporaries of tendencies and movements that are leading towards alternative politics, activism, hacktivism, and even an alternative organization of life in terms of the current theoretical paradigms shift. Rather than through intrinsic events in the autopoeitic system of contemporary art, changes in this field are influenced by science, new technologies, new concepts of politics and activism. In addition to the already mentioned project "The Transborder Immigrant Tool," let us also mention two historical examples of new media art: the Slovenian artist Marko Peljhan's "Makrolab" and Critical Art Ensemble's project "Free Range Grain" (2003-2004).

Marko Peljhan's "Makrolab," first presented at the documenta X, 1997, is arranged as laboratory based on the model of the Russian MIR station in order to tap communications data streams emanating from police radio to satellite telephones. This arouses in equal measure the suspicion of official bodies and the curiosity of professional surveillance institutions. Peljhan has been working on the "Makrolab" from 1997 to 2007, as a project that focuses on telecommunications, migrations, and weather systems research in an intersection of art and science. Critical Art Ensemble's "Free Range Grain" (2003-2004) was created as a live, performative action that used basic molecular biology techniques to test for genetically modified food available worldwide in the global food trade. CAE, in collaboration with Beatriz da Costa and Shyh-shiun Shyu constructed a portable, public laboratory to test foods that others deemed suspicious of "contamination" caused by the common genetic modifications. Members of the audience was invited bring pieces of foods to te gallery that they found suspect for whatever reason, and artists tested them over a 72-hour period to see if their suspicions were justified.

The point of this project is that science should not be left fully to scientists and that by using an artistic apparatus and artistic non-profit driven approach one can set up more responsible research. The point is similar to the "Transborder Immigrant Tool," in that this device, which had been developed in an artistic context, would perform a role that corrects politics and those national institutions that are protecting the integrity of the individual. In the field of new media art we are also contemporaries of a number of practices that are critical of broader social issues and of contemporary technological advances. An important direction within it is precisely the demonstration of the malfunctioning of high-tech. Such a direction, in terms of bigger social critique, is much less noticeable in the case of e-literature. Only feminist hypertext and a few rare pieces that deal with the critique of high tech advances (especially of their promises) and with their malfunctioning (e. g. Eugenio Tisseli's Degenerative) hold a more important role in this context. In addition, we should mention also the topic of vanishing text, which draws upon insecure existence of electronic literary text.

However, there are many commonalities that are essential for new media art and e-literature:

1. Both fields are connected by smart technologies, new media, new areas of presentation (beyond the gallery's white cube and printed book, and thus, for example, similar spaces in clubs and at conferences and festivals), and new dissemination possibilities (the web, mobile and locative media). Rather than being a production of a single author, meaning in both fields is created between the user and the system (platform, interface, network)

2. Both place the research value of their practices in the foreground (and not the cult, aesthetic or exhibition one). While e-literature focuses on the fate of the letter, word, text, narrative, and storytelling in the age of new media, various new media art genres absolutely free the movement and image from their representative functions and focus them to pure movement and the composition of vision (see Lazzarato's focus on video as an art which crystallize time and simulate the perception).

3. Both fields are closely associated with theory, and participation between the artists and theoreticians is essential. A good statement, which an author attaches to a project, is conditio sine qua non for successfully addressing an audience. Consequently one of the conditions for the artists is that they are familiar with the contemporary theoretical paradigms that define their fields. In both fields, festivals and conferences alike are platforms at which theoreticians and practitioners (artists, e-writers) meet.

4. Even in a quantitative sense, the surplus of theory over artistic and especially e-literary production is not a negative and disruptive affair. E-literature as practice is one thing, while the theory of it is another. Theory produces its own subject of

knowledge, which is not identical to the "artistic/literary object." Precisely due to their pioneering in and investigating of new media shaped perception, a reference to e-literary and new media works of art is appropriate in various theoretical discussions of new media and the individual's experience in an augmented reality.

5. Both fields are focused more on performances, actions and services than on finished works. Their user is directed to problem-solving activity; she also interferes with e-literary projects, defined as processes, in real time. Thus both fields belong to the broader context of algorithmic culture.

6. Essential for production in both fields are artistic and e-literary platforms and cooperation, based on networking. The concept of the artist as genius has definitely been surpassed. Furthermore, in this field the criterion of national literatures functions only to a limited extent. One can come across artists/e-writers from different countries particularly in the case of projects with collective authorship. English as the lingua franca of the globalized world also has a prevailing role in e-literature. Only in countries with a rich e-literature tradition (e.g. Brazil and France) do national languages hold an important role.

7. Projects of new media art and e-literature are also useful for educating people for new media (digital) literacy, as they expand the knowledge of media and its behavior outside of by the routine of everyday practice shaped situations.

8. A great role in the reception, perception and familiarization with these works is given to the hybrid viewer-reader-listener in the role of the user, which is associated with the very ontological structure of projects and performances, which often have the nature of schematic structures (for instance, the "textual instrument" in e-literature) that invite users (or other artists) to individualized concretizations. The most competent users (in the case of e-literature also readers) are experts (including programmers), authors who have a certain surplus of knowledge in comparison with the traditional artistic and literary audience.

9. Characteristic of both fields is great uncertainty, instantaneousness, difficulty in definition, and weak institutionalization. Each project blurs the boundaries of an individual field and authors are forced to invent new genres and to redefine the boundaries of their fields. E-literary and the new media art pieces are processes, relations, programs, in-between realities, instruments, and performances. Their stable, object-like nature is at stake: "the art happens between the pieces, less in them" (Harm van den Dorpel).

10. Neither field has developed critique in the form that we are familiar with in the literature-as-we-know it and in modern and contemporary art. Critique as we know it in the case of printed literature is being replaced by merely precise descriptions and presentations of individual works or these projects appear as the subject of a broader theoretical analysis that is focused on the conceptualization of certain paradigms. It seems as though the less important and unsuccessful works are being ignored, while the important ones (those that invent their own genre) deserve wider attention. Particularly in the e-field, greater critique should be given to works that burn out in a spectacle, that exaggerate the use of special effects, and deploy a highly abstract and McDonaldized concept of language.

In the first chapter, referring to the post-object world, we saw that new movements, forms, and directions in the field of e-literature (and the new media art) are not alien to the key cultural, philosophical and social paradigms in the present, but belong even to its forefront. It seems that in the present the world become artistic in particular sense (and e-literary), whereas artificial and fictional worlds, as well as the realm of aesthetics, have shifted to popular culture, sport, fashion, and even science. Today we are witnessing new media art and Post-Internet art as new movements, as new media shaped art enters the fields of science, politics, economics, and the social, all in order to make some significant social changes in alternative worlds, communities, tactical media, activism, and social design. Avant-garde concepts (e.g. gesamtkunstwerk/total work of art), lifelike art (Allan Kaprow,) and society considered as artwork (Herbert Marcuse), are included in broader discussions that take into account electronic civil disobedience (Critical Art Ensemble), temporary autonomous zones (Hakim Bey), activism (The Yes Men), the issue of the conceptual artistic state (Neue Slowenishe Kunst), and space culturation (the Slovenian project tied to KSEVT)). The significant movements in contemporary new media art are engaged in the projects of changing the society. They are situated very close to the topics and goals addressed in contemporary critical theory (Hardt, Negri, Lazzarato, Virno, Agamben, Galloway, Thacker, Fuller, etc.).

The development of new technologies and media is very rapid. At the moment the current topics and trends include ubiquitous computing, the Internet of things, and—as mentioned above—Post-Internet art, locative, and mobile art. What is important in this kind of art is not related to a stable object: experiences are more valuable, and relations between objects and mobility. The question is no longer what the image, text, or music composition are, but what is happening with applications, platforms, and processes, and how they are disseminated online. Rather than being stored in a static database, art is somewhere in-between relations and events. The important component is also the link between the project and its technological context. For example Olia Lialina's project "Summer" (2013), where 21 shots of a girl are distributed over 21 websites, which means that the browser has to switch between servers. Animation of these images, therefore, depends on the individual Internet sites, Internet infrastructure and Internet speed and that is why the switch is not smooth at all and we are faced with delays and freezes.

Post-Internet art includes objects that are changeable and elusive, artists deal with their different versions, they pass between their physical mode and their Internet version. There are also changes in artist's position: today's practitioners are moving from institutions of the single author institution towards creative artistic platforms and ubiquitous authorship, which demands more and more active users that have to be familiar with this kind of artistic practices, or otherwise they may be rejected. We are faced by artworks that are shaped like non-trivial machines in motion, and their social context is as important as their functioning. It is not just about how the thing functions but how it behaves in a social environment and how it is spread via network.

Janez Strehovec

12 AN EXPANDED CONCEPT OF E-LITERARY CRITICISM

In this book, the basic notion of the e-literary changed significantly in comparison to its position in established scholarship, which was formed first and foremost within hypertext theory, as well as in the recent theories that are in the core of activities driven by organizations such as the ELO. While the e-literary text in this scholarship is analyzed and discussed with regard to the new media specificity of e-textuality and e-writing, we aim to address such a text in terms of its wide-spread interactions with new media art, popular culture, new lifestyles (e.g. clubbing), and new social paradigms. This means that we consider the e-literary as contextualized and deeply embedded in contemporary information society and the society of techno-spectacles. The book's title Text as Ride directs us toward the closeness of the e-literary and popular culture (e.g. theme parks and arcade rides); however such an approach does not mean addressing the e-literary text as trivial and profane. Our account of the e-literary is also an attempt at not reducing e-literary projects to textual artefacts but in addressing them in terms of process, program, and application, and as extremely demanding activity for one's perception. In this vein, the chapter Cycling as Reading a Cityscape explains the city as a textlike cityscape, e.g. as a material text shaped in terms of a spatial syntax, which is read as if it consisted of linguistic and non-linguistic signifiers.

E-literary text also stimulates the reader who is not familiar with printed fiction but is into geeky video games, VJing (e.g. Amy Alexander's performance CyberSpaceLand), hacker culture, new media art, and clubbing. The e-literary also challenges theoreticians from disciplines and fields that are not strictly bound to literary theory and criticism but which deal with new media art theory, mobile culture studies, software studies, epistemology of new media, digital literacy, digital humanities, and new media aesthetics. We also need to stress that e-literary criticism has gained much from the recent paradigm of ubiquitous and persuasive computing, as the e-literary is turned from the stationary computers to mobile screenic devices and starts deploying the data from locative mobile networks. Today, the convergence of global and local networks, online databases, and new tools for location-based mapping (from GPS to RFID) provokes great interest among artists dealing with the internet of things, locative art, and locative e-literature.

Such a shift in practice has a big aftermath in the theory, first and foremost due to a very intimate and corporeal link between the user and the cultural, artistic, and literary content (e.g. the digital tangible introduced in this book). Susan Kozel argues for ubiquitous computing "as relational and corporeal. It is temporal and intercorporeal. Embedded in our lives, it is touched, seen, lived in, or with." (338) Referring to convergences between artistic and daily performance, Kozel coined the term "ubiquitous corporeality," because "bodies are ubiquitous, they may be digital, distanced, or distracted, but they are present" (339). "Ubicorp" can be considered as a counterbalance to "ubicomp," as a precondition of later. In the world of mobile and locative media we can not escaped from embodiment. Writing on mobiles (phones, tablets) invents new bodily gestures and reinvents the hand as a bridging organ between the self and the screenic world.

One of the crucial notions presented in this book is that it is not sufficient to analyze the e-literary in a broader (cultural, social) if we analyze it solely through born digital criterion. We also need to call attention to born social, born political, and born corporeal (ubicorp) criteria as well as to crucial movements in contemporary philosophy and cultural studies. In a moment where new media specificity ceases to be central as the most talked about criterion of the e-literary, e-literary criticism can enter the broader field of contemporary humanities and social sciences. It means that along with the new media features of digital textuality, there are also issues addressing the fate of the letter, word, text and literacy being addressed in current discussions concerning embodiment, bio-politics, gender, tactical media, activism, feminism, spectacle, postpolitics, neoliberalism, and economics.

The e-literary also implies the conceptual (similar to several movements in contemporary and new media art), and that contemporary politics and economics are becoming more and more conceptual (e.g. derivative writing, discussed in a previous chapter). Along with algorithms, such derivatives can serve as a feature which links the e-literary with the key scopes of contemporary social (Strehovec 2013).

Derivative writing is only one of the new concepts that this author has introduced. Some of them have been found also in his previous scholarship. These concepts—spread between the theory of new media art and e-literary criticism—include word-image-movement, post-hypertext e-literature, digital tangible, nomadic cockpit, text as a ride, techno-suspense, techno-surprise, new media paratexts, closeness that grows toward the user, e-literary service, new media artwork as program and application, and the aesthetic of closeness. E-literary criticism is one of the most significant and at the same time questionable concepts of post-hypertext e-literature, as I discussed in "Text as Virtual Reality"—presented at the first Digital Arts and Culture conference in Bergen, Norway (1998). In fact, in that paper we mentioned the second order techno-literatures as the more conceptual and hybrid endeavors of several authors who deploy several new media tools (plug-ins) along with hypertext.

The most compelling and innovative projects of post-hypertext e-literature (only these and not the hypertext ones provoke our attention in this book) share the goal of calling into question the very specificity of literature as we know it. They also destabilize common ideas about digital writing and the smooth functioning of technological advances, foregrounded instead the malfunctioning of high-tech, vanishing text, noise, glitch, and networked disruption. They do so by opening new ways of textual organization (e.g. cinematic and riding ones), by reflecting on how the software conditions our basic understanding of on-line textuality with literary scripts, and by pointing to the changes caused by algorithmic culture. Whereas the hyperfiction (as the most significant movement of e-literature in 20th century) addresses narrative under new media conditions (e.g. Marie-Laure Ryan's Narrative as Virtual Reality, Ilana Snyder's Hypertext. The electronic labyrinth), post-hypertext e-literature is more conceptual and open to various new paradigms that it shares with new media art. Here we can mention Mark Amerika's Filmtext and Talan Memmott's Lexia to Perplexia as the seminal projects in which the fiction and non-fiction intertwine: textual units in them are formed as commentaries and theoretical reflections.

In this book some of the key applied concepts relate to new media art, because the crucial features of this field (i.e. the software controlled projects, databases, algorithms, processes, applications, along with the post-

215

object nature of its projects, customization, and big stress on the user's role) are put into force also in e-literature. Here we can mention Gene Young-blood's book Expanded Cinema (1970), in which the author's attention was directed to the issues of life, experience, process and synesthesia. By analyzing Michael Snow's experimental film Wavelength, he argued that:

> like all truly modern art, Wavelength is pure drama of confrontation. It has no "meaning" in the conventional sense. Its meaning is the relationship between film and viewer. We are interested more in what it does than what it is as an icon. The confrontation of art and spectator, and the spectator's resultant self-perception, is an experience rather than a meaning. (126)

This finding (the experience vs. meaning divide) is accomplished in the analysis of e-literature as the field in which the traditional way of reading gives way to the more sophisticated experiencing of a textual event shaped as a ride (see also my term not-just-reading). In dealing with e-literary pieces, we are interested in how they address the user and challenge their basic orientation and functioning (that is Youngblood's "what it does"). In digital text considered as a ride, meaning decoding is just one of components in a sophisticated experience of e-literary text accompanied with the new media paratexts.

The way in which Youngblood foregrounds experience at the expense of meaning is crucial here. Semantics in the narrow linguistic sense gives way to more complex process of meaning making in terms that includes various mental and physical procedures. It is in fact in-between meaning decoding and corporeal experience (riding), including various kinesthetic and motor activities. Mouseovers, clicks and drags, pinch-outs are also at play here. Due to the fact that the e-literary text deploys interfaces, art platforms (Goriunova), and software advances it can attract also the users dealing with the video games, new media art, VJing, and design.

What is most challenging in e-literature, if we consider only the born digital criterion, that is, if we address the e-literary in a narrow sense? What is in it of importance due to its very particular features that can not be found in other fields of new media creativity? By answering this question we draw upon e-literature's ability to push the textual to its limits, to provoke its most hidden affordances, to arrange text in a way that it starts to replicate itself or vanish or is transformed in unreadable fashion. Whereas the significant movements in new media art deploy glitches, crashes, malfunctions of high-tech (e.g. Jodi's play with the browser's crash in the OSS project), e-literature gives attention to vanishing and erased text (in the tradition of Gibson and Ashbaugh's **Agrippa**, 1992) and text transformations in the direction of unreadability. The user/reader's of e-literature is often not in charge (e.g. in Bouchardon's projects), she is not the master of the piece, and the author's grasp over her project is also diminished.

Some e-literary works, such as Geniwate's generative work **Concatenation**, require a patient, exploratory reader who builds up experience with the piece over a number of readings. In a generative work, the reader starts a process that results in an unpredictable output that neither author nor reader can preview. A piece of code, like the genetic code, is let loose on a lot of variables. No one knows what the specific output will be—they can only know the rules that constrain it (Strickland).

The e-literary is fixated on the limits and what lies beyond them: only such an extremely unsafe endeavor stimulates readers, scholars and critics in this field. On the other side, in the print literature blockbusters, the will to experiment with the textual is pushed aside. Many of these works are less demanding in terms of mental combinatorics and are integrated into entertainment industry.

In similar vein to Youngblood's writing on expanded cinema and synaesthetic cinema (and Joseph Beuys expanded concept of art introduced in the 1960 and 1970), we can also consider the expanded concept of e-literature (e. g. synaesthetic e-literature), which challenges e-literary criticism. The most recent development in e-literature stimulates novel theoretical approaches and blurs the boundaries between fields and disciplines engaged in analyzing the e-literary. By drawing from Manovich's views about "true cultural innovators of the last decades of the twentieth century" (Manovich, 2003: 16), we can state that e-literature and its theory (e-literary criticism) in first decades of 21st century are more innovative than traditional, print literature and its theory. In terms of a self-reflexive position and deployment of new concepts, devices, and paradigms, we can say that print literature is far behind the e-literature and its criticism. The novel experience of digital textuality stimulates e-literary criticism toward critical thinking on digital culture and introduces new theoretical devices, which can be deployed also in other fields (e.g. in digital literacy, technoculture studies, digital humanities).

As we have seen in previous chapters, this book foregrounds the critical interrogation of the e-literary in terms of shifting attention from solely born digital criterion to born social, born political, and born corporeal criteria that are profoundly addressed in the new media art. Along with the endeavors of scholars engaged in ELO, E-Poetry festivals, American English departments, and the European ELMCIP project and its Knowledge-Base, one needs to also follow voices beyond this stream, such as Kenneth Goldsmith's Uncreative Writing (2011), which searches for a position which differs from purely academic and controlled digital writing and e-literary practice. Another critical position is found in Florian Cramer's keynote speech at ELO 2012 conference in Morgantown, which defined e-literature as "islands of literary works within the massive writing/reading streams of the Internet" (a position close to that of Adorno and the Frankfurt school in addressing the fine arts vs. cultural industry issue), and a digital boutique and gated community of literary writing inside a sea of digital ephemera (a position resembling a fine art white cube shielded from the digital pop). He distinguished between writing shaped by distributed net.art practices, streaming and "netwurking" (the practice of Australian e-author Mez), on the one hand, and e-literature, on the other, focused to the notion of the oeuvre as it was addressed in the print literature.

Cramer critically refers to today's mainstream approach to the e-literary, which also accompanies the ELO and e-literature as an established field and institution. In broader context he mentions Brion Gysin's statement that literature was "fifty years behind painting." Today the painting in this syntagm can be replaced with new media art focused not only on software but on issues regarding networking, protocols, ubiquitous computing, malfunctioning of high-tech, performance, gender, activism, hactivism, bio-politics, and locative media. Although e-literature is not fifty years behind new media art, as noted above in "The Nomadic Cockpit," it is comparatively less radical than new media art in its scope of reference (e.g.

bio-politics, body, gender, tactical media, performance, locative media, and activism).

We also need to be aware that a significant portion of new media projects that deal with the fate of the letter, word, text and the narrative in the contemporary have been created beyond institutions of e-literature and have not been thoroughly discussed within the ELO conferences and E-Poetry festivals. Formed within other fields and traditions (e.g. Brazilian), they were presented in other venues and reviewed by scholars dealing with the new media art and contemporary art. Many practitioners of net. art and text-based installations created their projects without the purpose being listed among the e-literary authors.

The "netwurker" Mez (the nickname of Australian artist Mary Anne Breeze), who invented the "mezangelle" language crowded with square brackets, is just conditionally an e-writer, and Olia Lialina's piece My Boyfriend Came Back From the War (1996), which is an excellent model of storytelling in new media, is also considered a net.art project. In fact, some of the most compelling projects in the field of new media textuality are text based installation. Here we can mention Jeffrey Shaw's The Legible City, and Bill Seaman and Daniel C. Howe's Architecture of Associations; both are not intended for inclusion in e-literature and were presented at several art shows worldwide. The same destiny accompanies Eduardo Kac's holopoetry pieces and Julius Propp's bit.falls, as an intriguing installation which interrogates the digital textuality shaped by the search engine. Natalie Bookchin's The Intruder belongs first and foremost to the genre of video game patches, although this piece is a paradigmatic example of to the new media specificity adjusted storytelling.

Future movements in e-literature will demonstrate whether the born digital criterion will retrain value as a crucial measure or it will be replaced by new concepts, ideas, and expressions that are opened more to the political and the social. In any case the power of the e-literary, which steadily stimulates critical views (along Cramer's text we can also mention Eskelinen's The Four Corners of the E-lit World , 2013) is calling into question the entire field and its institutions through in its uncertainty, self-reflexivity, and shifting borders (toward games and postliterary projects, toward new media shaped storytelling and vanishing texts). Such an unsafe condition provokes theory, which finds challenge for its endeavors at the intersection of the e-literary with the new media art, video games, clubbing, cyberspectacle, derivative trading, software, and algorithmic cultures. The point is also a broadening the field toward issues addressed within digital humanities, ubiquitous computing, mobile and locative media, and digital literacy.

Many debates on the e-literary relate to its literariness, as well as other topics that are linked to the literary, e. g. the fate of the letter, storytelling, and literacy. In addressing these issues we need to pay attention to the feature that could be named "e-literariness." This feature relates to defamiliarization (e.g. making strange) under new media condition, which presupposes the arrangement of the digital text in a way that enables novel forms of perception and experience of digital tangible.

Addressing e-literariness today means questioning the e-literary in context such as: expanded digital textuality and postliterary projects on the place of literature; the visual and kinetic verbal (the author's concept word-image-movement); and temporary, self-erasing, and vanishing texts (e.g. Gibson's and Ashbaugh's Agrippa at the beginning of this movement). Such turns are accompanied by shifts in considering the field of meaning (e.g. Simanowski's Digital Art and Meaning, 2011), which needs to be approached anew, not in a traditional vein of meaning decoding in print literature. One needs to be aware that meaning is in the case of e-literature an outcome of several components engaged in digital text-making, and not just the verbal components. Meaning is also conveyed by silence, blanks, vanishing, crossed-out and illegible letters, punctuations, and interruptions. E-literariness presupposes compression (in terms of the elevator pitch effect explained in this book) and replacement of linear form of expressions (narrative, discourse) with the non-linear, shortened, and economical.

E-literariness should be found in between: on the insecure intersection of letters, words, html characters, words-images, textual and non-textual signifiers, vanishing and self-destructing signifiers, and algorithms, on one hand; and on the basic components of algorithmic, digital, spectacle, software, and interface culture on the other. E-literariness is generated also where there are bodily interactions with the textual as well as gestures like rotate, zooming out, clicks-and-drag, drags-and-drop, drag-touche-hold, pinch, flick, and tap. It means that categories and concepts that intersect with the human-computer interface should be understood as e-literary ones. They add value to the story, style, author's poetics, plot, and dissolve. Aya Karpinska's term "zoom narrative" is illustrative for such an understanding.

Rather than depending on e-literary production, the new movements and developments of e-literary criticism are also bound to new conceptual challenges and shifts of paradigms in other fields. Just as the concept of rectangle is not rectangular, so too e-literary criticism is its own story. There is no requirement that in the future e-literary criticism will go hand in hand with simultaneous e-literary production. It can gain significant stimuli for its endeavors from other fields as well (e. g. text-based new media art, post-internet art, software cultures, textual practices in social networking and mobile cultures). One can even speculate that e-literature as a practice is gone in its present form. It may be replaced by other practices of digital textuality and writing in mobile and locative media that will be shaped quite differently than the present ones and articulated in material form only for a limited time (and erased after). It is also possible that e-literary criticism will bloom in terms of an alternative theory, which does not need e-literary pieces (as we know them within the present e-literary movements) for its future investigations. Rather than close reading of such texts, its basic generator will be found in critical addressing other manifestations of text based digital cultures and their contextualizations.

Janez Strehovec

BIBLIOGRAPHY

Aarseth, Espen J. Cybertext: Perspectives on Ergodic Literature. Baltimore, London: The Johns Hopkins University Press, 1997.

Adorno, Theodor W. Aesthetic Theory. Minneapolis: University of Minnesota Press, 1998.

Agamben, Giorgio. Homo Sacer: Sovereign Power and Bare Life. Translated by Daniel Heller-Roazen. Stanford, California: Stanford University Press, 1998.

Amerika, Mark. "Filmtext". markamerika. 2002. Accessed November 13, 2013. http://www.markamerika.com/filmtext/.

Amerika, Mark. "Expanding the Concept of Writing: Notes on Net Art, Digital Narrative and Viral Ethics" . Leonardo. Vol. 37, (2004) No. 1, pp. 9-13.

Anders Sundnes Løvlie "Flâneur, a walkthrough: Locative Literature as Participation and Play". Dichtung Digital, No. 42. (2012-12-20)

"Anthology of European Electronic Literature". ELMCIP, 2012. Retrieved November 18, 2013. http://anthology.elmcip.net/works.html.

Baldwin, Sandy. "New Word Order: Basra". 2003. Accessed November 21, 2014. http://collection.eliterature.org/2/works/baldwin_basra.html.

Barbrook, Richard. "The High-tech Gift Economy". 2005. Accessed June 13, 2013. http://www.firstmonday.org/issues/issue3_12/barbrook/.

Banham, Reyner. Los Angeles: The Architecture of Four Ecologies. University of California Press, 2009.

Baudrillard, Jean. The transparency of Evil. London: Verso. 1993.

Bauer Rene, Suter Beat. "AndOrDada". 2008. Accessed February 24, 2013. http://elmcip.net/creative-work/andordada-0.

Bell, Daniel. The Coming of Post-Industrial Society: A Venture in Social Forecasting. Reissue ed. New York: Basic Books. [1973] 2001.

Beller, Jonathan. The Cinematic Mode of Production. Hanover and London: Dartmouth College Press, 2006.

Benjamin, Walter. The Work of Art in the Age of Mechanical Reproduction. Illuminations. Translated by H. Zohn. New York: Schocken Books, 1969.

Benjamin, Walter. One-Way Street. Gesammelte Schriften, IV, (Frankfurt/M: Suhrkamp). 1972.146-148.

Bey, Hakim. T. A. Z. The Temporary Autonomous Zone, Ontological Anarchy, Poetic Terrorism. New York: Autonomedia, 1985.

Bolter, J. D. & Grusin, R. Remediation: Understanding New Media. Cambridge, MA: The MIT Press, 2000.

Bookchin, Natalia. "Mass Ornament". Vimeo. 2009, Accessed May 9, 2012. http://vimeo.com/5403546 .

Bootz. Philippe. "Set of U". 2004, Accessed May 14, 2014. http://collection. eliterature.org/1/works/bootz_fremiot__the_set_of_u.html.

Bourchardon, S. & Volckaert, V. "Loss of Grasp". 2010. Accessed November 10, 2013. http://lossofgrasp.com/.

Bouchardon, S., Carpentier, K., & Spenlé. "Toucher. E-Literature Collection, 2". 2009. Accessed February 13, 2013. <http://collection.eliterature.org/2/works/bouchardon_toucher.html>.

Burroughs, William S. Word Virus: The William S. Burroughs Reader, Edited by Grauerholz, James and Silverberg, Ira. New York: Grove Press, 2000.

Caillois, Roger. Les jeux et les homes, Gallimard, Paris, 1967.

Carpenter, C. R. "Along the Briny Beach", Accessed February 13, 2012 .http://luckysoap.com/alongthebrinybeach/alongthebrinycredits. html

Castells, Manuel. The Internet Galaxy. Oxford, New York: Oxford University Press, 2002.

Cayley, John. "Writing to be Found and Writing Readers." Digital Humanities Quarterly 5.3. 2011, Accessed February 19, 2013. http://digital-humanities.org/dhq/.

Chaouli, Michel. "How interactive can fiction be?" Critical Inquiry, 2005. 31(3), 599–617.

Cheney-Lippold, John. "A New Algorithmic Identity. Soft Bio-politics and the Modulation of Control". Theory, Culture & Society. 2011 (SAGE, Los Angeles, London, New Delhi, and Singapore), Vol. 28 (6): 164-181.

CodeDoc Exhibition. 2003. Accessed April 13, 2004. http://artport.whitney.org/commissions/codedoc/ .

Cooley, Heidi. R.. "It's all about the fit: The hand, the mobile screenic device and tactile vision." Journal of Visual Culture, 3 (2), 2004.133-155.

Cramer, Florian. "Post-Digital Writing". Electronic Book Review. 2012. Accessed May 31, 2014. http://www.electronicbookreview.com/author/florian-cramer.

Cramer, Florian. Words Made Flesh, Code, Culture, Imagination. Rotterdam: Piet Zwart, 2005.

Critical Art Ensemble. Molecular Invasion. New York: Autonomedia, 2002.

Critical Art Ensemble. GM food. It's everywhere you want to be. Edited by M. Heinzelmann and M. Weinhard. Auf eigene Gefahr, Frankfurt/M: Revolver – Archiv für aktuelle Kunst, 2003.

Danet, Brenda. Cyberplay@.communicating online. Berg, Oxford and New York, 2001.

Danto, Arthur C. After the End of Art. Contemporary Art and the Pale of History. Princeton: Princeton University Press, 1997.

Darley, Andrew. Visual Digital Culture: Surface Play and Spectacle in New Media Genres. London und New York: Routledge, 2000.

De Certeau, Michel. The Practice of Everyday Life. Translated by Steven Rendall, Berkeley, Ca.: University of California Press, 1984.

Deleuze, Gilles. The Logic of Sense, Edited by C.V. Boundas. New York: Columbia University Press, 1990.

Droitcour, Brian. "Interview with Alexei Shulgin". Rhizome.org, November 19th, 2008, Accessed November 19, 2008. http://rhizome.org/editorial/2099.

"Electroboutique". 2005, Accessed October 21 .2008. /www.electroboutique.com/.

"Electronic Disturbance Theatre 2.0." 2007-2008. Accessed February 26, 2013. Transborder Immigrant Tool. <http://vimeo.com/27222287>.

"Electronic Literature Collection Vol.2". February 2011, Accessed September 10, 2013. Publication of Electronic Literature Organization. http://collection.eliterature.org/2/

"Electronic Literature Collection. Vol. 1". October 2006. Accessed September 10, 2013. Publication of Electronic Literature Organization. http://collection.eliterature.org/1/.

Eskelinen, Markku. "The Four Corners of the E-lit World; Textual Instruments, Operational Logics, Wetware Studies, and Cybertext Poetics." Primerjalna književnost (Ljubljana). 36.1 (2013), 15-24.

Eskelinen, Markku. Cybertext Poetics: The Critical Landscape of New Media Literary Theory. New York, London: Continuum, 2012.

Feyerabend, Paul. Die Natur als ein Kunstwerk, W. Welsch. Edited by Die Aktualität des Ästhetischen, München: Wilhelm Fink Publishing House, 1993.

Fink, Eugen. Studien zur Phänomenologie: 1930-1939 [Studies in phenomenology: 1930-1939]. The Hague, Netherlands: Martinus Nijhof, 1966.

Fink, Eugen. Spiel als Weltsymbol. Stuttgart: Kohlhammer Verlag, 1960.

Fuller, Matthew, "Foreword," in Throughout Art and Culture Emerging with Ubiquitous Computing. Edited by Ulrik Ekman. Cambridge, London: The MIT Press, 2013, xi-xxxiv.

Fuller, Mathew. "A means of Mutation," March 1998, Accessed October, 24, 2005. http://bak.spc.org/iod/mutation.html.

Funkhouser, Criss. New Directions in Digital Poetry. New York, London: Continuum, 2012

Gadamer, Hans-Georg. Truth and Method. London: Sheed & Ward, 1975.

Galloway, Alexander. R. The Interface Effect. Malden, MA.: Polity Press, 2012.

Galloway, Alexander R. Gaming: Essays on algorithmic culture. Minneapolis: University of Minnesota Press, 2006

Gandelman, Claude. Reading Pictures, Viewing Texts. Bloomington and Indianapolis: Indiana University Press, 1991.

Genette, Gerard. Paratexts: Thresholds of interpretation. Cambridge: Cambridge University Press, 1997.

Gibson, William. Neuromancer. New York: Ace, 1986.

Goldsmith, Kenneth. Uncreative Writing. New York: Columbia University Press, 2011.

Goriunova, Olga. "Autocreativity and Organisational Aesthetics in Art Platforms," Fibreculture Journal, 17/2011. Accessed April 12, 2012. http://seventeen.fibreculturejournal.org/fcj-115-autocreativity-and-orga.

Gray. Jonathan. "Hype, Paratexts, and Over-sized Smurfs: The Case of Avatar". 2010, Accessed October 22, 2013. http://www.fromthesquare.org/?p=833.

Groys, Boris. Google: Words beyond Grammar. Ostfildern: Hatje Cantz Verlag GmbH, 2012. (Collection dOCUMENTA (13): 100 Notizen - 100 Gedanken).

Hansen, Mark. New Philosophy for New Media. Cambridge Mass. The MIT Press, 2003.

Hegel, Georg Wilhelm. F. Aesthetics: Lectures on Fine Art. Translated by T. M. Knox, vol. 1, Oxford: Clarendon Press, 1975.

Heidegger, Martin. The Principle of Reason. Bloomington and Indianapolis, University of Indiana, 1996.

Heidegger, Martin. Parmenides. Translated by André Schuwer and Richard Rojcewicz. Bloomington: Indiana University Press, 1992.

Heidegger, Martin. The Question concerning Technology and Other Essays. Translated and with Introduction by William Lovitt. New York, London: Garland Publishing, 1977.

Hemment, Drew. "Locative Arts," August 2004. Accessed February 13, 2012. http://socialinterface.files.wordpress.com/2007/12/locativearts.pdf.

Hoover, Wesley A.and Gouch, Philip B. "The Simple View of Reading." Reading and Writing: An Interdisciplinary Journal, 1990, 2. pp.127-160.

Ingarden, Roman. The Cognition of Literary Work of Art. Evanston, Illinois: Northwestern University Press, 1973.

Ingarden, Roman. The Literary Work of Art. Translated by George G. Grabowicz. Evanston, Illinois: Northwestern University Press, 1973.

Ingarden, Roman. Erlebnis, Kunstwerk und Wert: Vorträge zur Ästhetik 1937-1967. Darmstadt, Germany: Wissenschaftliche Buchgesellschaft, 1969.

Iser, Wolfgang. The Act of Reading: A Theory of Aesthetic Response. Baltimore and London: The Johns Hopkins University Press, 1978

Jauss, Hans-Robert. "Literary History as a Challenge to Literary Theory." in Toward an Aesthetic of Reception. Translated by Timothy Bahti. Minneapolis: University of Minnesota Press, 1982. 3-45

Jodi. "ZXY." Accessed March 13, 2013. <http://zyx-app.com/>.

Johnson, Steven. Interface Culture. New York: HarperEdge, 1997.

Joyce, Michel. Afternoon, a Story. Cambridge, MA: Eastgate Systems, 1987.

Joyce, M. "Twelve Blue." Accessed September 19, 2004. http://eastgate.com/ TwelveBlue/sl1.html.

Kac, Eduardo, ed. Media Poetry: An International Anthology. Bristol, Chicago: Intellect, 2007.

Kane, Carolyn. "Dancing Machines: An Interview with Natalie Bookchin". Rhizome.org.May 27, 2009, Accessed June 13, 2012. <http://rhizome. org/editorial/2009/may/27/dancing-machines/>.

Kaprow, Allan. Essays on the Blurring of Art and Life. Berkeley: University of California Press, 1993.

Karpinska, Aya N. "The arrival of the beeBox: An Exploration of Spatial Text." 2003. Accessed March 11, 2009. http://technekai.com/box/ beeBoxPaper.pdf.

Karpinska, Aya N., and Daniel C. Howe. "open.ended." 2004. Accessed March 11, 2009. http://www.technekai.com/open/index.html.

Karpinska, Aya. "Shadows Never Sleep." 2008, Accessed February 29, 2014. www.technekai.com/shadow/shadow.html.

Kelly, Kevin. "Gossip is Philosophy". Wired 3.05. 1995, Accessed September 18, 2004. <http://www.wired.com/wired/3.05/eno. html?pg=4&topic=>.

Kittler, Friedrich. Gramophone, Film, Typewriter. Stanford, CA: Stanford University Press, 1999.

Kozel, Susan. "Sinews of Ubiquity: A Corporeal Ethics for Ubiquitous Computing" in Throughout. Art and Culture Emerging with Ubiquitous Computing. Edited by Ekman, Ulrik. Cambridge, London: The MIT Press, 2013. 337-349.

Kracauer, Siegfried. The Mass Ornament: Weimar Essays. Translated, edited and with an introduction by Thomas Y. Levin. Cambridge: Harvard University Press. 1995.

Landow, Georg P., ed. Hyper/Text/Theory. Baltimore: The John Hopkins University Press, 1994.

Lash, Scott. Sociology of Postmodernism. London and New York: Routledge, 1990.

Lemos, Andre. "Post-Mass Media Functions, Locative Media, and Informational Territories: New Ways of Thinking About Territory, Place, and Mobility in Contemporary Society." Space and Culture 13. Pp. 403-420.

Luesebrink, Marjorie C. "One + One = Zero – Vanishing Text in Electronic Literature". Electronic Book Review. Accessed April 5, 2014. http://www.electronicbookreview.com/thread/electropoetics/disappearing.

Lyotard, Jean-François. The Inhuman Reflections on Time. Stanford, California: Stanford University Press, 1991.

Mangen, Anne. "Hypertext fiction reading: haptics and immersion". Journal of Research in Reading, 31 (4), 2008. 404–419.

Manning, Erin. Politics of Touch. Sense. Movement, Sovereignty. Minneapolis: University. of Minnesota Press, 2007.

Manovich, Lev. The Language of New Media. Cambridge, MA: The MIT Press, 2001.

Manovich, Lev. "Software Takes Command." Released under CC. 2008, Accessed November 19, 2013. http://black2.fri.uni-lj.si/humbug/files/doktorat-vaupotic/zotero/storage/D22GEWS3/manovich_softbook_11_20_2008.pdf

Manovich, Lev. "New Media from Borges to HTML." in The New Media Reader. Edited by Noah Wardrip-Fruin and Nick Montfort. Cambridge, MA: The MIT Press, 2003, 13-25.

Marx, Karl. "Economic and Philosophic Manuscripts of 1844, Private Property and Communism", 1844, Accessed November 19, 2012. http://www.marxists.org/archive/marx/works/1844/manuscripts/comm.htm

McKeon, Michael, ed. Theory of the Novel: A Historical Approach, Baltimore and London: The John Hopkins University Press, 2000.
Merleau-Ponty, Maurice. Phenomenology of perception. Translated by C. Smith. London, UK: Routledge & Kegan Paul, 1998. (Original work published 1945.)

Merleau-Ponty, Maurice. The world of perception. Translated by Oliver Davis. London, UK & New York, NY: Routledge, 2004. (Original lectures delivered on French radio 1948.)

Massumi, Brian. Semblance and Event. Cambridge, Mass.: The MIT Press, 2011.

Mencia, Maria. "Cityscapes: Social Poetics/Public Textualities". 2007, Accessed March 11, 2009. http://www.epoetry2007.net/english/artiststxts/mencia.pdf.

Monfort, Nick. "ppg256-1". Electronic Literature Collection 2. Accessed September 23, 2013. http://collection.eliterature.org/2/works/montfort_ppg256.html.

Morris Adalaide and Swiss Thomas, eds. New Media Poetics: Contexts, Technotexts, and Theories. Cambridge, Mass.; London: MIT Press, 2006.

Murray, Janet H. Hamlet on the Holodeck. Cambridge, Mass.: The MIT Press, 1997.

Napier, Mark. "Feed." 2002, Accessed November 13, 2003 http://dian-network.com/con/feed/index.html

Negri, Antonio. Art and Multitude. Malden, MA : Polity, 2011

Nelson, Jason. "Nothing You Have Done Deserves Such Praise". Turbulence. 2013. Accessed October 30, 2013. http://www.turbulence.org/Works/nothing/.

O'Donnell, Kath. "Silence, infomania." Post to IDCmailing list. September 8, 2007, Accessed January 28, 2009. https://lists.thing.net/pipermail/idc/2007-September/002811.html

Paul, Christiane, ed. New Media in the White Cube and Beyond: Curatorial Models for Digital Art. Berkeley: University of California Press, 2008\

Quaranta, Domenico. "The Postmedia Perspective." Rhizome.org. Editorial, 2011. Accessed March 19, 2012. http://rhizome.org/editorial/2011/jan/12/the-postmedia-perspective/.

Rosenberg, Jim. "Diagram Series 6." Accessed March 13, 2013. http://www.inframergence.org/jr/d6/readMe.html.

San Cornelio, Gemma and Ardevol, Elisenda. "Practices of place-making through locative media artworks," Communications 36 (2011).

Schleiner, Anne-Marie. "Does Lara Croft Wear Fake Polygons? Gender and Gender-Role Subversion in Computer Adventure Games." Leonardo, 3:34, 2001.

Simanowski, Roberto, interview with Simon Biggs. "Technology, Aura, and the Self in New Media Art." Dichtung-digital. 2002. Accessed November 4, 2003. http://www.dichtung-digital.de/.

Simanowski, Roberto. Digital Art and Meaning. Minneapolis; University of Minnesota Press. 2011.

Snow, C.P. Two Cultures. Cambridge: Cambridge University Press, 1959.

Stanitzek, Georg. "Texts and Paratexts in Media." Critical Inquiry 32(1) 2005. 27-42.

Stefans, Brian Kim. "Language as Gameplay: toward a vocabulary for describing works of electronic literature." Electronic Book Review. March 9, 2012 Accessed January 24, 2013. http://www.electronic-bookreview.com/thread/electropoetics/gameplay.

Strehovec, Janez. "The Software Word: digital poetry as a new media-based language art," Digital Creativity, 15: 3, 2004, 143-158.

Strehovec, Janez. "Digital Poetry Beyond the Metaphysics of Projective Saying." In Regards Croises. Perspectives on Digital Literature, edited by Philippe Bootz and Sandy Baldwin. Morgantown: West Virginia University Press, 2010. 63-83.

Strehovec, Janez. "Digital Literary Text as a Play and a Ride." In Officina di Letteratura Elettronica: Lavori del Convegno. Napoli, Atelier Multimediale Edizioni, 2011. 381-393.

Strehovec, Janez. "Derivative Writing: E-Literature in the world of new social and economic paradigms." In Remediating the Social, edited by Simon Biggs. Bergen: ELMCIP, University of Bergen, 2012. 79-83.

Strehovec, Janez. "The Word/Image/Virtual Body: On the Techno-Aesthetics of Digital Literary Objects". Afterimage, 30:2, September/October 2002. 9-10

Strehovec, Janez. "Attitudes on the Move. On the Perception of Digital Poetry Objects." In CyberText Yearbook 2002-2003, edited by Eskelinen and Koskimaa. University of Jyväskylä, 39-55.

Strehovec, Janez. "The Digital Word in a Palm: Digital Poetry between Reading and immersive bodily Experience." E-Poetry 2007, Université Paris 8. Accessed May 13, 2011. http://epoetry.paragraphe.info/english/papers/strehovec.pdf.

Strehovec, Janez: "Stihovi za sedam tjedana. (Šesti komentar uz pjesme koje više ne postoje)". Quorum : časopis za književnost. Vol. XIX (2003), 5-6; 109-128.

Strickland, Stephanie. "Born Digital". Poetry Foundation. Accessed February 13, 2013. http://www.poetryfoundation.org/article/182942.

Thacker, Eugene. "After Life: swarms, demons and antinomies of immanence". In Theory After Theory, edited by Elliott Jane and Attridge Derek. London and New York: Routledge, 2011.

Thomson, Jon, and Alison Craighead. "Trigger Happy." Thomas & Craighead. 1998, Accessed April 27, 2014. http://www.thomson-craighead.net/docs/thap.html.

Thrift, Nigel. "Movement-space: The changing domain of thinking resulting from the development of new kinds of spatial awareness." Economy and Society, 33: 4 (2004): 582 — 604.

Tisseli, Eugenio. "Degenerative." nt2. http://nt2.uqam.ca/repertoire/degenerative_-_regenerative/media

Torres, Rui. "Poemas no meio do caminho." E-Literature Collection, 2. 2008, Accessed February 13, 2013. http://collection.eliterature.org/2/works/torres_poemas_caminho.html.

Turkle, Sherry. "Rethinking Identity Through Virtual Community." In Clicking In: Hot links to a digital culture, edited by Lynn Hershman Leeson. Seattle: Bay Press, 1996.

Turkle, Sherry. "Video Games and Computer Holding Power." In The New Media Reader, edited by N.Wardrip-Fruin and N. Montfort. Cambridge, London: The MIT Press, 2003

Vesna, Victoria. "Towards a Third Culture or Working in Between." Leonardo. 34.2. (2001): 121-125. Accessed December 9, 2014. http://vv.arts.ucla.edu/publications/publications/00-01/ThirdCulture/ThirdCulture.htm.

Virilio, Paul. Open Sky. Translated by Julie Rose. London: Verso, 1997.

Virno, Paolo. A Grammar of the Multitude. For an Analysis of Contemporary Forms of Life. Translated by Isabella Bertoletti et al. New York: Semiotext(e), 2004.

Wardrip-Fruin et al. Screen. Quicktime documentation. Accessed September 18, 2002.http://www.uiowa.edu/~iareview/tirweb/feature/cave/ScreenProfile20

Wardrip-Fruin. Interview. http://www.artificial.dk/articles/wardripfruin.htm

Wardrip-Fruin, N. Expressive Processing: Digital Fictions, Computer Games, and Software Studies. Cambridge, MA/London: The MIT Press, 2009.

Wardrip-Fruin, N. "From Instrumental Texts to Textual Instruments." Melbourne DAC. 2003, Accessed October 13, 2013. http://www.hyperfiction.org/texts/textualInstrumentsShort.pdf.

Wilson, Stephen. Information Arts. Cambridge, MA: The MIT Press, 2002.

Youngblood, Gene. Expanded Cinema. New York: E. P. Dutton, 1970.

Janez Strehovec

Index

A

B

E

F

G

H

I

J

N

O

T

U

V

TEXT AS RIDE

JANEZ STREHOVEC

EDITED BY
KWABENA OPOKU-AGYEMANG
AND SANDY BALDWIN

COMPUTING LITERATURE
MORGANTOWN, WV / ROCHESTER, NY

COMPUTING LITERATURE

A book series distributed by the West Virginia University Press.

Volume 1 Regards Croisés: Perspectives on Digital Literature
Edited by Philippe Bootz and Sandy Baldwin

Volume 2 Writing Under: Selections from the Internet Text
By Alan Sondheim. Edited and Introduced by Sandy Baldwin

Volume 3 Electronic Literature as a Model of Creativity and Innovation in Practice
A Report from the HERA Joint Research Project. Edited by Scott Rettberg and Sandy Baldwin

Volume 4 Po.Ex: Essays from Portugal on Cyberliterature and Intermedia
Edited by Rui Torres and Sandy Baldwin

Volume 5 Word Space Multiplicities, Openings, Andings
By Jim Rosenberg. Edited by Sandy Baldwin

Volume 6 Electronic Literature Communities
Edited by Scott Rettberg, Patricia Tomaszek, and Sandy Baldwin

Volume 7 Text as Ride
By Janez Strehovec. Edited by Kwabena Opoku-Agyemang and Sandy Baldwin